More praise for
The Atheist's Guide to Reality

"This eccentric, funny treatise on 'scientism' . . . takes a perverse delight in 'nice nihilism.' Rosenberg doesn't believe in free will, morality, or secular humanism, and apparently you shouldn't either, dummy." —*Village Voice*

"Undeniably brilliant." —*Kirkus Reviews*

"Rosenberg is admirably frank about the implications of scientism." —*Harper's*

"Fascinating and thought-provoking." —*Publishers Weekly*

"The section on biology, and [Rosenberg's] discussion of Darwin's theory of natural selection and its implications, is clear and sharp." —Doug Johnstone, *Independent on Sunday*

"Thought-provoking." —Manjit Kumar, *Independent*

"Rosenberg is doing something different. . . . He's bringing a few home truths to the table. . . . Rosenberg has written a provocative and clever book that is fresh, shocking and revelatory. . . . It'll make you think." —Richard Marshall, *3:AM* magazine

"This book is at once deeply disturbing and oddly comforting. . . . Tightly argued, it always carries a wry recursive humour." —Daniel Binney, *Times Higher Education*

"In his lively, provocative book, Rosenberg presents a philosophy that he describes as both scientistic and nihilistic. . . . Rosenberg's style is clear and forceful." —Anthony Kenny, *Times Literary Supplement*

Also by Alex Rosenberg

Microeconomic Laws: A Philosophical Analysis

Sociobiology and the Preemption of Social Science

Hume and the Problem of Causation
(with T. L. Beauchamp)

The Structure of Biological Science

Philosophy of Social Science

Economics: Mathematical Politics or Science of Diminishing Returns?

Instrumental Biology, or the Disunity of Science

Darwinism in Philosophy, Social Science and Policy

Philosophy of Science: A Contemporary Approach

*Darwinian Reductionism, or, How to
Stop Worrying and Love Molecular Biology*

Philosophy of Biology: A Contemporary Introduction
(with Daniel McShea)

THE ATHEIST'S GUIDE TO REALITY

Enjoying Life
without Illusions

ALEX ROSENBERG

W. W. NORTON & COMPANY
NEW YORK LONDON

For information about permission to reproduce
selections from this book,
write to Permissions, W. W. Norton & Company, Inc.,
500 Fifth Avenue, New York, NY 10110

For information about special discounts for bulk purchases,
please contact W. W. Norton Special Sales at
specialsales@wwnorton.com or 800-233-4830

Manufacturing by Courier Westford
Book design by Lovedog Studio
Production manager: Devon Zahn

Library of Congress Cataloging-in-Publication Data

Rosenberg, Alexander, 1946–
The atheist's guide to reality : enjoying life
without illusions / Alex Rosenberg. — 1st ed.
p. cm.
Includes bibliographical references and index.
ISBN 978-0-393-08023-0 (hardcover)
1. Atheism. 2. Scientism. I. Title.
BL2747.3.R67 2011
211'.8—dc23
2011019961

ISBN 978-0-393-34411-0 pbk.

W. W. Norton & Company, Inc.
500 Fifth Avenue, New York, N.Y. 10110
www.wwnorton.com

W. W. Norton & Company Ltd.
Castle House, 75/76 Wells Street, London W1T 3QT

1 2 3 4 5 6 7 8 9 0

CONTENTS

PREFACE

WHAT IS THE NATURE OF REALITY, THE PURPOSE of the universe, and the meaning of life? Is there any rhyme or reason to the course of human history? Why am I here? Do I have a soul, and if so, how long will it last? What happens when we die? Do we have free will? Why should I be moral? What is love, and why is it usually inconvenient?

These questions are unavoidable. But the answers aren't. Indeed, most people manage to avoid them completely—and do it quite intentionally. People who believe in religion are particularly adept at avoiding the answers. This is not a book for them. This is a book for those who want to face up to the real answers to these questions. It's a book for people who are comfortable with the truth about reality. This is a book for atheists.

Most people think of atheism as one big negative. Atheists perpetuate the stereotype by devoting so much time and energy to broadcasting the evidence against God's existence. But if atheism ever were a matter of evidence, it isn't any longer. Contemporary religious belief is immune to rational objection. Often we are wasting our time refuting it.

There is much more to atheism than its knockdown arguments that there is no God. There is the whole rest of the worldview that comes along with atheism. It's a demanding, rigorous, breathtaking grip on reality, one that has been vindicated beyond reasonable doubt. It's called science.

Science enables atheism to answer life's universal and relentless questions with evidence employing a real understanding of the natural world. Some of the answers it provides to these questions may disconcert you. Several will certainly surprise you. But they are all as certain as the science on which our atheism is grounded. An unblinking scientific worldview requires atheism. That's why 75 percent of the members of the National Academy of Sciences admit to being atheists. Four-fifths of the rest say they're agnostics—no opinion either way. It can't be a coincidence that 95 percent of the most distinguished scientists in America (along with their foreign associate members) don't believe in God.

If science made you an atheist, you are already as strongly committed to the serious scientific answers to the unavoidable questions as you are to atheism.

Science reveals a rough reality. But in its reliance on our capacity for experimentation, discovery, and cumulative knowledge, it solves all the great puzzles that people have tried to deal with through faith, philosophy, and alcohol and drugs. In doing so, science illuminates some of humanity's most remarkable qualities and unravels some of its deepest illusions. But atheists will find a surprising amount of consolation in this worldview, or at least a certain amount of relief from anxiety.

It was an American public radio humorist, Garrison Keillor, who first called the daunting problems that we all face "the persistent questions." I have adopted his label to emphasize the fact that they keep bothering us until we find the answers. In fact, science has found the answers—some of them 400 years ago, others in the nineteenth century, and several only quite recently. These answers are provided by the very same facts that atheism itself rests on. That's why they are a part—the positive part—of the atheist's worldview.

Science—especially physics and biology—reveals that reality is completely different from what most people think. It's not just different from what credulous religious believers think. Science reveals that reality is stranger than even many atheists recognize. From the nature of the reality uncovered by science, consequences follow. This book is about those consequences. It provides an uncompromising, hard-boiled, no-nonsense, unsentimental view of the nature of reality, the purpose of things, the meaning of life, the trajectory of human history, morality and mortality, the will, the mind, and the self.

REALITY IS ROUGH. But it could have been worse. We could have been faced with reality in all its roughness *plus* a God who made it that way. Take, for example, what the British historian Eric Hobsbawm called "the short twentieth century." It starts in 1914 with the beginning of trench warfare in the First World War and carries on through the worldwide influenza epidemic of 1918, the Russian civil war, collectivization, and great purge, the Great Depression of the 1930s, through the Second World War's Holocaust and the nuclear attacks on Japan, and all the way past the Chinese Great Leap Forward famine of 1958 to the collapse of the Berlin Wall in 1991—a 73-year century with enough horrors to last Earth a millennium. Now add to those horrors the God of the Abrahamic religions—Judaism, Christianity, and Islam—and you get an even worse reality; it's one just as rough as the real world, but it adds a moral monster who arranged for it all to happen.

In recent years, there have been a number of very popular books devoted to disapproving of as well as disproving religious belief. Some of them attack arguments for God's existence, and others show the harm—intellectual and moral—that religions do in the name of their respective deities. A Nobel Prize–winning physicist, Steven Weinberg, once said, "With or without religion, good people can behave well and bad people can do evil; but for good people to do evil, that takes religion." He had a point.

But it's not *my* point. I am not interested in hammering another nail into the intellectual coffin of theism. Enough of those arguments already exist. And the relative lack of originality in the arguments of the recent best sellers attacking religion (*The God Delusion*, *God Is Not Great*, *Letter to a Christian Nation*) shows that the arguments have been around for quite some time and have achieved little effect. The effort to argue most people out of religious belief was doomed by the very Darwinian evolutionary forces that the most fervent of Christians deny. The most sophisticated believers understand the arguments against theism. Yet they are still able to create clever excuses for harboring theistic convictions as logically self-consistent if ultimately unprovable. If they can do it, imagine how much easier it is for credulous people, who are neither as well informed nor as logically scrupulous, to continue to believe. There is little point in preaching to these unconverted.

This book doesn't preach to the converted either. Instead, its aim is to sketch out what we atheists really should believe about reality and our place in it. The picture painted here is subject to completion and modification. What is not debatable are the broad outlines of the sketch. They are the reasons we can be so confident about the nature of reality. All we need to understand its character are the parts of modern science that are no longer in doubt. These parts are so basic that nothing to be uncovered by physics or biology will make science take them back.

WHY MIGHT SUCH a book be of interest to people who have already, for one or another of the many good scientific reasons, given up all religious belief?

One reason is that you and I are assailed annually, even weekly, with books, articles, and television programs seeking to sow doubts about the completeness and credibility of science. There are apologists who suggest that science's findings are perfectly compatible with the higher superstitions, the morally and emotionally uplifting religions. Worse yet, some of the advocates of religion argue that science's teachings do not touch on these matters of "ultimate concern." Among the figures sowing these doubts about the reach of science are individuals with sturdy scientific credentials, like John Polkinghorne, Knight of the British Empire, member of the Royal Society, trained high-energy physicist, Cambridge professor, and Anglican vicar. And there are well-known theologians, like John Haught, Catholic defender of Darwin against intelligent design, making common cause with scientists as well known as everyone's favorite biologist, the late Stephen Jay Gould. Francis Collins, one-time head of the Human Genome Project and now director of the National Institutes of Health, joined this choir, writing a book claiming that there is no incompatibility between religion and what empirical inquiry has revealed. I am sure that Collins is sincere. But the claim that religion and science don't compete is good politics. It's also confused, as we'll see.

Atheists and our fellow travelers need some protection against this tide of impressively credentialed misunderstanding. In a way, this book may serve like one of those pamphlets that used to be available in Anglican Churches: "What to say when a Jehovah's Witness [substitute Mormon missionary, Seventh Day Adventist, representative of the Reverend Moon, and so forth] comes to your door." It aims to suggest how we scoffers should deal with reconcilers and mystery-mongers.

Most importantly, besides rebutting misrepresentations of science, we should be clear for ourselves about what our attachment to science, as the right description of the world, really commits us to. This book identifies science's answers to the perennial questions we humans pose to ourselves about reality and our place within it. These are the questions that vicars, visionaries, gurus, and all too many philosophers have tried to answer, often with ulterior motives and never with the kind of evidence that is worthy of a question of worldly importance. The right answers are ones that even some scientists have not been comfortable with and have sought to avoid or water down.

It's worth repeating that this book is written mainly for those of us who are already deniers, not just doubters and agnostics. Although we will address the foibles and fallacies (as well as the wishful thinking) of theists, we won't treat theism as a serious alternative that stills needs to be refuted. This book's intended readers have moved past that point. We know the truth.

Knowing the truth makes it hard not to sound patronizing of the benighted souls still under religion's spell. So from time to time, some of the tone of much that follows may sound a little smug. I fear I have to plead guilty to this charge, with mitigation. So far as I can see, belief in God is on a par with belief in Santa Claus.

How did I come to that conclusion and to the others in this book? That question is ambiguous. It could be a request for some autobiography—for the particular path that brought me personally to trust science's answers to the persistent questions. Or it could be a request for the facts and arguments that justify these answers. The answer to the second question is given in the 12 chapters that follow. But here is a brief answer to the first question—how I managed to find a way through the thicket of illusions about ourselves and the world that come along with religion. Make no mistake, my route was not the only route or even the most direct one.

I am a philosopher, or if that sounds pretentious, a philosophy professor. I didn't start out to be one. I wanted to study physics because I really wanted to understand the nature of reality. The more I learned, the more I was disappointed with the answers physics provided. They just didn't scratch the itch of curiosity that was keeping me up at night. If I was going to stop the itch, I was faced with two choices: therapy or philosophy. With enough psychotherapy, I thought, I might get over worrying about what the nature of reality really was. Psychotherapy was too expensive and philosophical therapy was too interesting.

So I switched to philosophy. I thought that if science couldn't answer my unavoidable questions, at least philosophy could tell me why not, and maybe it could even answer the questions.

Imagine how troubling it was for me to discover quite soon that the history of philosophy was mainly a matter of great minds wrestling with science! At least from the beginning of the seventeenth century onward, the agenda of every one of the great philosophers has been set by advances in physics and chemistry and later also in biology.

It took a few years, but by reading David Hume (1711–1776), I was able to figure out the mistake preventing science from satisfying me. The mistake, as Hume showed so powerfully, was to think that there is any more to reality than the laws of nature that science discovers.

For the past 40 years, I have been trying to work out exactly how advances, especially in biology, neuroscience, and evolutionary anthropology, fit together with what physical science has long told us. I spent a lot of that time on the foundations of economics and the other behavioral sciences. I even went back to grad school for a couple of years to study molecular biology. The results were a lot of books and papers on technical issues in the philosophy of science, matters of purely academic interest. Nobody gets tenure, in philosophy at any rate, for figuring out the nature of reality. Doing that turned out to be a by-product of all the thinking that went into those academic articles and scholarly books.

Now I have finally seen how all the pieces fit together to settle the daunting, unavoidable, relentless questions we all have about the nature of things and the nature of us. There is only one way all the pieces of the puzzle fit together. But there are lots of different ways in which to figure out that one way. The path I took to put the pieces together was just one path of many, and probably not the most efficient one. I hope this book will help you save a step or two in coming to the same conclusions.

THE
ATHEIST'S
GUIDE TO
REALITY

Chapter I

Answering Life's Persistent Questions: Do You Want Stories or Reality?

Everyone seems to know what life's persistent questions are. Almost all of us have been interested in answering them at one time or another, starting back sometime in our childhood when the lights were turned out and we found ourselves staring at the ceiling, unable to sleep. As time goes on, thinking about sex increasingly pushes these thoughts out of adolescent minds. This is fortunate. Otherwise there would be an even greater oversupply of philosophy and divinity students than there is of English majors. But the questions keep coming back, all too often right after sex.

The Persistent Questions

These are the questions that always bothered me as I stared at the ceiling after the lights were turned off. Maybe they're the same ones you've entertained in periods of insomnia. Besides *Is there a*

God? (everyone's favorite), there are lots of other persistent questions about the nature of reality, the purpose of the universe, the meaning of life, the nature of the self, what happens when we die, whether there is free will, or any will at all, and if so, does it have to go through probate? (That last one may keep you up nights but doesn't really count as persistent unless an apartment in Manhattan is at stake.)

Some people are troubled by immorality almost as much as they are by immortality. (Did you have to read that sentence twice?) Not as many are troubled by it as we might like. But almost everyone wants to know the nature of right and wrong, good and evil, why we should be moral, and whether abortion, euthanasia, cloning, or having fun is forbidden, permissible, or sometimes obligatory.

This book aims to provide the correct answers to most of the persistent questions. I hope to explain enough about reality so that, as the old textbooks used to say, answers to any remaining questions "can be left as an exercise to the reader."

Here is a list of some of the questions and their short answers. The rest of this book explains the answers in more detail. Given what we know from the sciences, the answers are all pretty obvious. The interesting thing is to recognize how totally unavoidable they are, provided you place your confidence in science to provide the answers.

Is there a God? No.
What is the nature of reality? What physics says it is.
What is the purpose of the universe? There is none.
What is the meaning of life? Ditto.
Why am I here? Just dumb luck.
Does prayer work? Of course not.

Is there a soul? Is it immortal? Are you kidding?

Is there free will? Not a chance!

What happens when we die? Everything pretty much goes
   on as before, except us.

*What is the difference between right and wrong, good and
   bad?* There is no moral difference between them.

Why should I be moral? Because it makes you feel better
   than being immoral.

*Is abortion, euthanasia, suicide, paying taxes, foreign aid,
   or anything else you don't like forbidden, permissible, or
   sometimes obligatory?* Anything goes.

What is love, and how can I find it? Love is the solution to
   a strategic interaction problem. Don't look for it; it will
   find you when you need it.

Does history have any meaning or purpose? It's full of sound
   and fury, but signifies nothing.

Does the human past have any lessons for our future? Fewer
   and fewer, if it ever had any to begin with.

The one persistent question not addressed directly in the pages
that follow (though we'll have some fun with it here and there)
is the very first one: *Is there a God?* We already know the correct
answer to that one. In the rest of this book, we will take the best
reason for atheism—science—and show what else it commits us
atheists to believing. There are compelling reasons to deny God's
existence, but those reasons don't just support a negative conclusion: no God, end of story. They provide everything we need to
answer all the other questions that inevitably come along with
the God question.

There are many reasons for not spending any more time on the
question, *Is there a God?* Here are three good ones:

First of all, lots of people have been there and done that—so many that most professional atheists long ago began to repeat their own and other people's solid arguments. In fact, we really haven't needed one since Hume wrote his *Dialogues Concerning Natural Religion*, first published, by his arrangement, three years after his death in 1779. (Is there a lesson here for us atheists?)

Second reason: Atheist tracts don't work. We all know what's wrong with the standard arguments for God's existence. The decisive arguments against God's existence are also well known. It's equally evident that the failure of the positive arguments for God's existence and the force of the negative arguments against it don't persuade theists. They know the knockdown arguments as well as we do, and still they believe. We are not going to convince them.

The third reason we won't bother to refute theism is that we have better things to do—like figuring out exactly what we ought to believe about a reality without a God. Once a person has become an atheist, a lot of questions become even more relentless than they were for the theist. After all, theists can just trust in God and see whether that works to answer these questions. At least for some believers, it does work, at least for some of the time. But for us atheists, *What, me worry?* is not a stopping place.

If you buy into that part of science that is pretty well fixed and not likely to be revised by even the most radical new discoveries, there is really only one challenge for the committed atheist: to understand the science that provides the obviously and irrefutably correct answers to the persistent questions. Understanding the science is a challenge because of the way science packages its discoveries. Our brain just didn't evolve to be able to unwrap the package easily. This is why most people have never been able to deal with science. And it's the main reason why there have always been far fewer atheists than believers.

What's in a Name? Would Atheism by Any Other Name Sound Sweeter?

Before tackling the persistent questions, we need a brief detour to talk about labels. The real problem for atheists is not a matter of what to believe. The real problem is finding a label that describes what we *do* believe instead of one that only announces what we *don't* believe.

Atheists have always faced a public relations problem, especially in the United States. Most Americans won't trust them. That's one reason why only one elected official, Pete Stark, the U.S. congressional representative from San Francisco—hotbed of Christian fundamentalism—has ever admitted to atheism. He did it because an atheist group offered a $1,000 reward to the highest-ranking elected official in the country willing to own up to atheism. The problem is less serious in Britain, where the last foreign minister announced he was an atheist without the prompting of a reward.

In recent years, some atheists have tried to deal with the public relations problem by finding a new label. Atheists, they argue, should call themselves "Brights." The word *bright*, with its connotations of intelligence and enlightenment, recalls the eighteenth-century period known as the Age of Reason, a time when the natural sciences and scientific philosophy flourished in Europe, before being eclipsed by Romanticism. Of course, there is now a Brights website and a *Wikipedia* article, too. They even have a logo.

But the label "Bright" has some obvious limitations. It's precious and self-congratulatory. It also offends theists, who can't help concluding that we "Brights" must think they are "dim."

Some atheists will also be unhappy with "Bright" because they are down on the Enlightenment. It ended badly—remember the reign of terror during the French Revolution? If that's a good reason, or if we worry that the label will provoke needless offense, let me suggest something else:

Scientism—noun; scientistic—adjective.

Scientism has two related meanings, both of them pejorative. According to one of these meanings, scientism names the improper or mistaken application of scientific methods or findings outside their appropriate domain, especially to questions treated by the humanities. The second meaning is more common: Scientism is the exaggerated confidence in the methods of science as the most (or the only) reliable tools of inquiry, and an equally unfounded belief that at least the most well established of its findings are the only objective truths there are.

If we are unhappy with "atheist" because it defines us by what we do not believe, and uncomfortable with "Bright" because it's too cute or too clever by half, we can take "scientism" away from our opponents. We have at least one good reason for trying.

"Scientism" is the pejorative label given to our positive view by those who really want to have their theistic cake and dine at the table of science's bounties, too. Opponents of scientism would never charge their cardiologists or auto mechanics or software engineers with "scientism" when their health, travel plans, or Web surfing are in danger. But just try subjecting their nonscientific mores and norms, their music or metaphysics, their literary theories or politics to scientific scrutiny. The immediate response of outraged humane letters is "scientism."

Let's expropriate the epithet. In the pages that follow, we won't use the label "Bright" as a variant on atheist. But we'll call the worldview that all us atheists (and even some agnostics) share "scientism." This is the conviction that the methods of science are the only reliable ways to secure knowledge of anything; that science's description of the world is correct in its fundamentals; and that when "complete," what science tells us will not be surprisingly different from what it tells us today. We'll often use the adjective "scientistic" in referring to the approaches, theories, methods, and descriptions of the nature of reality that all the sciences share. Science provides all the significant truths about reality, and knowing such truths is what real understanding is all about.

Most people don't understand science, and most Americans don't even believe its findings. They place the persistent questions in the hands of their pastors and try not to think about them. The trouble is, depositing these questions with your priest, vicar, imam, or rabbi never works. The questions persist. In America, every year you can find a new best-selling book devoted to answering these questions, usually in the Christian bookstores. They are published by people eager to make a buck on the combination of gullibility and anxiety that Americans seem to have so much of. A good example of the sort of book I mean is *The Purpose Driven Life*, written by a now very rich preacher who provides the pat Christian answers to the persistent questions. These answers, and their packaging, have made organized religion the most successful long-term growth industry in America since before the republic was founded. But the fact that there is a market for a new Christian self-help book every year shows that the pat answers don't really scratch the itch.

There are two differences between the real answers to the persistent questions and the ones religion keeps trying to get people to buy into. First, the answers that science provides are not particularly warm and fuzzy. Second, once you understand them, they stick. You are unlikely to give them up, so long as you insist that evidence govern your beliefs.

To answer these unavoidable questions correctly, we have to be scientistic. Being scientistic doesn't mean giving up anything we like to do—singing in a choir, volunteering for Habitat for Humanity, even enjoying literary criticism. It certainly doesn't require we become scientists. We don't even have to be scientific if that means being dispassionate, unemotional, number-crunching nerds. Being scientistic just means treating science as our exclusive guide to reality, to nature—both our own nature and everything else's.

How Mother Nature Made Things Difficult for Science

The most serious obstacle facing atheists when we set out to answer the persistent questions for ourselves is one erected by Mother Nature herself. Ironically, this barrier to scientism results from the very Darwinian evolutionary process that theism has to reject (as we'll see in Chapter 3). It's actually worse than ironic because the same Darwinian process that made it hard for anyone to understand science's answers to these questions made it easy to be seduced by religion's answers to them!

The big obstacle to accepting science's answers to life's relentless questions is deep, subtle, insidious, purely psychological, and probably hardwired into our genes. It's a problem that even the most scientistic among us must grapple with. It's not that some people will find the answers science gives scary or hard to follow. The problem doesn't even look like a problem. It has to do with the way we—educated or uneducated, atheist or theist, agnostic, deist, scientist—in fact, all human beings—like our information to be "packaged."

We are suckers for a good story—a description of events in the form of a plot with characters driven by motives. If information doesn't come in story form, we have trouble understanding it, remembering it, and believing it. Unfortunately for real science (and for science writers!), its real explanations never come in the form of stories. Luckily for religion, it almost always comes in the form of stories. So religion has a huge psychological advantage in the struggle to convince people of the answers to the relentless questions.

Science has three things going for it that religion doesn't have. First, the facts that make any story true, when it is true, are to be found in equations, theories, models, and laws. Second, most of religion's best stories are false. Third, and most important, science shows that the stories we tell one another to explain our own and other people's actions and to answer the persistent questions are all based on a series of illusions. That should be enough to forestall our innate penchant for stories.

We won't spend any time showing that religion's most important stories are false, but the chapters that follow will build the case against stories teaching us anything important about reality, history, or ourselves. By the time you get to the last chapter, you will understand why, no matter how enjoyable a story is, it's never much more than a story. Scientism requires that we be able to see through the superficial charms of narrative, the specious sense of closure provided by happy (or even sad) endings, the feeling of relief from curiosity when dots are connected into a plausible conspiracy. We need to begin to disentangle ourselves from our species' love affair with stories. That's the first challenge for scientism.

We prefer our information to come in a package with a natural starting place, an exciting, tension-filled middle, topped off by a satisfying finish. We prefer stories with plots that make sense of the order of events by revealing their meanings. The plot reveals how the outcome resulted from the motives, plans, and purposes of the heroes and heroines, the villains, and the bystanders that strut across the story's stage. It's not just that we find stories easy to remember or that they excite our emotions or even that they satisfy the psychological itch of curiosity better than anything else. Our attachment to stories is much stronger and more mischievous. Experiments show that when information comes to us any other way, we have trouble understanding it, remembering it, and believing it. When we have a choice between buying into a story versus believing anything that can be expressed as a lab report or a computer program or a mathematical model, we'll take the story every time. Think about humanity's greatest hits (they also used to be among the Humanities' greatest hits before "the canon" took a hit): the *Odyssey, Hamlet, War and Peace, Middlemarch, Sophie's Choice*—great narratives, sources of meaning and wisdom, because they are stories that move us emotionally. Stories, and only stories, "sell."

Why are we suckers for stories? Why is it that despite their appeal, stories—even true ones—never really convey any deep understanding of anything? The answer requires some of the story-free science that is so hard to keep in mind—Darwin's theory of natural selection and the most basic laws of physics. Chapter 2 will provide some of the details, and Chapters 6–9 the rest. But we can sketch some of them here.

Everyone loves narratives, across all cultures and all times, and all that is needed is language—any language at all that humans speak. As we'll see in Chapter 5, our brain was shaped by natural selection to take on board very early in life, or maybe even innately, a set of guesses about how other people operate. The guesses eventually take the shape of a sort of theory about what people want, what they think is going on around them, and how those wants and beliefs work together to determine people's choices and actions. One reason to think that this "theory of mind" is almost innate is that infants begin to use it when they are only 6 or 7 months old. If it is not innate, then we are primed to learn it early in life with only very little experience. When we get to Chapters 6 and 7, we'll see what's profoundly wrong about this theory of mind and how and why consciousness seduces us into believing it anyway. Wrong or not, it was crucial to the evolution of *Homo sapiens* that we be equipped and predisposed to imbibe this theory at our mother's breasts if we didn't already know it at birth.

There are a few other species whose behavior shows that they have at least an incipient, basic theory of mind. Elephants, dolphins, and of course other primates treat one another in ways that strongly suggest that some device in their heads enables them to figure out and predict the behavior of others. It's a trait that goes along with large brain size and great intelligence. In our hominin ancestors, the ability to predict the behavior of others got better and better over the evolutionary time scale.

A theory of mind is part of nature's quick and dirty solution to a huge challenge for our species' survival—a "design problem" that faced our hominin ancestors over the last few million years. Given our puny size, our conspicuous lack of speed or strength, we would have been easy pickings for African megafauna (lions and tigers and bears, oh my). The only way we were going to survive was through cooperation, coordination, and collaboration: warning each other and ganging up to protect ourselves or chase the predators away so we could scavenge their kills. That requires the sort of rudimentary ability to predict other people's behavior that a theory of mind provides. It turns out that having a theory of mind is not having a set of thoughts about other organisms' beliefs and wants and how they shape their behavior. It's having a set of abilities as a result of the evolution and development of certain neural circuits. As the ability got more refined and enhanced by natural selection, our ancestors moved up the carnivore food chain until they had become the top predators everywhere.

When our ancestors lived in small family groups, predicting what family members were going to do made the difference between life and death and eventually between feast and famine. Later, when populations became large enough so that you were meeting strangers, there had to be further selection for the ability to predict behavior. In the evolutionary past, if other people could pose a threat, then you needed to know what they wanted to do to you so that you could prevent them from doing it. If other people could do something nice for you, you needed to figure out how to motivate them to do it. Predicting other people's actions is no easy matter. We're probably not much better at it than our late Pleistocene ancestors.

Long ago, these facts about the benefits and threats people pose to each other put further selective pressure on refining the theory of mind into a practice of plotting out other people's actions, to figure out their motives, their desires and goals, and their beliefs about how to realize them. There was, in effect, selection pressure on our ancestors that resulted in their telling themselves "whodunit" stories.

Natural selection uses carrots along with sticks to get its way. So, sooner or later, it started to reward the tactic of working out other people's motives by watching their actions. Doing so began to produce a pleasurable feeling of relief from curiosity or even from anxiety. That very special "aha!" feeling.

How did Mother Nature manage to match up good guesses about why people act the way they do with the satisfying experience of curiosity allayed? Roughly the same way it got us to think about sex all the time—by natural selection. Among our distant ancestors, some were hardwired to feel nothing when they had sex, some to feel a little pleasure, some to feel a lot. Some may have even felt some pain. Such variation is the way of the world. No prize for guessing which of these creatures had more offspring and which went extinct. After long enough, the only mammals left were the ones hardwired the way most of us are—to have orgasms during intercourse. The same goes for coupling together the ability to guess the plot and getting that feeling of curiosity satisfied.

Natural selection doesn't have time to wander through all the variations that might just randomly emerge, looking for the perfect solution to a survival problem. Instead it makes do with the first quick and dirty solution that comes along. In the time it would take to find a perfect solution, our ancestors would have all died out. In this case, natural selection hit on a solution that is imperfect in two different ways. On the one hand, the theory of mind it endowed our species with has profound limitations: Too often we are completely floored by the behavior of others. Our theory of mind fails in its job of enabling us to predict behavior. Our theory of mind also reflects another of natural selection's imperfections: To ensure survival, Mother Nature overshoots. Instead of building the exact solution to the problem of figuring out other people's motives, Mother Nature selected for people who see plots everywhere: *conspiracy theorists*. The simplest way to create someone who is good at reading motives from other people's behavior is to overdo it: endow them with a penchant for seeing motives everywhere—in human behavior and animal behavior, but also in the seasons, the weather, health and illness, the sunrise, lightning storms, earthquakes, droughts, beavers coming out of their lodges in the spring—everything.

Humans tend to see everything in nature as organized by agents with motives, often malevolent ones. We are all natural-born conspiracy theorists. That's why we don't need to be taught how to suss out other people's motives. That's why the same grand conspiracy theory operates in all cultures and why we can often appreciate stories from other cultures almost as much as our own. That's why we remember narratives and think of them as naturally easy to understand without any special knowledge or information. We all have a strong incentive to force anything we need to remember into a story with a plot. Once we make sense of a chain of events—by finding the motives of agents behind the events that make it into a story—we get that familiar feeling of relief from curiosity or anxiety about how the story turned out.

People have been making a sport of our insistence on seeing everything this way for a long time now. There is a famous joke about Talleyrand, the sinister foreign minister who managed to serve Louis XVI, then Napoleon, and then the restored French kings who followed him. When he died in 1838, the story goes that the Austrian foreign minister, Prince Metternich, asked himself, "I wonder what he meant by that."

A lot more of the details of why nature forced us to be conspiracy theorists are found in Chapter 6. But enough has been said here to see why we are not really psychologically satisfied by an explanation unless it's a good story. The drive to force events into the mold of a story with a plot is a hangover from our evolutionary past. That drive has been around for so long that it's practically hardwired into our brain.

It's unfortunate for science that no matter how imaginative we are, we just can't convey the content of science in stories with plots (even if we employ such convenient but misleading metaphors as "Mother Nature" and "design problem"). That makes the human penchant for stories the greatest barrier to understanding what science actually tells us about reality. At the same time, it is the slippery slope down which people slide into superstition.

It's Not Story Time Anymore

Real science isn't a set of stories, not even true ones, and it can't be packaged into stories either. Real science is much more a matter of blueprints, recipes, formulas, wiring diagrams, systems of equations, and geometrical proofs. That's why we have a hard time following it, understanding it, accepting it, applying it, or even remembering it. And that's why most people don't much like it either.

Science doesn't deny that it's sometimes important to get right what actually happened in the past. There are even some sciences in which the right chronology is crucial: biology, geology, even cosmology. They give us the sequence of events that actually happened: biologists need to know the order of events in evolution, geology can tell us about the process that made the continents, and cosmology chronicles the major events in the history of the universe since the big bang.

But these three kinds of history show us that in science the real work of explanation is not achieved by the chronology—the before and the after, the earlier and the later. The events that make up reality are ordered by processes that are completely reversible. With only one exception, the most basic laws of physics work the same way forward in time as backward. As far back as Isaac Newton's discoveries in the seventeenth century, scientists have recognized that the fundamental laws that stitch up every sequence of events—big and small—don't care about time order! That means that when it comes to science's understanding of reality, stories have to give way to equations, models, laws, and theories in which there is no preferred time order of events from earlier to later.

Think about how the dinosaurs became extinct. Over the last 50 years, a vast amount of evidence has revealed what really happened. The evidence from geology, paleontology, climate science, and several other independent lines of inquiry suggest that 65 million years ago, a large asteroid hit the Yucatán peninsula with the force of about 100 trillion tons of TNT and kicked up enough dust to produce several atmospheric changes that blocked the sunlight for at least a year. The result was the disappearance of most of the herbivorous dinosaurs' plant food, leading to their starvation. Then came the death of their carnivorous predators and their eventual conversion to petroleum. But what makes this the right story of why the dinosaurs disappeared? It's because the basic links in this chain of events are forged together by a set of fundamental laws of chemistry and physics. But these very same laws could have produced exactly the reverse sequence of events. It's perfectly compatible with the laws of motion—Newton's, Einstein's, even the laws of quantum mechanics—for each and every atom and molecule in the whole vast process to move in exactly the reverse direction. Starting from the petroleum, the atoms and molecules can move in trajectories that produce the dinosaurs from their rotting corpses, that grow the plants back from straw into bloom, that send the atmospheric dust clouds back down to fill up the crater in the Yucatán, and that reconstitute the asteroid and even push it back into space. I know it sounds absurd, but it's true. The basic laws of motion that govern everything that happens to everything in the universe work both ways. They are what hold everything together. They tell no stories because they are completely indifferent to which event is the beginning and which is the end, so long as the sequences are mirror images of one another. What's more, there is no story anyone can tell about why the basic laws are true.

Scientism doesn't have an easy task. Mother Nature built our minds for other purposes than understanding reality. She was trying to solve the problem of equipping us to work with one another. Solving that problem ensured that when it comes to the real nature of the world and our place in it, most people just wouldn't get it. That means that scientism's answers to life's persistent questions are going to be hard to accept, and not just because they come without a sugar coating. The answers science provides—based on time-reversible laws—just can't be turned into stories with plots. Scientism has to face the fact that most people aren't going to have the patience for the full answers that science gives to these questions.

Despite all that natural selection for preferring stories, some of us have managed to get past the biggest conspiracy theory of them all: the story of how God put us here. We have the capacity to break through and understand the real answers that science provides. The next chapter will begin the process, explaining why physics tells us everything we need to know about the nature of reality. Once we have a handle on the fundamental nature of reality, we'll then be able to see exactly how physics, by itself, makes the process Darwin discovered the only way that any life, and ultimately intelligent life, could have emerged in the universe. We'll learn why the purposelessness of the physical universe also pervades biology, neuroscience, social life, and even conscious thought. By the time we get to the end of this book, we'll see that science beats stories.

We'll have to accept that the answers to the relentless questions won't come packaged in a lot of stories. And understanding the answers won't produce that sudden relief from curiosity we all experience from a good bedtime story. But if we can work through the details, we'll get something much better—a real understanding of life, the universe, everything, warts and all.

HERE IS A BRIEF GUIDE to the landscape of scientism we will travel through on the way to the (story-free) scientific answers to the persistent questions. I'll admit here and now that sometimes the tour guide will break down and tell a story or two. Remember, when I do, it's just to help you remember things, not to help you understand them.

Scientism starts by taking physics seriously as the basic description of reality. Fortunately, we don't need to know much physics to answer our unrelenting questions. Even more fortunately, what we do need is relatively easy to understand and not at any risk of being overturned by future discoveries in physics. The slogan of Chapter 2, that the physical facts fix all the facts, will get repeated throughout the rest of the tour.

First, we see how these facts determine the biological ones, and then through biology, how physics fixes the rest of the facts about us.

Taking physics seriously has the surprising consequence that you have to accept Darwin's theory of natural selection as the only possible way that the appearance of purpose, design, or intelligence could have emerged anywhere in the universe. We'll see exactly why this is so and what this means for the persistent questions about the meaning of life in Chapters 3 and 4.

Scientism dictates a thoroughly Darwinian understanding of humans and of our evolution—biological and cultural. But that does not in any way commit us to thinking about human nature or human culture as hardwired, or in our genes. It does mean that when it comes to ethics, morality, and value, we have to embrace an unpopular position that will strike many people as immoral as well as impious. So be it. Chapter 6 takes the sting out of the charge, however, without denying its basic accuracy. If you are going to be scientistic, you will have to be comfortable with a certain amount of nihilism. But as we'll see, it's a nice sort of nihilism.

Adopting nihilism isn't even the hardest thing scientism will force on us. If physics fixes all the facts and fixes the biological ones via natural selection, then it will fix the psychological facts about us the same way. Consciousness tells us that we are exceptions to the physical world order, but science requires us to give up consciousness as a guide to the truth about us. Chapter 7 catalogs some of the empirical discoveries of the last 50 years that make this conclusion inescapable. Freed from the snares of introspection, in Chapters 8–10 we will be able to put together the whole "story," showing how our own mind seduces us into being relentless conspiracy theorists. The love of stories comes to us in a package that also includes the illusion of free will, the fiction of an enduring self, and the myth of human purpose. A scientistic worldview has to give up all of that. In exchange, at least you get correct answers to life's questions.

So, individual human life is meaningless, without a purpose, and without ultimate moral value. How about human history or human culture, civilization, or the advancement of our species as a whole? It's even easier for science to show that human history has no such trajectory than it is to show that individual lives lack one. Seeing why this is so is again really just a matter of working out how the physical facts, by fixing the biological and psychological processes, also fix the social, political, economic, and broadly cultural ones, too. This makes history bunk, as Chapter 11 headlines.

It's true that scientism asks us to surrender a lot of complacent beliefs in exchange for the correct answers to the persistent questions. If this seems hard to take, the last chapter cushions the blow, showing that we can surrender all the illusions of common sense, religion, and new-age and traditional mystery mongering, along with the meretricious allure of storytelling; indeed, physics, chemistry, biology, and neurology have shaped most of us to survive very nicely without them. And just in case, there's always Prozac.

Chapter 2

◆

THE NATURE OF REALITY: THE PHYSICAL FACTS FIX ALL THE FACTS

IF WE'RE GOING TO BE SCIENTISTIC, THEN WE HAVE to attain our view of reality from what physics tells us about it. Actually, we'll have to do more than that: we'll have to embrace physics as *the whole truth about reality*.

Why buy the picture of reality that physics paints? Well, it's simple, really. We trust science as the only way to acquire knowledge. That is why we are so confident about atheism. The basis of our confidence, ironically, is the *fallibility* of scientists as continually demonstrated by other scientists. In science, nothing is taken for granted. Every significant new claim, and a lot of insignificant ones, are sooner or later checked and almost never completely replicated. More often, they are corrected, refined, and improved on—assuming the claims aren't refuted altogether. Because of this error-reducing process, the further back you go from the research frontier, the more the claims have been refined, reformulated, tested, and grounded. Grounded where? In physics.

Everything in the universe is made up of the stuff that physics tells us fills up space, including the spaces that we fill up. And physics can tell us how everything in the universe works, in principle and in practice, better than anything else. Physics catalogs all the basic kinds of things that there are and all the things that can happen to them.

The basic things everything is made up of are fermions and bosons. That's it. Perhaps you thought the basic stuff was electrons, protons, neutrons, and maybe quarks. Besides those particles, there are also leptons, neutrinos, muons, tauons, gluons, photons, and probably a lot more elementary particles that make up stuff. But all these elementary particles come in only one of two kinds. Some of them are fermions; the rest are bosons. There is no third kind of subatomic particle. And everything is made up of these two kinds of things. Roughly speaking, fermions are what matter is composed of, while bosons are what fields of force are made of.

Fermions and bosons. All the processes in the universe, from atomic to bodily to mental, are purely physical processes involving fermions and bosons interacting with one another. Eventually, science will have to show the details of how the basic physical processes bring about us, our brain, and our behavior. But the broad outlines of how they do so are already well understood.

Physics is by no means "finished." But the part of it that explains almost everything in the universe—including us—*is* finished, and much of it has been finished for a century or more. This includes all the physics that we are going to need. Nothing at the unsettled frontiers of physics challenges the parts we're going to make use of. What's more, the physics we need is easy to understand, certainly far easier than quantum mechanics, general relativity, or string theory.

WHY TRUST PHYSICS?

Before getting to the physics that we need, we should get clear about our reasons for attaching so much confidence to it. Why suppose that all the other facts about the world are just complex combinations of physical facts?

For the last 350 years, physics has been has been telling us more and more about the world, both at the level of the cosmological—stars, black holes, galaxies—and at the level of the microphysical—the fermions and bosons. It has continually revealed realms of nature that we had no reason to expect existed. It has told us how those realms affect us with a degree of accuracy that is breathtaking. The latest physical theories explain and predict what happens in regions of space and time that are so small that further division seems pointless or impossible. They do the same for quantities of space-time that are so large that we cannot gauge their enormity. Mostly we take for granted the startling precision of physics' predictive power across an amazing range of phenomena. Few people realize that physical theory explains and predicts almost everything to inconceivably precise values over the entire body of data available. Few are prepared to see exactly how, from a small number of laws, physics can neatly explain the whole trajectory of the universe and everything in it. The reach of physics runs from before the initial big bang and "inflationary" expansion of the universe 13.7 billion years ago to its end a 100 billion years from now. And yet its theories, along with the scenario they mandate, are confirmed more and more strongly by every new scientific instrument we send into space and by every new linear accelerator that goes online underground (even if it breaks down the first couple of times it's switched on, like the Large Hadron Collider in Geneva).

Physics has been demonstrating its explanatory, predictive,

and technological power for quite a long time now, since about 1660, when Newton got things rolling, and it has been proving its powers at an accelerating rate over the last century. It's not just that physics predicts what will happen to more and more decimal places. Physics has been predicting completely unexpected events, processes, and phenomena for a hundred years or more.

For example, scientifically sophisticated people may have first heard of black holes a few decades ago. We sometimes forget that Einstein's general theory of relativity predicted their existence in 1917. And while some people know about antimatter, few realize that in 1929, long before there was any evidence for its existence, a physicist named Paul Dirac showed that there had to be antimatter just by looking at the equations expressing the quantum physics of electrons. It's a surprise to people that the solid-state physics underlying every computer chip in our houses, cars, and mobile phones dates back to the 1930s and '40s. And only physics groupies know or care that quantum electrodynamics predicts the mass and charge of subatomic particles to 12 decimal places. As Richard Feynman famously noted, that's like predicting the distance between New York and Los Angeles to the accuracy of one hair's width. And of course, physics has built most of the tools that the other natural sciences employ to expand their grasp on nature—X-rays, electron microscopes, spectrographs, DNA sequencers and gene chips, radio telescopes, fMRI brain readers, and supercomputers that can beat most people at *Jeopardy!*, just to tick off the obvious ones. The technological success of physics is by itself enough to convince anyone with anxiety about scientism that if physics isn't "finished," it certainly has the broad outlines of reality well understood.

The physicist's picture of the universe is the one on which all bets should be placed. The bets are not only that it's correct as far as it goes, but that it will eventually go all the way and be *com-*

pletely correct. When finished, it will leave nothing out as unexplained from physical first principles (besides those principles themselves). And it's not just the correctness of the predictions and the reliability of technology that requires us to place our confidence in physics' description of reality. Because physics' predictions are so accurate, the methods that produced the description must be equally reliable. Otherwise, our technological powers would be a miracle. We have the best of reasons to believe that the methods of physics—combining controlled experiment and careful observation with mainly mathematical requirements on the shape theories can take—are the right ones for acquiring *all* knowledge. Carving out some area of "inquiry" or "belief" as exempt from exploration by the methods of physics is special pleading or self-deception.

It took the nineteenth and twentieth centuries to show not only that physics is correct about the basic stuff and how it works, but to begin to uncover the details of how the basic stuff can explain everything about all the rest of reality, including biology.

Remember the periodic table from your high school chemistry class? The nineteenth-century Russian chemist Dmitri Mendeleev came up with this table. But how could we be sure that Mendeleev got it right? His taxonomy of the fundamental elements was shown to be correct by physics, by the atomic theory and the electron theory that physicists discovered in the first half of the twentieth century. Atomic theory showed why each element had to have exactly the place in the table Mendeleev gave it as a result of the number of protons, electrons, and neutrons its atoms contain. For a hundred years or so, chemists had been painstakingly weighing and measuring the amounts of each element needed to make a compound. Suddenly all those recipes emerged from the numbers of electrons an atom of each element contains. Physics explains chemistry.

And chemistry explains biology. Respiration, reproduction, muscle movement, the nervous system, heredity and development—all of these components of our biology are now well understood as chemical processes, and these in turn are understood as physical processes. The history of the Nobel Prize in Physiology or Medicine, as it is formally called, along with the one in chemistry, is a century-long catalog of awards to scientists who have figured out which physical and chemical facts fix all those wonderfully complicated biological facts that constitute life.

On his television series in the 1970s, astronomer Carl Sagan used to say that we are all "star stuff." Though he was ridiculed for it, he was of course exactly right: the human body is nothing but complex arrangements of "billions and billions" of atoms; and every atom in every one of our bodies was produced by reactions deep inside stars light-years away from Earth. These reactions have been chugging out the chemical elements for 13 billion years now. We literally are all just part of a physical universe. It's a universe in which everything happens as a result of pushes and pulls of bits of matter and fields of force that physics understands almost completely and in enough quantitative detail to enable us to build space stations, pacemakers, robot vacuum cleaners, molecular soccer balls, and artificial chromosomes.

The phenomenal accuracy of its prediction, the unimaginable power of its technological application, and the breathtaking extent and detail of its explanations are powerful reasons to believe that physics is the whole truth about reality. As for the rest of reality above the subatomic, all we need to know is what things are physically composed of and how the parts are arranged in order to explain and predict their behavior to equal detail and precision. That goes for people, too.

Physics is *causally closed* and *causally complete*. The only causes in the universe are physical, and everything in the universe that has a cause has a physical cause. In fact, we can go further and confidently assert that the physical facts *fix* all the facts.

Let's unpack that slogan—*The physical facts fix all the facts.* It means that the physical facts constitute or determine or bring about all the rest of the facts. Here's a graphic way of thinking about it. There is some corner of space-time far from here and now, so far in fact that light signals have not yet reached us from that corner of the universe. Imagine that by some cosmic coincidence, every molecule, every atom in that distant region just happens to be arranged in a distribution or configuration that is a perfect duplicate of the current distribution of the molecules and atoms in our own corner of the universe—the region of Earth and its moon. So we are to imagine two distinct regions of the universe many millions of light-years apart, each several hundred thousand miles across, that are physically identical, fermion by fermion and boson by boson.

With these two regions in mind, we can see what it means for the physical facts to fix all the facts—including the chemical, biological, psychological, social, economic, political, and other human facts. In the distant duplicate of our Earth-and-moon region, there are also animals and people, cities and shops, libraries full of books, paintings on the walls and refrigerators full of food, in every way physically indistinguishable from our own region of space-time. It would have to be the case that the distant arrangement of all the molecules, atoms, and their parts would also have to have a duplicate in it for everything that exists in our world. This must include every single biological creature, every human being, with all the same relationships in it that exist here and now in our own corner of the universe. What is more, since each of the brains of all the inhabitants of this distant world have to be identical to one and only one of the brains in this world, they would have all the same emotions, attitudes, and memories (or the feeling that they remembered) that the brains in our world have.

That distant region would have to be *exactly* like ours, no matter what the actual history of that distant chunk of matter and energy had been up to just before the moment of perfect duplication. It would have to be a duplicate of our region of space even if it had been organized and synthesized in a few moments of random fluctuation as opposed to the 4 billion years it took to produce us and our memories. A perfect physical duplicate of our world would have to be a perfect chemical, biological, neurological, psychological, social, economic, and political duplicate, too. It would have to—if the physical facts fix all the facts.

Before you reject this idea of a physically duplicate region of space-time, there are two observations to be made. First, no one is saying this really happens—ever. We are using this idea to illustrate what we mean when we say that the physical facts in our little corner of the universe (and every little corner, for that matter), fix, determine, establish, create, bring about, generate (or whatever word you want to use) all the other facts about it—including the biological, psychological, and social ones that obtain here and now.

Second, as a disquieting aside, the idea that there *might be* a duplicate corner of a distant part of the vast universe is, I regret to say, something that a number of cosmologists actually think is physically possible and has a nonzero probability (try Googling "Boltzmann brains"). Take the arrangement of all the atoms that compose your body and, in particular, your brain. If our actual universe is infinitely large, there is a tiny probability that all the fundamental particles in some other distant but finite part of it will, just by chance, take on exactly the same arrangement as the atoms that make up your brain right now. If the universe is infinitely large, there are an infinite number of such regions, each with a tiny nonzero probability of duplicating your brain. When you add up an infinite number of such infinitesimally small but positive probabilities, the sum has to approach 1. Ergo, for any brain that exists around here and that has, for example, consciousness, it's an almost 100 percent chance that there is a duplicate arrangement of molecules somewhere else in the universe having exactly the same conscious thoughts. Of course, if the universe is not infinite but just huge, the probability of a duplicate of you somewhere else will be smaller.

So the argument goes. I am not going to take sides on this cosmological speculation. All I can say is that it gives the philosopher's use of science fiction a good name.

THE SECOND LAW OF THERMODYNAMICS ... AND YOU

Scientism commits us to physics as the complete description of reality. But what exactly does it tell us about the answers to our persistent questions? Almost everything. The fundamental piece of physics that we need in order to answer the persistent questions is the second law of thermodynamics. Physics has accepted this law throughout all the developments of the discipline since its discovery in the nineteenth century. It is a law that much in physics—including all of relativity and quantum mechanics—has continued to support and that nothing in physics—be it ever so shocking—has challenged. Here we'll take a little time to try to explain what the second law says and how it relates to the rest of physics and our inevitable questions about life, the universe, and everything in between.

The usual way to put physics across is to tell a story about how the second law was discovered in the 1800s. Start by making some noises about the age-long quest to understand heat; sketch the ancient physics of the four elements—earth, air, fire, and water; then invoke the "caloric" theory of heat as a very fine fluid that flows from hot things to cool ones; after that comes Lavoisier's idea that heat is a substance that can mix with ice to produce water; next bring in Count Rumford from stage right (Germany) showing that horses going round and round turning huge drill-bits to bore cannon barrels would also boil buckets full of water left on top of the cannons; until at last William Thomson becomes Lord Kelvin for figuring out that in a gas, at least, heat is just the motion of molecules. But science isn't stories, and no story can teach the second law of thermodynamics. Let's do enough of the science to get a grip on it.

The second law tells us that in any region of space left to itself, differences in the amount of energy will very, very, very probably even out until the whole region is uniform in energy, in temperature, in disorder. Suppose you are trying to pump air into your flat bicycle tire. You attach the hose to the valve on the tire and start to pump. Notice the increasing resistance as you push the handle down. The sources of that resistance are the air molecules being pressed together into a small space at the bottom of the pump. And of course some are entering the tire through the narrow opening where the hose connects to the tire. If you keep pumping, the bottom of the pump gets warmer and warmer to the touch. This increased heat is the molecules moving around faster and faster, bumping into one another and into the container walls more and more as a result of your pushing them. The cause of this increase in warmth is the same as the cause of the increased resistance to the handle: the air molecules are bouncing against the sides and bottom of the pump faster and more frequently as you push them into a more and more confined space. If you closed off the hose to the tire, you would soon be unable to overcome the push-back of the air molecules in the small space at the bottom of the pump. They would be more than a match for the strength of your arms. In fact, if you let go of the handle at the bottom, it would rise a bit, being pushed up by the air molecules, allowing the space in which the molecules move to increase. The handle would not go up as high as it was at the beginning of your last downstroke, however. Some of your downstroke effort will have been wasted.

The reason some of your effort gets wasted is easy to see. Not all of the molecules you pushed down have hit the bottom and bounded straight back up at the piston head. Some of the molecules were not headed down to the bottom when you started to pump; some bumped into one another or headed to the sides of the pump instead. So some of that energy that your pumping added to each molecule will not be sent back toward the handle when you stop pressing. This energy is just wasted, and that is the second law of thermodynamics at work.

Whenever heat—that is, the motion of molecules—does any useful work, some of the heat is wasted. In fact, wasting energy is the ruling principle of this universe, and that is the second law. To see why, suppose you squeeze all the air molecules in the pump into a single layer at the bottom of it, or as close as you can get to a single layer. Now let go of the handle. It goes up, of course, as the air molecules come bouncing off the bottom. As they do, the molecules will spread out evenly throughout the cylinder, or at least it's fantastically probable that they will do so. Suppose there are a million air molecules at the bottom of the pump. When they push the pump piston up and spread out evenly in the cylinder, there will be many more than a million times a million different ways the 1 million air molecules can be arranged throughout the cylinder. All of these arrangements are equally possible. And of course there is no reason why the molecules will end up distributed evenly throughout the cylinder except that an even distribution is the most probable one. The starting point, when all the molecules are flat against the bottom of the cylinder, is one of the most *improbable* distributions of air molecules in the pump. The second law tells us that in our universe, the arrangement of everything goes from more improbable distributions (with more useful energy) to less improbable ones (with less useful energy). And the same goes for any self-contained part of the universe.

The more improbable distributions are the ones that are more neatly arranged, better organized, than others. The less improbable distributions are the more disorderly, less organized ones. The most probable distribution of matter and energy in the universe is the completely even distribution of everything. This is the one in which there is no region left with more energy, more order than others. The even distribution of energy and disorder in the universe is the state toward which, according to the second law, everything is moving, some places slower, some places faster, but almost inexorably. This evening-out of things—from molecules to galaxies—from less probable to more probable distributions is the rule of the universe. Increasing disorganization is inevitable, or almost so.

The physicist's term for disorder is *entropy*. The entropy of a region measures how much order there is in the region. But it measures orderliness backward, because the more disorganized a region, the higher its entropy. The second law says that entropy, or disorder, almost always increases. The "almost" is important. Lord Kelvin thought that the second law was a strict statement of invariable entropy increase. Thanks to the work of three nineteenth-century geniuses—James Clerk Maxwell, Ludwig Boltzmann, and J. Willard Gibbs—the increase in entropy has been recognized to be only very, very, very probable, not everywhere and not always inevitable. It's barely possible (but extremely improbable) that the cream poured into a cup of coffee will stay right where it hits the coffee and not spread out. All that is needed is that the cream molecules collide with the coffee molecules and with each other in such a way that one after another they bounce back in the direction they came from instead of wandering out into the hot liquid. Possible, but very, very, very improbable.

The second law can't be a statement of the absolute inevitability of increasingly disordered states everywhere and always. It requires only the extremely probable increase of entropy from moment to moment in a closed system—the whole universe or some isolated part of it. Of course, in this universe there are some areas of very low entropy: the insides of stars, the cylinder heads of gas-guzzling internal combustion engines, and of course the highly organized biological systems on this planet—from single cells to plants to us, for example. These are not counterexamples to the second law. Nor are they just some of the improbable outcomes that it permits. These are regions of the universe in which the maintenance of order is being paid for by using much more energy to produce the orderly things than the amount of order they produce or store. Each region of local order is part of a bigger region in which there is almost always a net increase in entropy. Take, for example, a reference library whose books are put back in the right place every night. The amount of energy needed to restore order is always greater than the amount used up in creating disorder, but thanks to the input of organized energy by librarians, the next day it's ready to be disordered all over again. As we'll see, most biological order is preserved for long periods, but at the cost of vast increases in disorder elsewhere.

Now, it is crucial to note a significant feature of the second law. Unlike the other basic laws of nature, it's asymmetrical. It tells us that when it comes to the amount of entropy in a region, and in the universe as a whole, the future is different from the past. Future states of the universe will almost always be different from past ones because entropy (disorder) very, very, very probably increases as time goes on. The second law is fundamentally different from all the other basic laws of physics that govern reality. All the other fundamental laws of the universe are *time symmetrical*. They work just as well to determine the order of events back in time as they do forward in time. Every process in the universe is reversible—except entropy increases.

Here are a couple of simple examples of this symmetry: You can predict all the solar eclipses to come. But you can also "post-dict" or "retrodict" all the solar eclipses there have ever been. Film the motions of the balls on a billiard table after the initial break: one is struck and starts a chain of balls successively striking other balls. Now run the film backward. Nothing unexpected, funny, or weird will leap out at you. After a while, you won't even remember which was the rewind and which was the forward direction of events. Any trajectory, or path, taken by a set of atoms or molecules is reversible. It can run back the other way in accordance with the same laws of motion. Except for the second law, all the basic laws of physics allow the past states of things to be fixed as much by their future states as they allow future states to be fixed by past states. And if the facts about atoms and molecules fix all the other facts, then any process can go both ways—including the painting of the Sistine chapel. When viewed as a whole bunch of trajectories of individual paint molecules, they could have gone from the ceiling back into the paint pots—*could have* except for the second law. All the other laws of physics will allow it. The same goes for our example of the extinction of the dinosaurs in Chapter 1. Except for its entropy increase, it could have gone in the other direction.

Hard to believe, but the second law is where the direction of time, its asymmetry, comes from. It cannot come from anywhere else in physics. By process of elimination, the time order of events from earlier to later is a consequence of the second law. The universe started in a highly improbable state—an incredibly hot, highly energetic sphere smaller than a Ping-Pong ball—and then expanded into a ball that was no bigger than an orange when it was a millionth of a second old and has been spreading out ever since. With each second, it has attained a more and more probable state, and so have almost all of the regions of space within the universe, no matter how small they are. Had the universe started in a highly disorganized state, one of the most probable distributions of matter, energy, and heat, it would have moved to other states of equally high probability, states in which all the mass in the universe is spread out evenly, along with all the energy and heat.

All this means that the second law is really the result of applying the symmetrical "forward or backward" laws to the universe at its starting place, which just happens to have been very orderly, very concentrated, and very small. The result was the spreading out and cooling off that is, and will be, the history of our universe.

So long as our best physics tells us that the other fundamental laws are symmetrical and that the universe started in a highly improbable, very energetic, concentrated state, it is going to behave as the second law says it does. This will also hold for all the regions of the universe as well. In the short run, there will be some regions of space, like your body, where energy is stored and not immediately wasted. But in the long run and as the regions of space under consideration enlarge, the probability of energy loss will approach certainty as closely as anything can.

Of course, we experience time as a fixed past, an instantaneous present, and an unfixed future. In our experience, things can only happen in one direction: a match can't go from being put out to being lit to being struck. But at the basement level of reality, the opposite of any sequence of events can and does happen. Given the present state of the universe, the basic laws of physics can't determine in which temporal direction we are headed. You can't read off which way is past and which way is future from these laws and the sequence of events can go in either direction from the present. At least none of the basic laws of physics do this except for one: the second law of thermodynamics. It makes a difference between earlier times and later times: the later it gets, the more entropy, or disorder, there is. In fact, the second law creates the direction of time from earlier to later.

No Room among the Physical Facts for Purpose or Design

With that, we can turn to some of the persistent questions that physics answers.

Where did the universe come from, how long ago, and where is it going? These are questions to which physicists are getting more and more precise answers, both through cosmology—studying the universe as a whole—and through high-energy physics—studying the basic building blocks of matter and fields that had to exist at the beginning of the universe. There is general agreement that the current universe began with a big bang about 13.75 ± 0.11 billion years ago (and every few years cosmologists increase the precision of the date by another decimal point). As noted, it started out as something smaller than a Ping-Pong ball, and a lot denser, but then expanded. Once it got to orange-size, something happened called "inflation," and during the next 300,000 years, all the subatomic particles—the fermions and bosons—were formed and matter started to take shape in the form of hydrogen atoms. Even now, 13.69 billion years later, there is still a great deal of evidence for these events left in the cosmic background radiation. In any direction we point microwave detectors, the amount they detect is always the same except for one small region of slightly greater intensity—the source of the big bang. The better our detection gear, the more we learn about the big bang by examining its debris. What's more, the recent evidence, from other kinds of radiation from distant galaxies, suggests not only that space is still expanding, but that the expansion is accelerating . . . with no end in sight.

So reality is an unimaginably large number of stars. By the fall of 2010, the best estimate was 70,000,000,000,000,000,000,000 of them (that's 7×10^{21} stars, 70 sextillion) clumped together in galaxies—125 billion of them, all moving away from each other in every direction at vast speeds that are getting ever faster. Recent astronomical observations of the most distant regions of space suggest the number might be three times higher.

Where did the big bang come from? The best current theory suggests that our universe is just one universe in a "multiverse"—a vast number of universes, each bubbling up randomly out of the foam on the surface of the multiverse, like so many bubbles in the bathwater, each one the result of some totally random event. Some pop immediately. Others expand for a while till they pop. Still others keep expanding. The ones that pop immediately are unstable: the values of their basic physical constants don't allow them to last very long or even get started. Other universes last longer.

Our universe is one whose basic physical constants—the gravitational constant, the size of the positive and negative charges on electrons and protons, the ratio of the strong, weak, and electromagnetic forces—have allowed it to last a long time (by our standards). It still shows no sign of collapsing. It has been around long enough to produce its 70 sextillion stars after about 13 billion years. On one minor rock circling one below-average star, it resulted in us *Homo sapiens* and some other stuff. One remarkable thing about this best current cosmological theory is the degree to which physicists have been able to subject it to many empirical tests, including tests of its claims about things that happened even before the big bang, let alone before the formation of Earth, our sun, or even our galaxy, the Milky Way. One of the most striking was the successful prediction of where to look for radiation from stars that went supernova and exploded as far back as 10 billion years ago. These tests came out so favorably to the big-bang theory that physicists decided to risk several billion euros on the Large Hadron Collider at CERN (the European Organization for Nuclear Research), outside Geneva, to test the big-bang theory directly by creating the very conditions that occurred just after the big bang.

The multiverse theory seems to provide an opportunity seized upon by wishful thinkers, theologians, and their fellow travelers among the physicists and philosophers. First they ask, "If our universe is just one of many in a multiverse, where did the multiverse come from? And where did the multiverse's cause come from, and where did *its* cause come from?" And so on, ad infinitum. Once they have convinced themselves and others that this series of questions has no stopping point in physics, they play what they imagine is a trump card, a question whose only answer they think has to be the God hypothesis.

It is certainly true that if physics has to move back farther and farther in the regress from universe to multiverse to something that gave rise to the multiverse, to something even more basic than that, it will never reach any point labeled "last stop, all off" (or rather "starting point" for all destinations). By the same token, if it has to move down to smaller and more fundamental components of reality than even fermions or bosons, it won't ever know whether it has reached the "basement level" of reality. At this point, the theologians and mystery-mongering physicists play their trump card. It doesn't matter whether there are infinite regresses in these two lines of inquiry or finite ones. Either way, they insist, physics can't answer the question, Why is there anything at all? or as the question is famously put, Why is there something rather than nothing?

Physics, especially quantum physics, shows that the correct answer to this question is: No reason, no reason at all. Things could have turned out differently. There could have been nothing at all. Our universe is just one of those random events that "sometimes" occur and at other "times" don't ("times" in quotes because quantum cosmology is going to eventually explain time, along with space, as a feature generated by the multiverse). The same goes for fermions and bosons. Their existence is just the way the cookie of quantum randomness crumbled. The fundamental constituents of matter and fields could have turned out differently. They could have been the antimatter versions of these particles. There could have been nothing at all. Why is that?

A hundred years ago, it became clear that most events at the level of the subatomic are random, uncaused, indeterministic quantum events—merely matters of probability. Locate an electron on one side of a steel barrier it doesn't have the energy to penetrate. There is some probability that the next time you detect it, the electron will be on the other side of the barrier it can't penetrate. But there are no facts about the electron that explain why sometimes it does this and sometimes it doesn't. At the basement level of reality, there are just probabilities. In the last 30 years, physicists have increasingly been able to translate the randomness and indeterminism of the subatomic particles into weird quantum behavior by tabletop-sized apparatus so that it can be detected on the laboratory bench. Since the big bang is just such a quantum event, it, too, is a wholly indeterministic one. It is an event that just springs up out of the multiverse's foam of universes without any cause at all. Why is there a universe at all? No reason at all. Why is there a multiverse in which universes pop into existence for no reason at all? No reason at all! It's just another quantum event. What science and scientism tell those who hanker for more is "Get over it!"

Dissatisfaction with this answer is practically built into our genes. As Chapter 1 sketched and Chapters 5–7 will make clear, conspiracy theorizing was bred in our bones. That makes it difficult to accept the right answer to the "Why is there something rather than nothing" question. Combine the psychologically natural refusal to take "No reason" for an answer and the fact that physics faces the prospect of a regress of ever more prior causes and ever more fundamental particles, and the question gets asked with increasing urgency: *Why is there something rather than nothing?*

Into the vacuum of psychologically satisfying answers to this question steps the Goldilocks theory, aka the anthropic principle. Why did the multiverse come into being? So that the universe could come into being. Why did the universe come into being? In order to produce us. And of course we know who arranged matters this way, blessed be his name. The universe was brought into existence and arranged to be hospitable to man . . . uh, make that humans. Whence the name *anthropic principle*. It's also called the Goldilocks theory because it cites as evidence for the presence of purpose in the universe's existence the fact that the basic physical constants of our universe are "just right" for us. If the constants are just right for human life, they must have been arranged that way on purpose. The gravitational constant, the strength of the strong, weak, and electromagnetic forces, the charge on the electron are not too strong, not too weak, but "just right"—finetuned to make human life as we know it possible. Had they been even slightly different, we couldn't have happened. And that's the evidence for the anthropic principle, for the theory that there is something rather than nothing owing to some very, very, very powerful agent's purposes, plans, or designs. (The universe and multiverse turn out to be a conspiracy of one.)

Physics ruled out this sort of reasoning right at the start of its success. Ever since physics hit its stride with Newton, it has excluded purposes, goals, ends, or designs in nature. It firmly bans all explanations that are *teleological* (from the Greek *telos*, meaning "end" or "goal" or "purpose" that some process aims at or is good at achieving). At each of the obstacles to its development, physics could have helped itself to purpose or design. No explanation of heat in Newton's laws? God must have added heat in separately. Why do electric fields produce magnetic fields and vice versa? God's clever design. Gravity is so mysterious, the way it moves through total vacuums at infinite speed and penetrates any barrier at all. How come? God made it that way to keep us from floating away from the ground.

Theories about purposes at work in the universe could have gotten physics off the hook every time it faced a challenge. But physicists have always refused to shirk the hard work of crafting theory that increases explanatory precision and predictive application. Since Newton 350 years ago, it has always succeeded in providing a nonteleological theory to deal with each of the new explanatory and experimental challenges it has faced. That track record is tremendously strong evidence for concluding that its still-unsolved problems will submit to nonteleological theories.

There are several such outstanding problems that physics faces. Among the empirical ones are the problems of "dark matter" and "dark energy"; the universe is expanding much faster than it would if all the matter and energy in it were the stuff we can currently detect. In fact, its actual rate of expansion could only be driven by many times more matter and energy than our instruments can locate. This is a big problem for experimental physicists and for astronomers. Then there is the huge theoretical problem: the two best theories in physics, the ones most accurate in their predictions—general relativity and quantum mechanics—are incompatible. They disagree on such basic matters as what happens when two particles come into contact. No one has yet figured out a more general theory that will combine the strengths of both theories.

No matter how physics eventually deals with these problems, there are two things we can be sure of. In solving them, physics will not give up the second law. And it will not give up the ban on purpose or design. That goes for the universe, the multiverse, or whatever gave rise to them. It also holds for anything it may discover more fundamental than fermions and bosons. Physics' long track record of successes is the strongest argument for the exclusion of purpose or design from its account of reality.

The banishment of purpose and the operation of the second law go together to a certain extent. A purpose is some goal or an end out there in the future for which events taking place earlier are a means of some kind, and these earlier events occur at least in part because they are a means to their ends. The second part—that the purpose or goal is part of what brings about its means—is crucial to anything being a purpose. It's hard to see how there could be purposes or teleology in a physical universe governed by the second law. To begin with, the second law tells us that the universe is headed to complete disorder. For the universe as a whole, the only end state is its heat death. It will be a flat, energyless jumble of patternlessness, at which everything will be a uniform temperature—probably somewhere near 273 degrees below zero Celsius. No purpose or goal can be secured permanently under such circumstances. Besides, if purposes were things out there in the future guiding processes in the past, we'd have another asymmetry competing with the second law's asymmetry:

purposes out there in the distant future and none back there at the beginning of things. That asymmetry is something else physics won't allow without at least as good an explanation as the second law has. What is worse, unless every future goal is somehow paid for by an increase in entropy in its neighborhood, its existence would violate the second law itself. And if it looks like some purposeful arrangement is paid for by net entropy increase, then maybe the whole process, one part of which looks like a purpose, is really just a well-disguised but purely physical process. (Hold that thought till we turn to biology.)

We might be able to avoid the incompatibility of teleology with the second law if those future states—the ends toward which physical processes are supposed be the means—could somehow be "written into" the past. "Writing" a purpose or future goal into the past is how designs work. The future state thus has a great deal to do with explaining the earlier means that bring it about. That's what qualifies it as a purpose. Then there could be physical processes that are "directed" by these earlier designs to achieve the designs. That way there could be future purposes bringing about past events as their means. An imaginative idea, but the only way this could happen is if there really were, out there in space, free-floating designs for the future, thoughts about how things were going to be arranged and how to organize the means to bring them about. These free-floating thoughts have to control physical processes to attain their aims—a sort of psycho-kinesis, spoon bending on a cosmic scale. But that wouldn't be enough. For there to be thoughts anywhere in the universe carrying around designs for the future, there are going to have be those Boltzmann brains all over the place, too. For one chunk of matter (say, a blueprint) to be a design for another chunk of matter (perhaps the house it is the blueprint of), there has already got to be a mind around to be the designer, the architect, to interpret the lines and squiggles. This is one point the famous "watchmaker" argument from design for God's existence got right. No chunk of matter (lines and squiggles) can just by itself be about another chunk of matter (bricks and mortar, arranged house-wise), without a mind to interpret the first chunk of matter as being *about* the second chunk.

Now physics tells us that for most of the first 13.69 billion years of this universe, there was nothing but fermions, bosons, and the atoms being made out of them inside stars (nothing more complicated than uranium atoms). Minds (that is, brains) have to be made up of fermions and bosons. However, they are much more complicated arrangements of fermions and bosons than a uranium atom. No brains, no Boltzmann brains. Without even a single Boltzmann brain around at the beginning of the big bang or for the next several billion years, designs and purposes couldn't get off the ground and do anything. If the only sapient life in the universe is ours, physics can't invoke minds in its explanations of anything until matters have proceeded at least 13.69 billion years after the big bang. (Even if there were minds in the universe before we came into the picture, it wouldn't help, as we'll see in Chapters 8–10.)

Let's be absolutely clear: no teleology, no purposes, goals, or ends. For that matter, no free-floating thoughts carrying around designs. Scientism cannot emphasize this self-denying ordinance of physics more strongly.

So, the answer to the persistent question, *What is the purpose of the universe?* is quite simply: There is none.

Why does our universe have the laws of nature and the physical parameters that make intelligent life possible? With an indefinitely large number of different universes being created all the time, some of them will just happen to have the mix of things and forces that brings us about. To demand any more of an answer than that is like winning a lottery and demanding to know why you won. Every ticket holder had the same chance. Someone had to win. It was you. End of story. (Stories again!)

EVEN IF WE accept physics' explanation of reality and the absence of purpose in the physical facts, we might still wonder if the emergence of living, sentient, and even sometimes sapient creatures like us can *put* purpose into a universe otherwise devoid of meaning. Seeing whether life can do this in a universe otherwise devoid of purpose will require some biology, of course.

Biology is usually a lot more fun that physics. It's a lot easier to understand, and there's sex. But no one should get their hopes up that its answers will be any more accommodating to the wishful thinkers or mystery mongers among us. It turns out that Darwin banished real purposes from the realm of the living as thoroughly as Newton drove it out of physical reality.

Chapter 3

◆◉◆

How Physics
Fakes Design

THE TEMPLETON FOUNDATION WAS CREATED BY John Templeton, a billionaire who managed international mutual funds. The foundation mainly supports academics and especially scientists who seek to reconcile religion with science. So the Templeton Foundation gives a single prize of 1,000,000 pounds sterling (a lot more than the Nobel Prize) every year to some worthy scientist or savant for "affirming life's spiritual dimension . . . through insight, discovery, or practical works." That worthy person usually turns out to be a physicist (almost never a biologist, for reasons that will become obvious) who has aided and abetted the reconciliation of science and God. Sometimes it's done by trading on the present incomplete state of physics, other times by invoking quantum indeterminism, and in a few cases by appealing to unintelligible mysteries. There's no chance that candidates for the prize will ever be in short supply.

In late 2007, there was apparently enough money left over after giving the 1,000,000 pound prize for the Templeton Foundation to take out a double-page ad in the *New York Times*. At the top in bold was the question, *Does the universe have a purpose?* and there followed the beginnings of 12 answers (all continued on a website): 6 yes votes, mainly from scientists (but no biologist), 3 noes, an "I hope so," and a couple of not sures.

But as we saw in the last chapter, the issue is not in doubt if you have any confidence in science. The banishment of purpose from the universe as a whole also provides for the banishment of purposes that are supposed to make sense of human and other biological activities. When physics disposed of purposes, it did so for biology as well. It is the causal completeness of physics that purges purpose from all living things and their lives. It does so by deploying the process that Darwin discovered. Because all biologists embrace Darwin's theory and understand its implications, the Templeton Foundation has a hard time finding a prizewinner among biologists. (The only biologist ever to win, a distinguished evolutionary biologist and ex-Catholic priest named Francisco Ayala, was honored for insisting that science can answer all questions except the ones about meaning, purpose, and moral values. What he really meant was that he just can't accept the answers science provides.)

When it comes to the biological realm, all that is needed to banish purpose is the recognition that the process of natural selection Darwin discovered is just physics at work among the organic molecules.

No Newton for the Blade of Grass?

Outside of physics, for a long time it was hard to see how nature could get by without purpose or design. The biological realm seems replete with beautifully, intricately designed objects and processes. There was no way science could deny this, nor, apparently, any way physics could explain it.

Even the most hardened Newtonian couldn't figure out how physics alone brings about the exquisite suitability of means to ends that we find everywhere in biology. Perhaps the greatest of Newton's defenders among philosophers was the late-eighteenth-century philosopher Immanuel Kant. In *The Critique of Pure Reason*, Kant tried to show that when it came to physics, Newtonian mechanics was the only game in town. But, he insisted, no one could ever do for biology what Newton did for physics—banish purpose and design from it. In 1790, he famously wrote, "It is absurd to hope that another Newton will arise in the future who shall make comprehensible by us the production of a blade of grass according to natural laws which no design has ordered."

"No Newton for the blade of grass" became the slogan of those who drew a line in the sand of science and dared physics to cross it. What Kant meant was that when we get past physics and into biology, the physics of matter and fields was not going to be enough to explain things. Only purposes could do the job. As in so many other areas of science and philosophy, Kant managed to get this one badly wrong. Only about 20 years after he wrote those immortal words, the Newton of the blade of grass was born to the Darwin family in Shropshire, England.

Kant was not alone in making this mistake. It continues to be made right down to the present. Its source is people's love of stories with plots. That's how explanations that invoke purposes or designs work: they are stories with plots. Because only such explanations provide relief from the psychological discomfort of curiosity, we seek them everywhere. Because they are absent in physics, most people have very little interest in it. Not only is physics too hard—too much math—what it explains is either boringly obvious (the motion of billiard balls on a table), absolutely scary (nuclear explosions), or completely unintelligible (quantum superpositions). Worst of all, it's not stories. What most people are really interested in is biology. And the reason biology is so interesting is how neatly and often how weirdly things are arranged to look like the happy ending of a story. Nature seems to show the obvious marks of purpose or hand of design everywhere.

Biologists have a label for the neat tricks that enable living things to take care of the four Fs of survival—feeding, fighting, flight, and . . . reproducing. The label for these traits is "adaptation." Adaptations are everywhere, apparent in the match between living things and their environments. Think of the nocturnal bat and its echo-locating sonar or the leathery cactus with its waterproof skin optimized for survival in the desert. Adaptation is equally to be found in the coordination and cooperation of the parts that enable living things to exploit their environment. There is no point in birds soaring high above their prey without the visual acuity to see it.

Camouflage often provides the most compelling illustrations of adaptations to the environment. Photos like the one in Figure 1 are all over the Internet. What you see here is an insect, not a leaf, even though it's green, flat, and broad, with the veins and segments of an oak leaf.

Many adaptations are so perfect, so intricate in their operation, so essential to survival, and so obvious that we take them for granted. The next time you are at a fish market, take a look at the whole flounders. Notice that each one has both eyes on the same side of the body. Why? The flounder is a bottom-dweller. It has no need of an eye looking down at the seafloor right beneath it and a great need to watch for predators and prey above it. Now you see why both eyes are on the same side of its body, the side it keeps facing up.

Job number one for biology is to explain both kinds of adap-

FIGURE 1. Phyllium giganteum

tations: organ to organism and organism to environment. From Aristotle in the third century BC to Kant in the eighteenth AD, the only way anyone could imagine explaining adaptations was by citing someone or something's purposes. As noted in Chapter 2, such explanations are teleological.

Over the last 150 years, the eye has certainly been the most overworked example in debates about how to explain the adaptation of parts to the wholes they make up. We know whom to blame for dragging it into the debate. Darwin made it the biggest challenge to his own theory. In *On the Origin of Species*, he identified the eye as "an organ of extreme perfection." There Darwin asserted, without qualification, that if natural selection could not explain the origin of its parts, their persistence, improvement, and how they gradually were put together into the complex organ they make up, then his theory of adaptation stood refuted.

It's obvious that scientism needs to explain adaptation. The supposed impossibility of a purely physical explanation of adap-

tation is thrown up at us most often and most forcefully by theists. Since time immemorial, the economy of means to ends, vivid
everywhere in nature, has been the strongest argument for the
existence of their sort of God—the one who made man in his
own image, along with making everything else. His design and
his execution of that design are the only things that could ever
explain adaptations. That was the idea Kant was pushing about
blades of grass.

By the same token, nothing more powerfully threatens theism
than an explanation of adaptation that meets Kant's challenge.
Nothing more powerfully vindicates scientism than an explanation of adaptation of just the kind Kant said couldn't be given,
one that invokes only physics.

Scientism needs more than an explanation of this or that
particular adaptation—white fur in polar bears or the fact that
bottom-dwelling fish have both eyes on the side of their bodies
facing away from the bottom. We need an explanation of how,
starting from zero adaptations, any adaptation at all ever comes
about. The explanation we need can't start with even a tiny
amount of adaptation already present. Furthermore, the explanation can't help itself to anything but physics. We can't even leave
room for "stupid design," let alone "intelligent design," to creep
in. If scientism needs a first slight adaptation, it surrenders to
design. It gives up the claim that the physical facts (none of which
is an adaptation) fix all the other facts. As we'll see, Darwin's theory faces the same requirement.

This is a very stringent demand. It goes far beyond the requirement that biology be compatible with physics, not disagree
with it. Scientists have long demanded consistency with well-
established physics as a requirement on all other theories in science. In fact, the nineteenth-century critics of Darwin's theory
were eager to adopt the standard of consistency with physics as

a way to blow the theory of evolution out of the water. One of these opponents was Lord Kelvin, of second law fame. Soon after the publication of *On the Origin of Species*, Kelvin argued that the Darwinian theory of natural selection had to be false. Darwin estimated that at least 300 million years had been required for natural selection to provide the level of adaptation we see around us. (He was off by an order of magnitude—1,000 percent.) But Kelvin thought that he could prove that the sun was no more than 20 million years old. Given the amount of energy it generated and the best theory of heat production available at the time (Kelvin's own theory), the upper limit on the sun's age was 40 million years. So there could not have been enough time for natural selection to provide adaptations by the process of natural selection.

Of course, Kelvin didn't have the slightest idea what the real source of the sun's energy is. It was only after World War II that Hans Bethe won the Nobel Prize in Physics for figuring out that the sun is a very long-lasting hydrogen-fusion-driven explosion. But in 1870, Kelvin's objection had to be taken pretty seriously. Explanations of adaptation must be compatible with the correct physical theory, and in 1870, Kelvin's was the best-informed guess about the physics of solar energy. Darwin himself owned up to being very worried about this problem, since he accepted the constraint of consistency with physics as a requirement on any theory of adaptation.

Kelvin was wrong about the age of the sun (and therefore wrong about Darwin). He was, of course, right about the second law of thermodynamics. Since the nineteenth century, Kelvin's discoveries about the nature of heat, as reflected in the first and second laws of thermodynamics, have become established physics. Any explanation of adaptation had better not fall afoul of them.

But as noted, scientism requires more than just logical compatibility. If the physical facts fix all the facts, then the emergence and persistence of adaptations had better result from the laws of physics alone. In fact, they had better be the result of the operation of thermodynamics. Otherwise we will have to admit that there is more going on in the universe than what physics tells us there is. Some physicists may be okay with this, but scientism has to reject it. We need an explanation of adaptation that makes it the consequence of purely physical processes. We need to show that the process Darwin discovered starts with zero adaptations and builds them all as a result of the laws of physics alone. Otherwise we will find ourselves on a slippery slope. If we have to add a separate and independent Darwinian theory to physics for completeness's sake, who's to say completeness won't require us to add Sigmund Freud's, or Karl Marx's, or, for that matter, Jacques Derrida's theory to physics. Worst of all, what if completing the picture requires the theism of the Abrahamic religions—Judaism, Christianity, and Islam?

We have to satisfy ourselves not just that Darwin's theory is true, but that physics is enough to make it true. And we need to show that when it comes to explaining adaptation, the causal closure of physics makes Darwinism the only game in town.

Although Darwinian biologists have not noticed, their theory also needs the causal closure of physics. It's not enough to show that Darwinian theory gets it mostly right but for a few exceptions, a couple of adaptations produced by non-Darwinian processes at work in biology. That leaves too much wiggle room for compromises with theism. The official Roman Catholic view, for example, revels in this wiggle room. Their religion is much more erudite than crude Protestant Fundamentalism (think how much Roman Catholicism owes to Aristotle and Augustine). The Pope allows that Darwin got it right from the beginning of organic life 3.5 billion years ago right up to the primates. The only exceptions are humans, who have been given souls one by one through divine spark for about 250,000 years now. If Darwinian biology allows a few exceptions, it won't be able to keep the floodgates closed against intelligent design, special creation, or even biblical inerrancy.

To close down the wiggle room, Darwinism (and, of course, scientism) needs to show that the only way adaptations can ever happen—even the most trivial and earliest of adaptation—is by natural selection working on zero adaptation. We must demonstrate that given the constraints of physics, adaptation can have no source other than natural selection. To do this, first we'll show that natural selection doesn't need any prior adaptation at all to get started; beginning with zero adaptations, it can produce all the rest by physical processes alone. The previous chapter gave us the two core ideas we need for this task: the causal completeness of physics and the second law of thermodynamics. The rest of this chapter shows how the physical facts can produce all the adaptation Darwinism needs from a zero-adaptation starting point.

With these two starting points—the second law and the completeness of physics—we can do more. We can close down the wiggle room. We can also show that the process Darwin discovered is necessarily the *only* way adaptations can emerge, persist, and be enhanced in a world where the physical facts fix all the facts. That is the task for the next chapter.

THE PASSIVE FILTER AND THE SLIGHTLY ERRATIC COOKIE CUTTER

To show how the process of natural selection follows directly from physics, we first need to state Darwin's discovery properly. One neat, simple, and very general description of the process was originally advanced in the 1970s by the well-known biologist Richard Lewontin. It's not perfect, but adding further details wouldn't affect the derivation of all Darwinian processes from physics.

According to Lewontin's version, adaptative evolution occurs when there are heritable variations in fitness. Lewontin identifies three conditions, each of which is necessary and when taken together are sufficient for the evolution of adaptations:

1. There is always variation in the traits of organisms, genes, hives, groups, or whatever it is that replicates or reproduces.
2. The variant traits differ in fitness.
3. The fitness differences among some of the traits are inherited.

The process that exploits these three conditions is natural selection. This is not the whole of Darwin's theory or its later modification by a century of discoveries that refine it in many ways. But it is the essence of how the means/ends economy of nature emerges, without purpose ever intervening. The process takes the variant traits in each generation and *filters* them for fitness differences. It allows those attaining a minimum level of fitness to survive at least long enough to be replicated in the next generation.

The replication isn't always perfect. Once in every hundred copies, or every thousand, or every million, something goes slightly or badly "wrong" in the copying process. It's as though you had an animal cracker cookie cutter that changed shape slightly (sometimes even not so slightly) and unpredictably once in every 10 or 20 or 100 cookies it cut. Every so often, out comes a cookie different from all the rest. Sometimes it's better—less burned because it's thicker, less likely to break because it has fewer sharp edges, showing more clearly the shape of the animal the cookie is supposed to look like. But most of these unpredictable, uncontrollable changes in the cookie cutter produce a result that even a baker with low standards would just get rid of. Every genetic trait of every organism on this planet is produced by a copying process that is rather like this.

The consequence is that there is always at least some variation in hereditary traits. This was the great insight Darwin brought home from his five-year voyage around South America on HMS *Beagle*. Variation in traits is the rule throughout biology. In chemistry, by contrast, variations within the periodic table of the elements (the isotopes) are rare exceptions. Before Darwin, biologists thought that species were more like the chemical elements, in which individual variations were exceptions, special cases, deformations, defective cases. The *Beagle* voyage convinced Darwin that in the biological domain, variation is the rule. He was right.

The result of repeated filtering by the environment of the many old and the few new variants in every generation is the emergence and enhancement of adaptive traits, traits that work well enough in their environments for the things that bear them to survive long enough to reproduce again. This was the idea Darwin found in Thomas Malthus's *Essay on Population*. He called this filtering by the environment "natural selection." He should have called it "environmental filtration," for the process that Darwin envisioned gives nature only a passive role. The local environment allows some organisms to live a little longer and have a few more offspring, while it prevents others from doing either. There is, in Darwin's view, no active "picking and choosing" or active "selecting" by nature of those variations that meet some preestablished criteria for survival and reproduction.

Most important, in this process there is absolutely no *foresight* about what variants will be useful to their bearers in the future. The absence of foresight in nature is better captured by the label "blind variation" than the more usual "random variation." As we'll see, the lack of foresight that Darwin attributed to nature has always been his theory's greatest strength. At the same time, it has been the theory's biggest sticking point for skeptics. The theory suggests that nature is rather like a driver navigating through a frantically busy and complex maze of streets in rush-hour traffic, relying only on a narrow rearview mirror. It seems like it would be a miracle if the driver survived, let alone ever arrived, safe and sound, at home.

The essence of natural selection is nature's passivity and lack of foresight. Darwin realized that passive processes with no foresight are what build all the incredible adaptations that seem to show such exquisite purpose. He saw clearly that the biological realm is as free of purpose as the physical realm. There is really no alternative but to treat purpose as just an illusion. It turns out to be an anthropomorphic overlay, fostered in large part by our talent for seeing conspiracies—malign and benign—everywhere. The appearance of purpose is a trick. Natural selection is physics faking design.

Physics is so good at faking design that even after Darwin pulled the curtain down and revealed the trickery, people still have had a hard time not reverting to a purposive view of nature. Every spoken language is rife with the images of nature as a cunning agent, knowingly taking a hand in shaping the outcome of biological processes. It is really no surprise that even the most dyed-in-the-wool Darwinian still invokes images of Mother Nature and the design problems she imposes on organisms, groups, and species. This is harmless, perhaps even helpful—a convenient metaphor. We made use of it ourselves in previous chapters. In the chapters to come, we will find even more convenient these and similar shorthand descriptions for processes that combine randomness and filtration to produce the simulacrum of design. Such expressions, which credit purely physical processes with volition, intention, and foresight, not to mention intelligence and wisdom, can always be cashed in for descriptions that deprive nature of these capacities. It would be tedious to unpack "a design problem Mother Nature faces" into a list of facts about the environment ("threats" and "opportunities" are the metaphors here) that have an impact on a species' likelihood of persistence. So would translating the description of a "solution" into terms that reveal it to be a "quick and dirty" one (more anthropomorphic metaphor), the result of the first blind variation that happened to combine with some feature of the environment (the "problem") to enhance survival and reproduction.

"Mother Nature" is just the disguise natural selection "wears" (there's that volitional metaphor again) when its results look particularly nurturing to us. In the rest of this book, hold me to the promise that any talk about purposes is harmless metaphor. Intentions, volitions, designs, solutions, or any other kinds of actions in nature—implied or expressed—must always be cashed in for the mindless process Darwin discovered.

Natural selection explains the blade of grass in just the way Kant thought was impossible. It explains the emergence and persistence of the most intricate adaptation by a prior sequence of lesser and lesser adaptations. In turn, that sequence can be traced back to a starting point with zero adaptation. The most complex and impressive adaptations are the result of a chain of events that starts with no adaptations at all, just molecules in random motion. That leaves nothing for purposes, ends, goals, to do anywhere in nature. Darwin figured out the only process for producing adaptation that is allowed by the laws Lord Kelvin discovered. It's ironic that despite Kelvin's attack on Darwin, his great contribution to physics—the second law—makes natural selection inevitable.

To review a bit from the previous chapter, the second law of thermodynamics tells us that with very high probability, entropy, the disorder of things, increases over time. The second law's consequences are almost as familiar to us as any physical process. Hold a cup while someone pours coffee into it, and you feel the cup getting warmer. Meanwhile, as it is poured into the cup, the coffee gets cooler. Pour some cream in the cup of coffee and watch it spread out on the top. Add a sugar cube. It dissolves. All these effects—the cooling of the coffee, the heating of the cup, the spread of cream, and the sugar's dissolving—demonstrate the second law's requirement that disorder increases almost everywhere almost all the time.

The second law is, of course, not restricted to milk protein molecules in coffee cups. It has the sobering implication that, just like in the coffee cup, eventually everything is going to even out everywhere.

But the biological realm seems to show the opposite of second-law disorder. It reflects persistent orderliness: start out with some mud and seeds, end up with a garden of beautiful flowers. The ever-increasing adaptation of plants' and animals' traits to local environments looks like the long-term increase in order and decrease in entropy. So we have to square the emergence and persistence of adaptation with the second law's requirement that entropy increases.

You may be thinking that if adaptation is orderly and increases in it are decreases in entropy, then evolution must be impossible. Some creationists have actually argued this way. This line of reasoning makes a slight mistake about entropy and magnifies it into a major mistake about evolution. The second law requires that evolution produce a *net* increase in entropy. Increases in order or its persistence are permitted. But they must be paid for by more increases in disorder elsewhere. Any process of emergence, persistence, or enhancement of adaptation must be accompanied by increases in disorder that are almost always greater than the increases in order. The "almost" is added because, as we have seen, increases in entropy are just very, very probable, not absolutely invariable. It won't be difficult to show that Darwin's explanation of adaptation, and only Darwin's explanation, can do this.

Just to repeat, explaining how Darwinian processes are really second-law processes shows that physics can fake design. Scientism is going to require more, however. We'll also have to show that second-law processes are the only way adaptations can happen. The only way appearances of design emerge is through the fakery of physics. We'll show that in the next chapter.

MOLECULAR SELECTION: NATURE'S OWN NANOTECHNOLOGY

Natural selection requires three processes: reproduction, variation, and inheritance. It doesn't really care how any of these three things get done, just so long as each one goes on long enough to get some adaptations. Reproduction doesn't have to be sexual or even asexual or even easily recognized by us to be reproduction. Any kind of replication is enough. In chemistry, replication occurs whenever a molecule's own chemical structure causes the chemical synthesis of another molecule with the same structure— when it makes copies of itself or helps something else make copies of it. This can and does happen several different ways, both in the test tube and in nature. The way most directly relevant for evolution on Earth is called template matching—the method DNA uses to make copies of itself.

First step: When atoms bounce around, some bind to one another strongly or weakly, depending on the kind of attraction there is between them—their chemical bond. When the bond is strong, the results are stable molecules. These molecules can only be broken up by forces that are stronger than the bonds. Such forces require more energy than is stored in the stable bond between the atoms in the molecule. Breaking down a stable molecule takes more energy than keeping it together.

Second step: Occasionally, these relatively stable molecules can be templates for copies of themselves. Their atoms attract other atoms to themselves and to each other so that the attracted atoms bond together to make another molecule with the same structure. The process is familiar in crystal growth. Start out with a cube of eight atoms in a solution of other atoms of the same kind. They attract another four on each side, and suddenly the molecule is a three-dimensional cross. As it attracts more and more atoms, the crystal grows from a small cube into a large one. The crystal grows in a solution through "thermodynamic noise": the increasingly uneven and disorderly distribution of atoms just randomly bouncing around in the solution as mandated by the second law. The atoms already in the crystal latch onto ones in solution in the only orientation chemically possible, making the nice shape we can see when they get big enough.

A crystal molecule doesn't just have to grow bigger and bigger. Instead the molecule can set up chemical forces that make two or more other unattached atoms that are just bouncing around bond with one another, making new copies of the original crystal. Instead of getting bigger, it makes more copies of itself.

The process could involve more steps than just simple one-step replication. It could involve intermediate steps between copies. Think of a cookie that is stale enough to be used as a mold to make a cookie cutter that takes the stale cookie's shape. It's a template to make a new cookie. Make the new cookie, then throw away the cookie cutter, let the new cookie go stale, and use it to make a new cookie cutter. Make lots of copies of the same cookie using one-use cookie cutters. You get the idea. (In a way, this is just how DNA is copied in the cell, using each cookie cutter once, except the cookie cutter is not thrown away. It's used for something else.)

Physical chemists and organic chemists are discovering more and more about how such complicated structures arise among molecules. They are applying that knowledge in nanotechnology—the engineering of individual molecules. Pretty soon they'll be able to induce molecules to build any geometrical shape they choose. Often the molecule of choice in nanotechnology experiments is DNA. Inevitably, there are people like the late Michael Crichton who warn us that we will soon be overrun by self-replicating nano-robots. The reason they claim to be worried is the role of "self-assembly" in building nanomachines.

Chemically building these structures molecule by molecule is remarkable in itself. What is truly amazing is that the structures assemble themselves. In fact, this is the only way nanotechnology works. There are very few molecules chemists can manipulate one at a time, putting one next to another and then gluing them together. All they can do is set up the right soup of molecules milling around randomly ("thermodynamic noise") and then wait while the desired structures are built by processes that emerge from the operation of the laws of physics. Just by changing the flexibility of small molecules of DNA in the starting soup at the bottom of the test tube and changing their concentrations, chemists can produce many different three-dimentional objects, including tetrahedrons, dodecahedrons, and buckyballs—soccer ball shapes built out of DNA molecules. Of course, what we can do in the lab, unguided nature can do better, given world enough and time.

Replication by template matching is even easier than self-assembly. And it works particularly well under conditions that the second law of thermodynamics encourages: the larger the number of molecules and the more randomly the molecules of different kinds are distributed, the better. These conditions increase the chances that each of the different atoms needed by a template will sooner or later bounce into it to help make a copy. In fact, "works well" is an understatement for how completely template replication exploits the second law.

Let's assume that the mixture of atoms bouncing around in a test tube or in nature is very disorderly and getting more so all the time, as the second law requires. As the disorderly distribution of atoms increases, the chances of different atoms landing on the template increase, too. Most of the time, an atom bouncing into a template of other atoms is too big or too small or too strongly charged to make a copy molecule that survives. Even if the new atom bonds to the others, the whole copy may break apart due to differences in size or charge or whatever, sending its constituent atoms off to drift around some more, increasing entropy, of course. In most cases, in the lab and out of it, this disorderly outcome of instability in copying is the rule, not the exception. The exception is a successfully duplicated molecule.

Now let's add some variation to the replication. In effect, we are introducing mutation in template copying. Variation is even easier to get going than replication at the level of molecules. It's imposed on molecules during the process of replication by some obvious chemical facts working together with the second law of thermodynamics.

One look at the columns of the periodic table of the elements (Figure 2) is enough to see how disorder makes chemically similar but slightly different molecules. In the table, fluorine is just above chlorine in the same column. They are in the same column because they react with exactly the same elements to make stuff. Chlorine and sodium atoms bond together and make table salt;

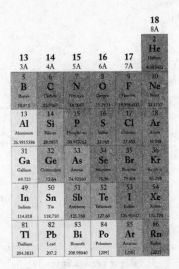

FIGURE 2. The right side of the periodic table of the elements

that means that fluorine and sodium atoms will bond together, too (the resulting molecule is a tooth decay preventer). The reason fluorine and chlorine atoms combine with sodium equally well is that they have the same arrangements of electrons that do the bonding. All that means is that if a chlorine and a fluorine molecule are both bouncing around and bump into the same template, they may both bond the same way with other atoms on the template to make similar, but slightly different molecules. A template with chlorine molecules in it could easily produce a copy molecule that differs only in having a fluorine or two where a chlorine would normally go. *Voilà!* Variation.

Here is an example of slight molecular variation with vast consequences. Sugar has a somewhat complicated molecular structure, one that packs a lot of calories of energy that the human digestive system can extract, and it tastes good, too. Splenda is a popular sugar substitute. It differs from sugar at only three points

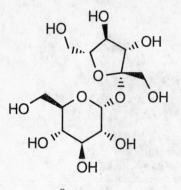
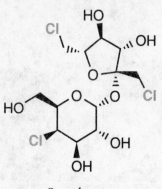

Sucrose

Sucralose
(Splenda®)

FIGURE 3. Molecular variation in action:
sugar versus Splenda

in its molecular structure. Where sugar has a hydroxyl molecule (an OH), Splenda has a chlorine molecule (Cl). It makes only a slight difference in taste. However, the enzymes in the human digestive system can't latch on to Splenda molecules and extract the calories from the molecule. That's why Splenda is a popular sugar substitute.

When chemical reactions happen billions of times in small regions of space and time, even a small percentage of exact copies quickly come to number in the millions, as does the percentage of slightly varied copies, with one or two atoms of different elements in place of the original atoms. Most of the time, the outcome of this is process is wastage—a molecule that doesn't replicate itself or that falls apart, just as the second law requires. But sometimes—very rarely—variation produces a molecule that is slightly better at replicating or one that is just a little more stable.

Now we have replication and variation. What about fitness differences, the last of the three requirements for evolution by natural selection? Fitness is easiest to understand at the level of molecules bouncing around in a world controlled by the second law. Molecules that form from atoms are stable for a certain length of time. Some break apart right after forming because their bonding is too weak to withstand the force of other atoms that bounce into them or even just pass by. Some "fragile" molecules will remain intact for a while. They just happen by chance to avoid bouncing up against other molecules, ones with stronger charges that pull atoms away from their neighbors. Here again the second law rears its head. As molecules bounce around, any amount of order, structure, pattern almost always gives way to disorder, to entropy. Hardly any molecule is stable for extremely long periods, with the exception of the bonded carbon atoms in a diamond crystal.

There are differences in stability among molecules owing to the variations that inexact replication permits. Differences in stability have an impact on the replication of different types of molecules. A template molecule produces copies just by random interaction with atoms that bounce into it or pass close enough to be attracted. The longer the original templating molecule stays in one piece—that is, the more stable it is, the more copies it can make. Most of its copies will be just as stable as the original template molecule, since they will be exact duplicates. They will serve as templates for more copies, and so on, multiplying copies of the original.

Of course, just as there are differences in the stability of different molecules, there are differences in their rates of replication. Both the number of copies of their templates that can be made and their stability will depend on their "environment"—the temperature, the local electric and magnetic fields, the concentration of other atoms and molecules around them. Consider two molecules that differ from one another along the two dimensions of stability and ease of replication. The first remains intact on average twice as long as the second; the second templates twice as many copies per unit of time as the first. Over the same period, they will produce exactly the same number of copies. What will be the long-term proportions of molecules of the two types? It will be 1 to 1. As far as producing copies are concerned, the two different molecules will have equal *reproductive fitness*. And of course, if their differences in stability and replicability don't perfectly balance out, then after a time there are going to be more copies of one type of molecule than of the other.

Molecules randomly bouncing around a region of space and bonding to form larger molecules will eventually, randomly, result in a few stable and replicating structures. Their structures will vary, and the variations will affect the molecules' stability and replication rates. These differences in the ability of molecules to stay intact (stability) and to allow for copies of themselves to form (replicability) will change the proportions of molecules in any region of space. If chemical and physical conditions in that region remain unchanged for long enough, the ratios of the different types of replicating molecules will eventually settle down to a fixed proportion. At that point, all the remaining replicating molecules in the region will be equally fit to survive—whether owing to their stability or replicability or varying combinations of both. In other words, a purely physical process has produced molecular adaptation: the appearance, persistence, and enhancement of molecules with chemical and physical properties that enable them to persist or replicate or both. Then, at some point, the chemical environment changes, slightly or greatly: temperatures rise or fall, new and different molecules diffuse through the region, the magnetic field strengthens or weakens. The process of adaptive evolution starts again, thermodynamically filtering for new stable, replicating molecules adapted to the new conditions.

As this process goes on, two other phenomena become inevitable: the size and complexity of the replicating molecules will increase. Eventually, molecules will emerge that enhance each other's stability or replication through their chemical relations to each other. There are no limits to the repetition of this process, making bigger and more complicated and more diverse molecules. If conditions are favorable, the result will be really big assemblies of stable and replicating molecules—for instance, RNA and eventually DNA sequences and strings of amino acids (that is, genes and proteins).

The rest is history—that is, natural history. The process we have described begins with zero adaptations and produces the first adaptation by dumb luck, sheer random chance that the second law makes possible. Molecular biologists don't yet know all the details of this natural history, or even many of them. Some have been known for a long time. It was in the early 1950s that two scientists—Stanley Miller and Harold Urey—showed how easy it is to get proteins, sugar, lipids, and the building blocks of DNA from simple ingredients available early in Earth's history. All they did was run an electric current through some water, methane, ammonia, and carbon. Chemists have been designing similar experiments ever since, getting more and more of the building blocks of terrestrial life. Biologists have discovered that the simplest and oldest of organisms on the planet—the archaebacteria—probably first emerged at least 2.8 billion years ago and still survive in volcanoes at the bottom of the sea. It is there, in volcanoes at the bottom of the ocean, under the highest temperatures and greatest pressure, that we find chemical reactions spewing out boiling lava and producing the largest quantities of entropy on the planet. This is just what the second law requires to drive thermodynamic noise, and through it to find stable and replicating molecules in a world of random mixing.

How much like the evolution of recognizably biological things—genes, cells, replicating organisms—is the molecular process we have described? Well, recognizably biological evolution has three distinctive features.

First, natural selection usually finds quick and dirty solutions to immediate and pressing environmental challenges. More often than not, these solutions get locked in. Then, when new problems arise, the solutions to old problems constrain and channel the random search for adaptations that deal with the newer problems. The results are jury-rigged solutions permanently entrenched everywhere in nature.

A second feature of biological evolution is the emergence of complexity and diversity in the structure and behavior of organisms. Different environments select among variations in different adaptations, producing diversity even among related lineages of organisms. The longer evolution proceeds, the greater the opportunities for more complicated solutions to continuing design problems.

A third feature of biological evolution is the appearance of cooperative adaptations and competing adaptations. The cooperative ones are sometimes packaged together in the same organism, sometimes separated in two quite distinct ones living symbiotically (like us and the *E. coli* bacteria in our guts). But natural selection also, and more frequently, produces competition between genes, individuals, lineages, populations, and species. There is always the chance that an "arms race" will break out between evolving lineages of traits: a new random variation in one trait may get selected for and exploit the other traits it has been cooperating with, or a new variation may randomly appear in a trait that enables it to suddenly break up a competitive stalemate it was locked into. We will be hearing a lot more about arms races in later chapters.

Each of these three features is found in the nano-evolution of the molecules. And each persists as molecular assemblies grow in size, stability, complexity, and diversity to produce organic life.

Lock in of quick and dirty solutions: Only a few molecular shapes will ever allow for their own self-assembly and copying (by templating or otherwise). These shapes begin the lock-in that second-law processes will have to work with in building the more stable, more replicable, bigger, and more complicated molecules.

Increasing diversity and complexity: Thermodynamic noise constantly makes more and more different environments—different temperatures, different pH, different concentrations of chemicals, different amounts of water or carbon dioxide or nitrogen, or more complicated acids and bases, magnetic fields, and radiation. As a result, there will be a corresponding selection for more and more different molecules. However, they will still be variations on the themes locked in by the earliest stages of molecular evolution.

Cooperation and competition: Some of these molecules will even start to work together, just by luck having structures that enhance one another's stability or replicability. Others will explode or dissolve or change their structures when they combine with one another. They will produce new environments that will select for new chemical combinations, ones that cooperate, ones that compete. And so on up the ladder of complexity and diversity that produces assemblies of molecules so big they become recognizable as genes, viruses, organelles, cells, tissues, organs, organisms, . . . our pets, our parasites, our prey, our predators . . . and us.

MOLECULES BOUNCING against one another inevitably follow a scenario dictated by the second law. Purely physical and chemical processes in that scenario are all that is needed for the emergence, persistence, and enhancement of adaptation through natural selection at the molecular level. Where and when molecules of some minimal size emerge, there will be some natural selection for chemical structures that confer more stability and replicability than other chemical structures confer. These chemical properties are *adaptations*. They have functions for the molecules that exhibit them. They enable the molecules to survive longer than less stable ones in the same chemical bath and to make more copies of themselves than other ones in the same bath. As a result of molecular natural selection, these molecules are better adapted to their molecular environment than others are.

This is an important outcome. Remember, scientism faces the demand of showing how to get the merest sliver of an adaptation from zero adaptation by purely physical, chemical, thermodynamic processes. Mother Nature can build on that sliver of an adaptation to get more adaptations and eventually more robust adaptations. But she can't cheat. She can't just assume the existence of that first sliver. The second law makes the first sliver possible. Variation and selection can take it from there. Now we have to show that this is the *only* way adaptations—molecular or otherwise—can emerge.

Chapter 4

—◆—

IKEA Didn't Make
Natural History:
Good Design Is Rare,
Expensive,
and Accidental

THE SECOND LAW MAKES THE MEREST SLIVER OF
an initial adaptation just barely possible. But it makes no
guarantees. For all we know, it might happen only once every
13.7 billion years in an entire universe. If the first adaptation survives long enough, the second law allows for improvements, but
only if they are rare, energetically costly, and just dumb luck. No
one said adaptation would be easy.

So far so good. But scientism needs more from physics than
just the possibility of adaptation. Physics won't fix all the facts,
it won't be causally closed, unless the second law's way of getting
adaptations is the only way to get them. Scientism needs to show
that blind variation together with environmental filtration is the
sole route through which life can emerge in any universe. We
have to understand why, in a universe made only by physics, the
process that Darwin discovered is the only game in town.

There are only two things we need to keep in mind to do this.

First, if we are out to explain how any adaptation at all can ever happen, we can't help ourselves to some prior adaptation, no matter how slight, puny, or insignificant. Second, the second law requires that the emergence and persistence of orderliness of any kind be energetically expensive. An explanation of adaptation's emergence and persistence is going to have to show that the process is wasteful. The more wasteful the better so far as the second law is concerned.

ADAPTATION HAS TO BE A BAD BET

The very first adaptation has to be a matter of nothing more than dumb luck. It has to be the random result of a very, very mindless process, like a monkey hitting the keys of a typewriter randomly and producing a word. Given world enough and time, the bouncing around of things just fortuitously produces adaptations. The second law insists that initial adaptations—no matter how slight, small, or brief—can't happen very often. And the same goes for subsequent adaptations that build on these. They will have to be rare and random as well. So any theory that explains adaptation in general will have to have this feature: that the first adaptation is a fluke, the luck of the draw, just an accident, simply the result of the law of averages. The inevitability of a first adaptation is ruled out by the second law. To begin with, the second law says that nothing is inevitable, even the heat death of the universe. More important, the appearance of the merest sliver of an adaptation is an increase in order and so at most improbable.

None of this is a surprise to Darwinian theory, of course. That's just what the theory says will happen: variations are random, they are almost always small, in fact they are almost always molecular; the first ones come out of nowhere, just as a matter of shuffling the cards; mostly they are maladaptive, and only rarely are they adaptive.

The second law also requires that the process through which later adaptations emerge out of earlier ones be energetically expensive and wasteful: expensive because building more and more order has to cost more and more disorder; wasteful because the early steps—the original adaptations on which later ones are built—will be locked in, so energetically less costly ways of building the later adaptations are not available. Every explanation of adaptation will have to share this feature, too. It will have to harness a wasteful process to create order.

We need only examine natural selection as it has played out on Earth to see how expensive and wasteful it is. The combination of blind variation and environmental filtration is great at increasing entropy. In fact, the right way to look at the emergence of adaptation on Earth is to recognize that it is the most wasteful, most energetically expensive, most entropy-producing process that occurs on the planet. The evolution and maintenance of adaptations by natural selection wins the prize for greatest efficiency in carrying out the second law's mandate to create disorder. Forget design; evolution is a mess. This is a fact about natural selection insufficiently realized and not widely enough publicized in biology.

Examples are all around us. A female leopard frog will lay up to 6,000 eggs at a time—each carrying exactly half of all the order required for an almost perfect duplicate offspring. Yet out of that 6,000, the frog will produce on average only two surviving offspring. Some fish are even more inefficient, laying millions of eggs at one time just to make two more fish. Compared to that, a dandelion is miserly with seeds. It will spread only 1,000 seeds and produce, on average, one copy of itself. But the human male competes well with profligate fishes. He ejaculates millions of sperm, full of information about how to build a person, almost all capable of fertilizing an egg, and yet 999,999 sperm out of 1,000,000 fail to do it. A high proportion of most organisms go through an entire life cycle building and maintaining order and then leaving no offspring at all. Everyone has one or two maiden aunts and bachelor uncles. Insofar as Darwinian processes make reproduction central to adaptation, they rely on a wonderfully wasteful process. It's hard to think of a better way to waste energy than to produce lots of energetically expensive copies of something and then destroy all of them except for the minimum number of copies that you need to do it all over again.

How about heredity? Another amazingly entropy-increasing process! Molecular biologists know that DNA copy fidelity is very high and therefore low in information loss compared to, say, RNA copy fidelity. But think of the costs of this much high fidelity. In every cell, there is a vast and complex apparatus whose sole function is to ensure copy fidelity: it cuts out hairpin turns when the very sticky DNA sticks to itself, it proofreads all the copies, removes mutations, breaks up molecules that could cause mutations, and so on. In *Homo sapiens*, at least 16 enzymes—polymerases—have so far been discovered whose sole functions are to repair different kinds of errors that thermodynamic processes produce in DNA sequences. The costs of high-fidelity heredity—both to build the equipment that protects and corrects the DNA sequences and to operate it—are very great. Just what the second law requires.

Now let's look at this energy waste on an even larger scale. The evolution of adaptations reflects environmental change over the course of Earth's history. The vast diversification of flora and fauna is also the result of differences between local environments in different places on Earth. Since long before continental drift and long after global warming, environments on Earth change over time and increase entropy as they do so. What is more, once natural selection kicks in, flora and fauna remake their environments in ways that further accelerate entropy increase. When nature started selecting molecules for stability and replicability, it began producing arms races more wasteful than anything the Americans and Soviets could ever have dreamed up. From that time on, there has been a succession of moves and countermoves in adaptatve space made at every level of organization. It has happened within and between all the descending lineage of molecules, genes, cells, and organisms. Each line of descent has forever searched for ways to exploit its collaborators' and its competitors' adaptations. All that jockeying for position is wasted when one organism, family, lineage, species is made extinct by the actions of another organism, family, lineage, species. This, of course, is what Darwin called the struggle for survival.

Add sexual reproduction to the struggle for survival and it's impossible to avoid the conclusion that Darwinian selection must be nature's favorite way of obeying the second law. Natural selection invests energy in the cumulative packaging of coadapted traits in individual organisms just to break them apart in meiosis—the division of the sex cells. Then it extinguishes the traits and their carriers in a persistent spiral of creative destruction. Think about this for a moment: 99 percent of the species that have been extant on this planet are now extinct. That's a lot of order relentlessly turned into entropy!

It's well known that every major change and many minor ones in the environment condemn hitherto fit creatures to death and their lineages to extinction. As environments change, yesterday's adaptation becomes tomorrow's maladaptation. In fact, it looks like three different cataclysmic events have repeatedly killed off most of the life-forms on Earth. The dinosaur extinction 65 million years ago, owing to an asteroid collision on the Yucatán peninsula, is well established. There are no dinosaur bones in any of the younger layers of stone around the world, but there is a layer of iridium—an element found in much higher concentrations in asteroids than on Earth—spread evenly around vast parts of Earth centered on the Yucatán in layers of rock 65 million years old. In that layer, the iridium is 1,000 times more concentrated than elsewhere above or below it in Earth's crust. At a stroke, or at least over only a few years, all the vast numbers of dinosaur species, which had been adapting to their environment beautifully for 225 million years, just disappeared. That's what made the world safe for the little shrewlike mammals from which we are descended. The fossil record reveals an even bigger extinction event on Earth 500 million years ago and an even more massive extinction after that, 225 million years ago: the Permian-Triassic extinction, in which three-fourths of all ocean-living genera and almost 100 percent of ocean-dwelling species along with 75 percent of land species became extinct. This is order-destroying waste on an enormous scale.

Long before all this, it was the buildup of oxygen in the oceans and in the atmosphere that killed off almost everything on Earth! Buildup of oxygen? How could oxygen be a poison? Remember, yesterday's adaptation can be today's maladaptation. Life started in the oceans with anaerobic bacteria—bacteria that don't need oxygen. In fact, they produce oxygen as a waste product the way we produce carbon dioxide. Just as the plants clean up our mess by converting carbon dioxide to oxygen and water, the environment cleaned up all that oxygen pollution by molecular action, binding the oxygen to iron and other metals. At some point, the amount of oxygen waste produced by the anaerobic creatures exceeded the absorption capacity of the environment. As a result, they all began to be poisoned by the increasing levels of oxygen around them. Around 2.4 billion years ago, these bacteria were almost completely wiped out, making enough space for the aerobic bacteria, the ones that live on oxygen and produce carbon dioxide as waste. We evolved from these bacteria.

Can any other process produce entropy as fast and on such a scale as natural selection? Just try to think of a better way of wasting energy than this: build a lot of complicated devices out of simpler things and then destroy all of them except the few you need to build more such devices. Leaving everything alone, not building anything, won't increase entropy nearly as fast. Building very stable things, like diamond crystals, will really slow it down, but building adaptations will use up prodigious amounts of energy. Adaptations are complicated devices; they don't fall apart spontaneously, and they repair themselves when they break down. They persistently get more complicated and so use even more energy to build and maintain themselves. Any long-term increase in the number of adapted devices without increased energy consumption would make a mockery of the second law. If such devices ever appear, besides being rare, they had better not persist and multiply, unless by doing so they inevitably generate more energy wastage than there would have been without them. This is the very process Darwin envisioned: in Tennyson's words, "nature red in tooth and claw."

Kelvin had the wrong end of the stick when he argued that there has not been enough time for natural selection to produce the adaptation, the order, we see on Earth. What really needs to be explained is the fact that adaptation here on Earth produces so much disorder. The second law does exactly this by allowing adaptations, but only on the condition that their appearance increases entropy. Any process competing with natural selection as the source of adaptations has to produce adaptations from nonadaptations, and every one of the adaptations it produces will have to be rare, expensive, and wasteful. We'll see that this requirement—that building and maintaining orderliness always has to cost more than it saves—rules out all of natural selection's competitors as the source of adaptation, diversity, and complexity.

Could there be a process that produces adaptations that is less wasteful than the particular way in which Darwinian natural selection operates on Earth? Probably. How wasteful such a process can be depends on the starting materials and on how much variation emerges in the adaptations built from them. But every one of these possible processes has to rely on dumb luck to produce the first sliver of an adaptation. In that respect, they would still just be more instances of the general process Darwin discovered—blind variation and environmental filtration. A process that explained every later adaptation by more dumb luck shuffling and filtering of the earlier adaptations would still be Darwinian natural selection. It would be Darwinian natural selection even if the process was so quick and so efficient as to suggest that the deck was stacked. So long as the deck wasn't stacked to produce some prearranged outcome, it's still just blind variation and environmental filtration. Any deck stacking—a process of adaptive evolution that started with some unexplained adaptation already in the cards—is ruled out by physics.

Only the Second Law Can Power Adaptive Evolution

The second law's demand for persistent increase in entropy makes natural selection the only game in town, but there is another, deeper reason why it does so. No matter what brings it about, the process of adaptation is different from the more basic physical and chemical processes in nature. They are all "time symmetrical." Adaptation is not. But the only way a time-asymmetrical process can happen is by harnessing the second law.

As you may recall from Chapter 2, a time-symmetrical process is reversible. Chapter 2 provided one example: any set of ricochets on a billiard table can be reproduced in exactly the opposite order. Here are some more examples: Hydrogen and oxygen can combine to produce water, but water can also release hydrogen and oxygen. Even the spreading circular waves made when a drop of liquid falls into a pool can be reversed to move inward and expel the drop upward from the surface. No matter in what order the basic chemical and physical processes go, they can go in the reverse order, too.

The second law creates all asymmetrical processes and gives them their direction in time. Now, the evolution of adaptations is a thoroughly asymmetrical process. Take a time-lapse film of a standard natural selection experiment. Grow bacteria in a petri dish. Drop some antibiotic material into the dish. Watch the bacterial slime shrink until a certain point, when it starts growing again as the antibiotic resistant strains of the bacteria are selected for.

Now try reversing the time-lapse video of the process of bacterial selection for resistance. What you will see just can't happen. You will watch the population of the most resistant strain diminish during the time the antibiotic is present. After a certain point, you will see the spread of the bacteria that can't resist the antibiotic, until the drops of the antibiotic leave the petri dish altogether. But that sequence is impossible. It's the evolution of maladaptation, the emergence, survival, and spread of the less fit.

There is only one physical process available to drive asymmetrical adaptive evolution. That is the asymmetrical entropy increase the second law of thermodynamics requires. Therefore, the second law must be the driving force in adaptive evolution. Every process of adaptive evolution—whether it's the one Darwin discovered or any other—has to be based on second law entropy increase.

The physical facts—the starting conditions at the big bang plus the laws of physics—fix all the other facts, including the chemical and biological ones. All the laws of physics except the second law work backward and forward. So every one-way process in the universe must be driven by the second law. That includes the expansion of the universe, the buildup of the chemical elements, the agglomeration of matter into dust motes, the appearance of stars, galaxies, solar systems, and planets, and all other one-way processes. And that will eventually include, on one or more of these planets, the emergence of things with even the slightest, merest sliver of an adaptation. We can put it even more simply. In a universe of things moving around and interacting on paths that could go in either direction, the only way any one-way pattern can emerge is by chance, here and there, when conditions just happen to be uneven enough to give the pattern a start.

These rare one-way patterns will eventually peter out to nothing. Trust the second law. Consider the one-way process that built our solar system and maintains it. It may last for several billion years. But eventually, the nice pattern will be destroyed by asteroids or comets or the explosion of the sun or the merging of the Milky Way with other galaxies, whichever comes first. That's entropy increase in action on a cosmic scale. On the local scale, entropy increase will occasionally and randomly result in adaptive evolution. And that is the only way adaptations can emerge in a universe where all the facts are fixed by the physical facts.

Because entropy increase is a one-way street, the second law is also going to prevent any adaptation-building process from retracing its steps and finding a better way to meet the challenge at hand. Once a local adaption appears, it can't be taken apart and put together in different, more efficient, less entropy-increasing ways. The only way to do that is to start over independently. Adaptation building produces outcomes that get locked in, to be worked around in the creation of new adaptations. Natural selection is famous for producing such examples of inferior design, Rube Goldberg complexity, and traits that could only have been "grandfathered in." It's not just the oft-cited example of the blind spot in the mammalian eye resulting from the optic nerve's coming right through the retina. An even more obvious case is the crossing of the trachea and the digestive system at the pharynx—convenient only if you like choking to death. We think of the giraffe's neck as an adaptation par excellence. But the nerve that travels from its brain to its larynx has to go all the way down the neck, under the aorta, and back up—a 20-foot detour it doesn't need to take.

Any adaptation-creating process has to produce suboptimal alternatives all the time. It has to do this not just to ensure entropy increase but to honor the one-way direction that the second law insists on. Perhaps our most powerful adaptation is the fact that our brain is very large. It has enabled us to get to the top of the carnivorous food chain everywhere on Earth. But this is only the result of a piece of atrocious design. The mammalian birth canal is too narrow to allow large-brained babies to pass through. This bit of locked-in bad design meant that the emergence of human intelligence had to await random changes that made the skull small and flexible at birth and thus delay brain growth till after birth. This is where the large fontanel—the space separating the three parts of the infant's skull—comes in. Now the kid has room to get through the birth canal and has a skull that will immediately expand afterward to allow a big brain to grow inside it. But brain growth after birth introduced another huge problem: the longest period of childhood dependence of any species on the planet. All this maladaptation, corner cutting, jury-rigging is required by the second law of any process that produces adaptations.

What does all this come to? The only way a recipe for building adaptations can get along with the second law is by employing it. The only recipe that can do that is the process that Darwin discovered: dumb luck variation, one-way filtering, and a very expensive copying machine.

To see how hard it is to build a real alternative consistent with the second law, let's consider the way the enlightened scientific theist explains the appearance of adaptations. It will turn out that all we need to do to turn the theistic recipe into a Darwinian one is modify it just enough to honor the second law!

You Can't Have Your Darwinian Cake and Eat Theism Too

So far in this book, there has been no effort to refute the God hypothesis. Our project is not to provide another argument for atheism, but to explore the God-free reality. Nevertheless, it will be worth showing that the second law makes reconciliation between theism and Darwin's discovery logically impossible. The demonstration has an added plus. It shows that when you actually try to combine Genesis and the second law, all you get is an extreme version of Darwin's explanation of how adaptations arise.

There has been a vast industry of attempts to reconcile God and Darwin's theory. It's an industry with a gold standard of achievement provided by John Templeton's 1,000,000-pound prize. Ever since Darwin, people have noticed that his theory makes God unnecessary, and they have jettisoned the hypothesis of God's existence. But some people also have lots of motives for hanging on to God along with their Darwinism, if they can. Motives, not grounds or evidence, mind you. For some people, chief among these motives is the desire to make science safe from religious fundamentalists—Jewish, Christian, or Muslim. The enlightened way to do that is to show that religion and Darwin's theory are perfectly compatible. If God and Darwin are compatible, we won't have to choose between them. We can give unto Darwin that which is Darwin's, and give unto Abraham, Jesus, or Muhammad that which is his. The budget for medical research will be safe from the troglodytes, and we'll be able to continue to teach evolution in Mississippi and Alabama, Jerusalem, Cairo, and Jakarta.

The strategy for reconciliation of Darwin and God is well known and well beloved, especially by high school science teachers. Here is how it works: Suppose there is a designer and he (theism pretty much insists on a *he*) created us, along with everything else, with all the nice adaptations we have. Suppose further that he did it intentionally, on purpose, with malice of forethought. Finally, suppose that he did so by using the mechanism of blind variation and natural selection that Darwin discovered.

Darwin didn't even mind encouraging this idea—kind of. In the first five editions of *On the Origin of Species*, there is no mention of God. In the sixth, he finally added a reference to "the creator" in the famous but originally deity-free peroration in the last paragraph of the last page of *On the Origin of Species*:

> There is grandeur in this view of life, with its several powers, having been originally breathed [added in the sixth edition: by the creator] into a few forms or into one; and that, whilst this planet has gone cycling on according to the fixed law of gravity, from so simple a beginning endless forms most beautiful and most wonderful have been, and are being, evolved.

The author of the most controversial theory in the history of science did everything in his power to maximize its acceptance by minimizing its radicalism. He shared credit, conciliated dissidents, and avoided bringing his theory into disrepute in every way possible. He kept his own atheism so quiet that people have been arguing about it ever since. And he sat still for attempts to reconcile the theory of natural selection with conventional pieties, as far as he could.

The reconciliation of deity-design theory and Darwin's theory of how adaptation happens looks breathtakingly simple and straightforward. It echoes Newton's view that the laws he discovered were God's commands to the universe he created. To reconcile Darwinism and theism, we need to give up a literal interpretation of the Old Testament, but we can still accept one essential tenet of the Abrahamic religions (Islam, Christianity, and Judaism): God created us (and everything else) in his own image—that is, according to a design he had in mind. The means he employed to create us could, for all we know, have been the very process Darwin discovered: blind variation and natural selection. This is almost the official Roman Catholic view. The Pope makes a slight fudge for the human soul, which being nonphysical cannot have been so created and was therefore "seeded" into each member of our species separately.

Even without the Catholic fudge, this reconciliation won't work. It's an illusion, based on a subtle misunderstanding of Darwin's theory and its foundations in the second law of thermodynamics.

The process of natural selection is a matter of probabilities in the same way the spread of gas molecules in the upstroke of a bicycle pump is a matter of probabilities, and for the same reason: the process of entropy increase is probable, not certain. This will be no surprise, given the role of the second law in generating evolutionary asymmetries. But even before this role became clear, the nature of evolutionary probabilities was well understood.

The theory tells us that fitness differences between organisms will *probably* lead to differences in their reproductive success. The Darwinian mechanism cannot guarantee the reproductive success of the fitter of two organisms, lineages, or populations. Therefore, it doesn't guarantee the evolution of adaptation. If it did claim that fitness differences guaranteed reproductive success, Darwin's theory would be false. Biologists are well aware of several quite rare circumstances under which, just through bad luck, the fittest among competing creatures do not survive at all, let alone have more offspring than the less fit ones.

The best-understood circumstance under which this happens is when populations are small. If there are only a handful of members of a species of varying fitness, then a bolt of lightning, a forest fire, a flash flood, a sudden earthquake, or an infrequent predator may by chance eliminate the fittest among these organisms before it has had the opportunity to convey its fitness-making traits to any offspring.

The small-number problem is of course much more serious in biology than in other domains, such as chemistry, for instance. Biology deals with organisms that number in the dozens or hundreds or thousands, while chemistry deals with molecules that number in the multiples of millions. Where many millions are concerned, the most probable outcome has a probability fantastically close to 1. Where only thousands are concerned, no outcome's chances ever reach anywhere near 1. When organisms are further divided up into small populations, lineages, and families interbreeding with one another, occupying different environments, subject to occasional environmental shocks that occur irregularly and infrequently, the highest probability outcome of selection is well below 1. In fact, there will often be several alternative outcomes tied for most probable.

Here is an example that should hit especially close to home.

About 200,000 years ago, we *Homo sapiens* were one of a relatively small number of primate species. Apparently, something not very good had been happening to our species' lineage for the million or so preceding years. Whatever it was that had been happening, by about 200,000 years ago, there were only something like 5,000 *Homo sapiens* individuals around. This definitely made us an endangered species, with a set of genes and traits that were quite improbable, given the presumably much larger set of genes shared in the hominin population before the bottleneck reduced us to such a small number. Geneticists know this by comparing mitochondrial and Y chromosome sequence variation among extant members of *Homo sapiens*. The comparison shows much less sequence diversity in humans than in practically any other mammal—even less than in the cheetah, the other African mammal that must have gone through a severe bottleneck, as its mitochondrial DNA sequences reveal.

Sometime later, about 80,000 years ago, give or take a few thousand years, some improbable event in one large family or small group prompted a handful of its members—certainly less than 150 people— to begin wandering north toward the Horn of Africa. What led to their departure we can only guess at—a feud, a theft, a refusal to share resources, a size too big to be supported by hunting in the area?

Perhaps a generation later, some of their descendants crossed the Red Sea (then much shallower than it is now and so dotted with islands). The ultimate result of this crossing over into Eurasia was the occupation by our species of almost every niche in the world, during which we killed off, directly or indirectly, all the other thousands of hominins whose ancestors had arrived there from Africa a million years before us. The point of this story is how a small number of improbable events moved our species from the threat of extinction to global dominance by taking an unrepresentative, improbable collection of its members out of Africa.

What does the role of low-probability events in evolution have to do with theism? Well, theism asserts the existence of a God of a certain kind, with certain important features. The "usual suspects" for this list of God's important properties are the three omnis—omnipotence, omniscience, omnipresence—along with benevolence, the will to do only good. This list of properties has been getting theism into trouble for a long time. The property that makes it impossible to reconcile theism and Darwinian natural selection is omniscience—God's complete knowledge of everything.

One feature is arguably indispensable to the theism of the Abrahamic religions—Judaism, Christianity, and Islam. They all say, "God created man in his own image. In God's image he created him; male and female he created them" (Genesis 27). One thing they all agree on is that we exist and have our features owing to God's design, based on an idea—an image, a design—of what he wanted. How literally to take this claim remains a matter of debate among the various sects, creeds, churches, divinity schools, madrassas, and biblical exegetes of the Abrahamic religions. There is a spectrum all the way from inerrancy—the Bible is to be taken literally and contains no errors—to a sort of minimal theism, according to which God created the world and everything in it, including us, in accordance with a design, but that thereafter his interventions have been minimal.

Any creed weaker than this minimal theism is hard to distinguish from atheism. Suppose that one holds that there is a God, but denies that God had any designs, intentions, or interests in setting the universe in motion and that our existence is just an interesting unintended by-product or side effect of his creative act. We may argue about whether this view, a kind of deism, differs in any significant way from that of the atheist, who holds that the universe was created by a quantum singularity. A version of theism worth believing must at a minimum attribute to God the *intention* to produce us and not just some intelligent creature or other, still less just any old life-form at all. Theism can give up on the omnis and maybe even surrender benevolence. Or it can just defend God's nature as beyond our ken. Theism can certainly deny to us any understanding of *why* God created us— you and me and every other pusillanimous creature that has ever crawled on Earth or slinked through slimy seas. What it can't give up is the credo that he created creatures like us, sapient creatures, and that he did so intentionally. Theism cannot accept the notion that we are a side effect, by-product, accident or coincidence, an unanticipated and unintended outcome.

Now, the standard reconciliation of Darwinism and theism goes like this. Everything *else* extant in zoology and botany might well be such a by-product, a side effect, an unintended but foreseen outcome of God's handiwork in creating us. Elephants and *E. coli* are by-products, since they were produced, along with us, by natural selection, and natural selection was the instrument, the means, the technique God used to produce his one intended outcome—*us*. A more ecumenical view might have it that all God's creatures, great and small, are equally intended outcomes, along with us, and all were produced by the device of blind variation and natural selection, just as the omniscient lord knew they and we would be so produced.

The trouble with this reconciliation is that it doesn't take Darwin's theory seriously. It just pretends to. Darwin's theory tells us that we, along with every other creature that roams Earth, are at best *improbable* outcomes of natural selection. It's not just that you and I might not have ever come into existence if different sperm had fertilized different eggs. Rather, sapient—

intelligent—life of any kind is an improbable outcome. Indeed, the theory of natural selection suggests that complex life of any sort is an improbable outcome; no wonder we haven't found it anywhere else in the universe. (The effort—SETI—the Search for Extraterrestrial Intelligence—has so far been pretty feeble.) In any case, the odds on finding anything that looks much like us elsewhere in the universe are vanishingly small, at least according to Darwinism.

Natural selection makes us highly improbable. It is therefore a highly *unreliable* means of making us or anything that looks like us. Indeed, it is an unreliable way of making intelligent life of any sort—or, for that matter, of making life of any sort. Any omnipotent deity (or other powerful agency) who decided to employ natural selection to produce us would almost certainly be disappointed many more than 99 times out of 100 attempts. If God had set his sights lower—say, to just producing any kind of intelligent life, or just any life at all, using the process of natural selection—he could have raised the probability of success a bit. But so long as you rely on natural selection, you can't raise the chances of ending up with life by very much. An omnipotent agency that employed natural selection to make *Homo sapiens* would certainly not be an omniscient one. He would have had to be rather dim. Even weak-minded creatures like us know that the combination of blind variation and environmental filtration is not a reliable way of making anything for which you already have a very definite design.

Theism, or at least a theism that makes the Abrahamic religions sensible, is just not compatible with Darwin's theory. You can't believe both. But if you are a true believer in theism, you can come close to reconciling them, perhaps close enough to deceive yourself. The trick is to believe that God is powerful enough, smart enough, and present at enough places and times to guide the process of evolution so that it *looks like* random variation and natural selection to anyone not in on the secret. Suppose God employed a method to obtain us—*Homo sapiens*—that was so complex, so subtle, and so difficult to uncover that the closest we could come to figuring it out is Darwin's theory of blind variation and environmental filtration. You might even go further and suppose that the closest any finite intelligence could come to uncovering God's method is Darwin's theory. You might even suppose that God designed our cognitive capacities so that the only scientific theory of evolution we could ever conceive of would be Darwin's. It would be, as Kant supposed of Newton's theory, the only game in town, not because it is true, but because its falsity is unthinkable by us once we see the evidence for it.

These suppositions would readily explain to a theist why so many smart scientists believe that Darwin's theory is true. For that matter, it would also explain why the smartest among them are atheists as well, since they recognize that theism and Darwinism are incompatible. But this stratagem won't reconcile theism and Darwinism.

In fact, one clear implication of this stratagem is that Darwinism is *false*. Darwinian theory tells us that evolutionary outcomes are the result of probabilities—chance reproduction, chance variation, chance environmental events operating on low population numbers. But the theist thinks that the process God chose was fiercely complicated and absolutely certain to have produced us. As such, the theist is committed to Darwin's theory being wrong, false, mistaken, erroneous, incorrect. Darwinian theory is false but just looks correct to smart people trying to figure out what caused adaptation. Saying it's false is no way to reconcile the truth of a theory with theism. Of course, the ways of God may be so far beyond our ken that the smartest and most knowledgeable of us *mistakenly* think adaptation is the result of natural selection. But that wouldn't reconcile theism and Darwinism. At most it shows how to be a theist and to treat Darwin's theory as a useful fiction, one that gets the mechanism of evolution completely wrong.

Actually, there is one way to reconcile second-law probabilities with theism. And maybe it will impress the prize-givers at the Templeton Foundation if they don't look too closely.

In the seventeenth century, an Irish theologian named Bishop Ussher, using the Old Testament, dated the creation of the world to October 23, 4004 BC. Later calculations by a Cambridge theologian refined this dating to 9:00 AM (Greenwich mean time?) on that date. Suppose they were right. Suppose that on that day, at that time of the morning, the entire Earth and everything in it, including our biblical ancestors as described in the Bible, spontaneously appeared, through no cause at all, as a quantum singularity. Call it the "Ussher event." That event would only be a little less probable than the sudden and entirely coincidental aggregation of matter into a Boltzmann brain somewhere in the universe (recall this possibility from Chapter 2). The sudden accidental, uncaused, spontaneous emergence of that much order in one place and time would satisfy physics, since it would have resulted from a state of the universe without any prior adaptation in the universe bringing it about. And all the "begetting" thereafter described by the Old Testament would have permitted the blind variants so created to pass through a certain amount of subsequent environment filtration.

The crucial thing to notice, however, is this: what we have imagined is really another case of the process Darwin discovered. Of course, it's just fantastically more improbable than the scenario that starts with a first tiny, minimal sliver of an adaptation appearing as a thermodynamic improbability. But the Ussher event is at least physically possible. And it would reconcile Genesis with natural selection. This would be a good thing for the

Bible, since, given the second law, Darwinism is the only game in town. Can I have the 1,000,000 pounds now, Mr. Templeton?

NEWTON EXPUNGED purpose from the physical world 350 years ago. Darwin did it for the biological realm 150 years ago. By now you'd think the message had gotten out. What is the purpose of the universe? There is none. What purposes are at work in the universe? Same answer: none.

Scientism means that we have to be nihilists about the purpose of things in general, about the purpose of biological life in particular, and the purpose of human life as well. In fact, wherever and whenever there is even the slightest appearance of purpose in the universe, the scientist's task is to figure out natural selection's sleight of hand. Take any biological process that looks like it's such an intelligent and flexible response to changes in the environment that it must be driven by a purpose, plan, or goal. Behind that appearance will be found some engine of blind variation and a filter passively screening for fitness, whether it's the building of the brain, navigating a freeway interchange, or keeping up your end of a conversation. We could fill a book with what is already known about how physics fakes design both on evolutionary time scales and from moment to moment. There is still a lot more to learn about Mother Nature's neat design-mimicking tricks. But we can be certain that natural selection is behind everything that seems to imply purpose, planning, goals, ends, and design.

There isn't any rhyme or reason to the universe. It's just one damn thing after the other. Real purpose has been ruled out by physics. And Darwinian natural selection is simply physics at work among the organic macromolecules. Many of us will treat this nihilism as a good thing. Remember the idea of God being responsible for the twentieth century?

Recognizing the fact of purposelessness in a world that is screaming design at us out of every niche and every organ is not easy. Even among people who accept scientism, the complete purposelessness of things is difficult to keep firmly in mind. That's because the teleological worldview is the second strongest illusion nature foists on us. We shall see that it does so as the side effect of an even deeper illusion, one that has itself a thoroughly Darwinian explanation. Exploring and exploding this last illusion is by far the biggest challenge scientism faces.

We'll start the task in the next chapter by asking where exactly this nihilism about purpose leaves human nature. Surely there is meaning and purpose in our lives, our actions, our history and institutions? We put it there. Surely we don't countenance nihilism about personal morality and social justice? If we did, others might rightly be anxious about our impact on culture and politics. And yet, doesn't nihilism about the physical and biological worlds put us on the slippery slope down to nihilism about the social and the psychological worlds, as well as the moral and the political ones?

Yup. But there's nothing to worry about.

Chapter 5

◀●▶

MORALITY:
THE BAD NEWS

IF YOU ARE LIKE MOST PEOPLE CONTEMPLATING SCI-
entism, it's the persistent questions about morality and mortality that grip you, not trivial topics like the nature of reality, the
purpose of the universe, or the inevitability of natural selection.

After all, the trouble most people have with atheism is that
if they really thought there were no God, human life would no
longer have any value, they wouldn't have much reason to go on
living, and even less reason to be decent people. The most persistent questions atheists get asked by theists are these two: In a
world you think is devoid of purpose, why do you bother getting
up in the morning? And in such a world, what stops you from
cutting all the moral corners you can? This chapter and the next
deal with the second question. The first one, about the meaning
of our lives, we'll take up in Chapter 9.

Scientism seems to make the unavoidable questions about
morality even more urgent. In a world where physics fixes all the

facts, it's hard to see how there could be room for moral facts. In a universe headed for its own heat death, there is no cosmic value to human life, your own or anyone else's. Why bother to be good?

We need to answer these questions. But we should also worry about the public relations nightmare for scientism produced by the answer theists try to foist on scientism. The militant exponents of the higher superstitions say that scientism has no room for morality and can't even condemn the wrongdoing of a monster like Hitler. Religious people especially argue that we cannot really have any values—things we stand up for just because they are right—and that we are not to be trusted to be good when we can get away with something. They complain that our worldview has no moral compass. These charges get redoubled once theists see how big a role Darwinian natural selection plays in scientism's view of reality. Many of the most vocal people who have taken sides against this scientific theory (for instance, the founders of the Discovery Institute, which advocates "intelligent design") have frankly done so because they think it's morally dangerous, not because it lacks evidence. If Darwinism is true, then anything goes!

You might think that we have to resist these conclusions or else we'll never get people to agree with us. Most people really do accept morality as a constraint on their conduct. The few who might agree privately with Darwinism about morality won't do so publicly because of the deep unpopularity of these views. "Anything goes" is nihilism, and nihilism has a bad name.

There is good news and bad news. The bad news first: We need to face the fact that nihilism is true. But there is good news here, too, and it's probably good enough to swamp most of the bad news about nihilism. The good news is that almost all of us, no matter what our scientific, scientistic, or theological beliefs, are committed to the same basic morality and values. The difference between the vast number of good people and the small number of bad ones isn't a matter of whether they believe in God or not. It's a difference no minister, imam, vicar, priest, or rabbi can do much about. Certainly, telling people lies about what will happen to them after they die has never done much to solve the problem of morally bad people. In addition to not working, it turns out not to be necessary either. By the same token, adopting nihilism as it applies to morality is not going to have any impact on anyone's conduct. Including ours.

There is really one bit of bad news that remains to trouble scientism. We have to acknowledge (to ourselves, at least) that many questions we want the "right" answers to just don't have any. These are questions about the morality of stem-cell research or abortion or affirmative action or gay marriage or our obligations to future generations. Many enlightened people, including many scientists, think that reasonable people can eventually find the right answers to such questions. Alas, it will turn out that all anyone can really find are the answers that they like. The same goes for those who disagree with them. Real moral disputes can be ended in lots of ways: by voting, by decree, by fatigue of the disputants, by the force of example that changes social mores. But they can never really be resolved by finding the correct answers. There are none.

Who Are You Calling a Nihilist, Anyway?

Nihilism was a word that was thrown around a lot in the nineteenth century. It often labeled bomb-throwing anarchists—think of Joseph Conrad's *Secret Agent* and people like Friedrich Nietzsche who rejected conventional morality. Today, nobody uses the word much. We can use it for a label, though we need to sharpen it up a bit, given the misuses to which it has also been put.

What exactly is nihilism? It's a good idea to start with what it isn't. Nihilism is not moral relativism. It doesn't hold that there are lots of equally good or equally right moral codes, each one appropriate to its particular ethnic group, culture, time period, or ecological niche. Nihilism doesn't agree with the relativist that capital punishment is okay at some times and places and not okay at other ones. It's also not moral skepticism, forever unsure about which among competing moral claims is right. Moral skepticism holds that capital punishment is definitely right or definitely wrong, but alas we can't ever know which.

Nor does nihilism claim that everything is permitted, that nothing is forbidden. Still less does it hold that destructive behavior is obligatory, that figurative or literal bomb throwing is good or makes the world better in any way at all. These are all charges made against nihilism, or at least they are often attributed to people the establishment wants to call nihilists. But they don't stick to nihilism, or at least not to our brand.

These charges fail because nihilism is deeper and more fundamental than any moral code. Nihilism is not in competition with other codes of moral conduct about what is morally permitted, forbidden, and obligatory. Nor does it disagree with other conceptions of value or goodness—what is good or the best, what end we ought to seek as a matter of morality.

Nihilism rejects the distinction between acts that are morally permitted, morally forbidden, and morally required. Nihilism tells us not that we can't know which moral judgments are right, but that they are all wrong. More exactly, it claims, they are all based on false, groundless presuppositions. Nihilism says that the whole idea of "morally permissible" is untenable nonsense. As such, it can hardly be accused of holding that "everything is morally permissible." That, too, is untenable nonsense.

Moreover, nihilism denies that there is really any such thing as intrinsic moral value. People think that there are things that are instrinsically valuable, not just as a means to something else: human life or the ecology of the planet or the master race or elevated states of consciousness, for example. But nothing can have that sort of intrinsic value—the very kind of value morality requires. Nihilism denies that there is anything at all that is good in itself or, for that matter, bad in itself. Therefore, nihilism can't be accused of advocating the moral goodness of, say, political violence or anything else.

Even correctly understood, there seem to be serious reasons to abstain from nihilism if we can. Here are three:

First, nihilism can't condemn Hitler, Stalin, Mao, Pol Pot, or those who fomented the Armenian genocide or the Rwandan one. If there is no such thing as "morally forbidden," then what Mohamed Atta did on September 11, 2001, was not morally forbidden. Of course, it was not permitted either. But still, don't we want to have grounds to condemn these monsters? Nihilism seems to cut that ground out from under us.

Second, if we admit to being nihilists, then people won't trust us. We won't be left alone when there is loose change around. We won't be relied on to be sure small children stay out of trouble.

Third, and worst of all, if nihilism gets any traction, society will be destroyed. We will find ourselves back in Thomas Hobbes's famous state of nature, where "the life of man is solitary, mean, nasty, brutish and short." Surely, we don't want to be nihilists if we can possibly avoid it. (Or at least, we don't want the other people around us to be nihilists.)

Scientism can't avoid nihilism. We need to make the best of it. For our own self-respect, we need to show that nihilism doesn't have the three problems just mentioned—no grounds to condemn Hitler, lots of reasons for other people to distrust us, and even reasons why no one should trust anyone else. We need to be convinced that these unacceptable outcomes are not ones that atheism and scientism are committed to. Such outcomes would be more than merely a public relations nightmare for scientism. They might prevent us from swallowing nihilism ourselves, and that would start unraveling scientism.

To avoid these outcomes, people have been searching for scientifically respectable justification of morality for least a century and a half. The trouble is that over the same 150 years or so, the reasons for nihilism have continued to mount. Both the failure to find an ethics that everyone can agree on and the scientific explanation of the origin and persistence of moral norms have made nihilism more and more plausible while remaining just as unappetizing.

PLATO'S PROBLEM FOR SERMONIZING ABOUT MORALITY

The problem of justifying morality—any morality—is a serious one for everybody—theist, atheist, agnostic. The difficulty of grounding ethics is one Plato wrote about in his very first Socratic dialogue—the *Euthyphro*. Ever since, it's been a thorn in the side of Sunday sermon writers.

In the *Euthyphro*, Plato invites us to identify our favorite moral norm—say, "Thou shalt not commit abortion" or "Homosexual acts between consenting adults are permissible." Assume that this norm—either one—is approved, sanctioned, even chosen by God.

Now, Plato says, if this norm is both the morally correct one and also the one chosen for us by God, ask yourself the following question: Is it correct because it is chosen by God, or is it chosen by God because it is correct? It has to be one or the other if religion and morality have anything to do with each other. It just can't be a coincidence that the norm is both the right one and chosen for us by God. Theism rules out coincidences like this.

Consider the first alternative: what makes the norm correct is that God chose it. If he had chosen the opposite one (a pro-choice or anti-gay norm), then the opposite one would be the morally right one.

Now consider the second alternative: God chose the pro-life or pro-gay norm, or whatever your favorite moral norm is, because it is the right one, and he was smart enough to discern that fact about it.

Pretty much everybody, including the dyed-in-the-wool theists among us, prefers the second alternative. No one wants to admit that our most cherished moral norms are the right, correct, true morality solely because they were dictated to us by God, even a benevolent, omniscient God. After all, he is omniscient, so he knows which norm is right; and he is benevolent, so he will choose the norm he knows to be morally best for us. If it's just a matter of whatever he says goes, then he could have made the opposite norm the right one just by choosing it. That can't be right.

It must be that the norms God imposes on us were ones he chose because they are the right ones. Whatever it is that makes them right, it's some *fact* about the norms, not some fact about God. But what is that fact about the right moral norms that makes them right? All we can tell so far is that it was some fact about them that God in his omniscient wisdom was able to see.

Atheists and agnostics, too, will make common cause with the theists in seeking this right-making property of any moral norm that we all share in common (and there are many such norms). Plato's argument should convince us all that finding this right-making property of the moral norms we accept is an urgent task.

There is one way for the theist to avoid this task, but it's not one people will have much intellectual respect for. The theist can always say that identifying the right-making property of the morally right norms is a task beyond our powers. They could claim that it is beyond the powers of any being less omniscient than God. So, we had better just take his word for what's morally right. We ought neither question it nor try to figure out what the right-making fact about the right morality is, the one that God can see but we can't. This is a blatant dodge that all but the least inquisitive theists will reject. After all, morality isn't rocket science. Why are its grounds beyond the ken of mortal humans?

What does Plato's problem for sermonizing about morality have to do with scientism, or nihilism for that matter? Two things. First, Plato's argument shows that our moral norms need to be justified and that religion is not up to the job. Second, it turns out that scientism faces a coincidence problem just like the one troubling the theists. No theist can accept that it's just a coincidence that a moral norm is the right one and that God just happened to choose it for us. One of these two things must explain the other. Similarly, scientism is going to be faced with its own intolerable coincidence. But unlike theism, it's going to have a solution: nihilism.

Nihilism maintains that there isn't anything that makes our moral norms the right ones or anyone else's norms the right ones either. It avoids the challenge Plato set for anyone who wants to reveal morality's rightness. Nihilism instead recognizes that Plato's challenge can't be met. But the nihilist doesn't need to deny that almost all people share the same core moral norms, theists and nihilists included. Ironically, almost everyone's sharing a core morality is just what nihilism needs to show that no morality can be justified. What's more, the reasons that make nihilism scientifically and scientistically unavoidable also reveal that it doesn't have the disturbing features scientistic people worry about. Public relations problem solved.

Two Easy Steps to Nihilism

We can establish the truth of nihilism by substantiating a couple of premises:

+ First premise: All cultures, and almost everyone in them, endorse most of the same core moral principles as binding on everyone.
+ Second premise: The core moral principles have significant consequences for humans' biological fitness—for our survival and reproduction.

Justifying the first premise is easier than it looks. It looks hard because few moral norms seem universal; most disagree somewhere or other. Some moral values seem incommensurable with each other—we don't even know how to compare them, let alone reconcile them. Moral norms are accepted in some localities but not in others: some cultures permit plural marriage, while others prohibit it; some require revenge taking and honor killing, while others forbid these acts. Adultery, divorce, abortion, and homosexual relations go in and out of moral fashion. At first glance, it looks like there is a lot of moral disagreement. It's enough to make some anthropologists into moral relativists (moral codes bind only within their cultures). It makes some philosophers into moral skeptics (there may be an absolute moral truth, but we can't be certain or don't know what it is).

On the other hand, in human culture there has long been a sustained effort to identify a core morality—one shared by the major religions, one that cuts across political differences and diverse legal codes. It is a core morality that has held constant or been refined over historical epochs. Soon after the founding of the United Nations in the late 1940s, there was enough consensus on core morality that it was enshrined in the Universal Declaration of Human Rights. Roughly the same core morality has been written into many more international conventions on rights and liberties that have been adopted by varying coalitions of nations ever since. Even countries that decline to be parties to these treaties have at least paid lip service to most of the norms they enshrine. These agreements don't prove that there is a core morality, but they're good evidence that most people think there is.

Thus, there is long-standing evidence for the existence of core morality in the overlap of ethical agreement by the major religions and in the lip service paid by international agreements. But wait, there's more. Neuroscience, in particular the techniques of fMRI (functioning magnetic resonance imaging of brain activity), increasingly shows that people's brains react the same way to ethical problems across cultures. This is just what the existence of core morality leads us to expect. If you are really worried about whether there is a core morality, you can jump to the next chapter, in which its existence is established beyond scientistic (if not scientific) doubt, and then come back.

At the base of the diverse moral codes out there in the world, there are fundamental principles endorsed in all cultures at all times. The difficulty lies in actually identifying the norms that compose this core morality. What is the difficulty? These almost universally agreed-on norms are so obvious that they are easy to miss when we set about trying to identify them. Instead we think of interesting norms such as "Thou shalt not kill" and immediately realize that each of us buys into a slightly different and highly qualified version of the norm. For some of us, "Thou shalt not kill" excludes and excuses self-defense, military activity, perhaps capital punishment, euthanasia, other cases of mercy killing, and killing other great apes, primates, mammals, and so forth. When we consider how pacifists, opponents of capital punishment, proponents of euthanasia, and so many others disagree on some or all of these qualifications, it's tempting to conclude that there is no core morality we all share, or else it's too thin to have any impact on conduct.

A more accurate way to think about core morality begins by recognizing those norms that no one has ever bothered to formulate because they never come into dispute. They might even be difficult to formulate if they cover every contingency and exclude all exceptions. If we set out to express them, we might start out with candidates like these:

> Don't cause gratuitous pain to a newborn baby, especially your own.
>
> Protect your children.
>
> If someone does something nice to you, then, other things being equal, you should return the favor if you can.
>
> Other things being equal, people should be treated the same way.
>
> On the whole, people's being better off is morally preferable to their being worse off.
>
> Beyond a certain point, self-interest becomes selfishness.
>
> If you earn something, you have a right to it.
>
> It's permissible to restrict complete strangers' access to your personal possessions.
>
> It's okay to punish people who intentionally do wrong.
>
> It's wrong to punish the innocent.

Some of these norms are so obvious that we are inclined to say that they are indisputably true because of the meaning of the words in them: having a right to something is part of what we mean by the words "earn it." Other norms are vague and hard to apply: when exactly are "other things equal"? And some norms could easily conflict with each other when applied: would you really treat your children and other people the same? This shows how difficult it is to actually tease out the norms we live by, to list all their explicit exceptions, establish their priorities over other norms, and show how they are to be reconciled when they come into conflict. Almost certainly, the actual norms we live by but can't state will be somewhat vague, will have a list of exceptions we can't complete, and will conflict with other equally important norms. But most of the time, none of these problems arise to bedevil the application of the norms of core morality.

The next step in understanding moral disagreement involves recognizing that such disagreements almost always result from the combination of core morality with different factual beliefs. When you combine the uncontroversial norms of the moral core with some of the wild and crazy beliefs people have about nature, human nature, and especially the supernatural, you get the ethical disagreements that are so familiar to cultural anthropology. For example, Europeans may deem female genital cutting and/or infibulation to be mutilation and a violation of the core moral principle that forbids torturing infants for no reason at all. West and East African Muslims and Animists will reject the condemnation, even while embracing the same core morality. They hold that doing these things is essential to young girls' welfare. In their local environments, some genital cutting makes them attractive to potential future husbands; some sewing up protects them from rape. The disagreement here turns on a disagreement about factual beliefs, not core morality.

Even Nazis thought themselves to share core morality with others, including the millions they annihilated, as the historian Claudia Koontz documents in *The Nazi Conscience*. Outside of the psychopaths among them, Nazis were right to think that to a large extent they shared our core morality. It was their wildly false *fac-*

tual beliefs about Jews, Roma, gays, and Communist Commissars, combined with a moral core they shared with others, that led to the moral catastrophe of the Third Reich. You may be tempted to reply that it couldn't be that the Nazis just got their facts wrong, since there was no way to convince them they were mistaken. You can't reason with such people; you just have to confine them. True enough. But that shows how difficult it is to pry apart factual beliefs from moral norms, values, and the emotions that get harnessed to them. It's what makes for the appearance of incommensurability of values we so often come up against.

In any case, the argument that we're developing here doesn't require that every part of the core morality of every culture, no matter how different the cultures, be exactly the same. What we really need to acknowledge is that there is a substantial overlap between the moral cores of all human cultures. The principles in the overlapping core are among the most important ones for regulating human conduct. They are the ones we'd "go to the mat for," the ones that are justified if any moral norms are justified. But as noted, they are also the ones that occasion the least argument, even across different cultures, and so hardly ever get explicitly articulated.

Along with everyone else, the most scientistic among us accept these core principles as binding. Such norms reveal their force on us by making our widely agreed-on moral judgments somehow *feel* correct, right, true, and enforceable on everyone else. And when we are completely honest with ourselves and others, we really do *sincerely endorse* some moral rules we can't fully state as being right, correct, true, or binding on everyone. Scientism is not going to require that we give up that feeling or withdraw the sincerity of the endorsement. In a fight with these emotionally driven commitments, they'll win every time, for reasons that will become clear in Chapter 6. But scientism does recognize that emotionally driven commitment is no sign of the correctness, rightness, or truth of what we are emotionally committed to. As we'll see, add that recognition to science's explanation of where the shared norms come from, and you get nihilism.

The second premise we need to acknowledge is that core morality, the fundamental moral norms we agree on, has serious consequences for survival and reproduction. This will be especially true when those norms get harnessed together with local beliefs under local conditions. The connection between morality and sex is so strong, in fact, that each may be the first word you think of when you hear the other. The connection makes for a lot of good jokes. (Did you hear the one about Moses descending from Sinai with the two tablets bearing the ten commandments? "I have good news and I have bad news," he says. The children of Israel ask, "What's the good news?" Moses replies, "I argued him down from 38." They ask, "And the bad news?" Moses replies, "Adultery is still one of them.")

The idea that the moral core has huge consequences for survival and reproduction should not be controversial. Any longstanding norm (and the behavior it mandates) must have been heavily influenced by natural selection. This will be true whether the behavior or its guiding norm is genetically inherited, like caring for your offspring, or culturally inherited, like marriage rules. That means that the moral codes people endorse today almost certainly must have been selected for in a long course of blind variation and environmental filtration. Because they had an impact on survival and reproduction, our core moral norms must have been passed through a selective process that filtered out many competing variations over the course of a history that goes back beyond *Homo erectus* to our mammalian ancestors.

Natural selection can't have been neutral on the core moralities of evolving human lineages. Whether biological or cultural, natural selection was relentlessly moving through the design space of alternative ways of treating other people, animals, and the human environment. What was that process selecting for? As with selection for everything else, the environment was filtering out variations in core morality that did not enhance hominin reproductive success well enough to survive as parts of core morality. (You'll find much more on how Darwinian processes operate in cultural evolution in Chapter 11.)

There is good reason to think that there is a moral core that is almost universal to almost all humans. Among competing core moralities, it was the one that somehow came closest to maximizing the average fitness of our ancestors over a long enough period that it became almost universal. For all we know, the environment to which our core morality constitutes an adaptation is still with us. Let's hope so, at any rate, since core morality is almost surely locked in by now.

If you are in any doubt about this point, you are in good company. Or rather, you were until the last 50 years of research in behavioral biology, cognitive social psychology, evolutionary game theory, and paleoanthropology. Until the recent past, no one thought that core morality was selected for. Now science knows better. If you are in doubt about this matter, the next chapter shows how natural selection made core morality inevitable. It's the key to taking the sting out of the unavoidable nihilism that this chapter is about to establish.

IF CORE MORALITY IS AN ADAPTATION, IT MUST BE GOOD FOR US. SO WHY NIHILISM?

Grant the two premises—moral norms make a difference to fitness and there is a universal core morality. Then the road to nihilism becomes a one-way street for science and for scientism.

The core morality almost everyone shares is the correct one, right? This core morality was selected for, right? Question: Is the correctness of core morality and its fitness a coincidence? Impossible. A million years or more of natural selection ends up giving us all roughly the same core morality, and it's just an accident that it gave us the right one, too? Can't be. That's too much of a coincidence.

Remember Plato's problem. God gave us core morality, and he gave us the right core morality. Coincidence? No. There are only two options for the theist. Either what makes core morality right is just the fact that God gave it to us, or God gave it to us because it is the right one.

Of course, there is no God, but science faces a very similar problem. Natural selection gave us morality, and it gave us the *right* morality, it seems. So, how did that happen? The question can't be avoided. We can't take seriously the idea that core morality is both correct and fitness maximizing and then claim that these two facts have nothing to do with each other. That's about as plausible as the idea that sex is fun and sex results in reproduction, but these two facts have nothing to do with each other.

Is natural selection so smart that it was able to filter out all the wrong, incorrect, false core moralities and end up with the only one that just happens to be true? Or is it the other way around: Natural selection filtered out all but one core morality, and winning the race is what made the last surviving core morality the right, correct, true one.

Which is it?

It can't be either one. The only way out of the puzzle is nihilism. Our core morality isn't true, right, correct, and neither is any other. Nature just seduced us into thinking it's right. It did that because that made core morality work better; our believing in its truth increases our individual genetic fitness.

Consider the second alternative first: Natural selection filtered out all the other variant core moralities, leaving just one core morality, ours. It won the race, and that's what made the last surviving core morality, our core morality, the right, correct, true one. This makes the rightness, correctness, truth of our core morality a result of its evolutionary fitness. But how could this possibly be the answer to the question of what makes our core morality right? There doesn't seem to be anything in itself morally right about having lots of kids, or grandchildren, or great grandchildren, or even doing things that make having kids more likely. But this is all the evolutionary fitness of anything comes to.

The first alternative is the explanation for the correlation that we'd *like* to accept: core morality is the right, binding, correct, true one and that is why humans have been selected for detecting that it is the right core morality. But natural selection couldn't have been discerning enough to pick out the core morality that was independently the right, true, or correct one. There are several reasons it had little chance of doing so.

First, there is lots of evidence that natural selection is not very good at picking out true beliefs, especially scientific ones. Natural selection shaped our brain to seek stories with plots. The result was, as we have been arguing since Chapter 1, the greatest impediment to finding the truth about reality. The difficulty that even atheists have understanding and accepting the right answers to the persistent questions shows how pervasively natural selection has obstructed true beliefs about reality.

Mother Nature's methods of foisting false beliefs on us were so subtle they have only recently begun to be detected. By the sixteenth century, some people were beginning to think about reality the right way. But natural selection had long before structured the brain to make science difficult. As we'll see in later chapters, the brain was selected for taking all sorts of shortcuts in reasoning. That was adaptive in a hostile world, but it makes valid logical reasoning, and especially statistical inference, difficult. Without the ability to reason from evidence, getting things right is a matter of good luck at best.

Second, there is strong evidence that natural selection produces lots of false but useful beliefs. Just think about religion, any religion. Every one of them is chock full of false beliefs. We won't shake any of them. There are so many, they are so long-lasting, that false religious beliefs must have conferred lots of adaptive advantages on believers. For example, it's widely thought that religious beliefs are among the devices that enforce niceness within social groups. The hypothesis that organized religion has adaptive functions for people and groups is backed up by a fair amount of evolutionary human biology. It couldn't have done so except through the false beliefs it inculcates. Of course, all the religious beliefs that natural selection foisted on people made acquiring scientific truths about the world much more difficult.

There is a third reason to doubt that natural selection arranged for us to acquire the true morality. It is really good at producing and enforcing norms that you and I think are immoral. It often selects for norms that we believe to be morally wrong, incorrect, and false. In fact, a good part of the arguments against many of these "immoral" beliefs rests on the fact that natural selection can explain why people still mistakenly hold them.

There are lots of moral values and ethical norms that enlightened people reject but which Mother Nature has strongly selected for. Racism and xenophobia are optimally adapted to maximize the representation of your genes in the next generation, instead of some stranger's genes. Consider the almost universal patriarchal norms of female subordination. They are all the result of Darwinian processes. We understand why natural selection makes the males of almost any mammalian species bigger than the females: male competition for access to females selects for the biggest, strongest males and so makes males on average bigger than females. The greater the male-male competition, the greater the male-female size difference. We also know that in general, there will be selection for individuals who are bigger and stronger and therefore impose their will on those who are weaker—especially when it comes to maximizing the representation of their genes in the next generation. But just because the patriarchy is an inevitable outcome of natural selection is no reason to think it is right, correct, or true.

In fact, once we see that sexism is the result of natural selection's search for solutions to the universal design problem of leaving the most viable and fertile offspring, some of us are on the way to rejecting its norms. We can now explain away sexism as a natural prejudice that enlightened people can see right through. In different environments, natural selection has produced other arrangements; consider, for example, the social insects, where the top of the hierarchy is always a female.

Natural selection sometimes selects for false beliefs and sometimes even selects against the acquisition of true beliefs. It sometimes selects for norms we reject as morally wrong. Therefore, it can't be a process that's reliable for providing us with what we consider correct moral beliefs. The fact that our moral core is the result of a long process of natural selection is no reason to think that our moral core is right, true, or correct.

Scientism looks like it faces a worse problem than the one Plato posed for theism. At least the theist can admit that there must be something that makes our moral core the right one; otherwise God would not have given it to us. The theist's problem is to figure out what that right-making property is. Faced with the widespread belief that the moral core is correct and faced with the fact that it was given to us by natural selection, scientism has to choose: did our moral code's correctness cause its selection, or did its selection make it the right moral core? As we've seen, scientism can't take either option.

Scientism cannot explain the fact that when it comes to the moral core, fitness and correctness seem to go together. But neither can it tolerate the unexplained coincidence. There is only one alternative. *We have to give up correctness.* We have to accept that core morality was selected for, but we have to give up the idea that core morality is true in any sense. Of course, obeying core morality is convenient for getting our genes copied in the next generation, useful for enhancing our fitness, a good thing to believe if all you care about is leaving a lot of offspring. If core morality is convenient, useful, good for any fitness-maximizing creature in an environment like ours to believe, then it doesn't matter whether it is really true, correct, or right. If the environment had been very different, another moral core would have been selected for, perhaps even the dog-eat-dog morality Herbert Spencer advocated under the mistaken label of social Darwinism. But it wouldn't have been made right, correct, or true by its fitness in that environment.

SCIENTISM STARTS WITH the idea that the physical facts fix all the facts, including the biological ones. These in turn have to fix the human facts—the facts about us, our psychology, and our morality. After all, we are biological creatures, the result of a biological process that Darwin discovered but that the physical facts ordained. As we have just seen, the biological facts can't guarantee that our core morality (or any other one, for that matter) is the right, true, or correct one. If the biological facts can't do it, then nothing can. No moral core is right, correct, true. That's nihilism. And we have to accept it.

Most people want to avoid nihilism if they can. And that includes a lot of people otherwise happy to accept scientism. Anti-nihilists, scientistic and otherwise, may challenge the two premises of this chapter's argument for nihilism: the notion that there is a core morality and the idea that it made a difference for survival and reproduction. The irony is that together these two premises, whose truth implies nihilism, also take the sting out of it. The next chapter sketches enough of what science now knows about human evolution to underwrite both premises and so make them unavoidable for scientism. At the same time, it shows that nihilism is nothing to worry about.

Chapter 6

◆

THE GOOD NEWS:
NICE NIHILISM

To NAIL DOWN NIHILISM, WE NEED TO BE VERY confident about how and why core morality is adaptive. We need to show why over the course of 3.5 billion years, relentless selection for fitness-maximizing creatures should have produced people with an almost universal commitment to a core morality. For evolutionary biology, this is the problem from heaven. Or at least it's the reason why more people prefer God's dominion to Darwin's hell of cutthroat competition.

For a long time after Darwin wrote *On the Origin of Species*, the existence of core morality made Darwinian natural selection apparently irrelevant to humanity's history, its prehistory, or its natural history for that matter. No one gave natural selection a chance to explain how our core moral code is possible, let alone actual. On the surface, core morality looks harmful to individual fitness. Think about all the cooperation, sharing, and self-sacrifice it enjoins. Consider its commitment to fairness, justice, equality, and other norms that obstruct looking out for number one and number one's offspring.

For over 100 years, Darwin's own difficulty explaining how core morality is even a possible result of natural selection was the single greatest obstacle to his influence in the social and behavioral sciences. Except for some racist kooks, no one took Darwin seriously in sociology, politics, economics, anthropology, psychology, or history.

All that has now changed. In the last 45 years or so, we have come to understand how natural selection gave us core morality. It turns out that doing so was integral and essential to the only adaptation that could have ensured our survival as a species. In fact, the adaptation that core morality constitutes enabled us to break out of that evolutionary bottleneck to which we were confined on the African savanna. We'll trace that process here in a little detail because of its attractive consequences for the nihilism to which we are committed. It is crucial to remember, however, that in this story, all the links in the chain are forged by the laws of nature that Darwin discovered. It is these that make the explanation convey real understanding.

When It Comes to Humans, Nature Had to Select for Niceness

Some components of core morality are easy explanatory targets for natural selection. Pretty much any norm that encourages good treatment of children and discourages bad doesn't need a very complicated evolutionary explanation. It's the components that encourage or require being nice to people genetically unrelated to you that has resisted evolutionary explanation. The most characteristic feature of human affairs is at the same time the one most recalcitrant to Darwinian explanation. The fact is, genetically unrelated people are nice to one another in many different ways, often without any guarantee or prospect of reward or reciprocation.

From the point of view of fitness maximization, this doesn't seem to make any sense. Of course, in small family groups of very closely related members, being nice to others will be selected for because it favors one's own (selfish) reproductive fitness; the people you are nice to will share your genes, and so their reproductive success will be yours, too. But once our hominin ancestors began to expand beyond the nuclear family, any tendency to niceness beyond the family should have been stamped out by natural selection, right?

This is not just a theoretical problem for human evolution. It was a concrete, life-or-death "design problem" faced by our hominin ancestors once they found themselves on the African savanna a few million years ago. They had been pushed out of the shrinking jungle rain forest by competition or because it was no longer capable of supporting them, or both. Our closet living relatives, the chimpanzees and gorillas, are still there, though hardly thriving themselves. It almost certainly was not intelligence or foresight that forced our ancestors onto the cooling, drying African plain. That's the lesson of Lucy, the 3-million-year-old fossil hominin found in Ethiopia in 1974; she was bipedal, but her brain was no larger than that of other primates. Survival on the savanna started to select for upright walking, both to see threats and keep cool, long before it started to select for increased intelligence.

More than a million years ago, our ancestors were beginning to differ from the other primates in at least three respects: they were living longer; they were having more offspring, owing to a much reduced interval between births compared to other primates; and the offspring were dependent for longer and longer periods than other primate babies. These changes, of course, had been gradual, probably caused by a change in diet that had other consequences. On the savanna, there was meat to scavenge from the carcasses that the megafaunal top predators were bringing down. It was mainly to be found encased by bone, in marrow and brain that the top predators couldn't get to. We could. Like chimps today, our ancestors were already using simple stone tools. Breaking bone was possible if they could only get to the carcasses quickly enough, then scare off the predator and keep it away. There wasn't much chance of that—but there must have been a little.

Over time, the increased access to protein would by itself have produced the three problems our ancestors faced. Increased protein enhances fertility, reduces birth intervals, and increases longevity. It also selects for reduction in the size of the digestive system of animals like us, since it is far easier to extract nutrients from marrow and brain than from vegetable matter. The same forces changed the shape of our molar teeth, the jaw, and jaw muscles needed to grind away at cellulose. Eventually, we ceased to require the ruminant capacities of bovines and other herbivores. No longer needing to build big guts for ruminant digestion released energy to make larger brains. The persistent increase in brain size led to longer childhood dependence. Recall the brain fontanel discussed in Chapter 4. To survive the narrow birth canal, the infant has to postpone most of its brain growth till after birth; whence the long period of childhood dependence.

This package of changes produced the design problem from hell: more mouths to feed over longer periods, but mothers prevented from providing for older offspring by the demands of younger ones; males living longer and so having still more offspring, putting further strains on available resources; and all those offspring needing literally years of protection and nourishment before they could fend for themselves. What a nightmare.

Some obvious solutions to this design problem are not attractive. Reducing maternal and paternal care will solve the resource problem by reducing infant survival. But it will expose lineages, groups, the species to extinction. Besides, it's not an available option, having been selected against among mammals for hundreds of millions of years. Increasing the birth interval may also have the same population-reducing risk. Besides, it's difficult to do. The only available method aside from abstinence (fat chance) is nursing the children for longer intervals. Lactation prevents menstruation, but it also puts further pressure on nutrition. Adults dying off earlier and offspring becoming self-supporting earlier are not available options.

Now, add in the presence of those megafauna predators on the savanna. In addition to the design problems already identified, our hominin ancestors also find themselves well down toward the very bottom of the carnivorous food chain. They were prey, not predators.

What could have solved the design problem faced by *Homo erectus*? Somehow the population explosion has to be put to use to increase resources instead of consuming them. Groups of adults might be able to protect populations against predators or even scare predators away from animal corpses with meat left to scavenge. Females could take turns caring for several offspring of relatives, freeing them to provide for the family group. Besides scaring megafauna away from carcasses, males could even work together to bring game down themselves. Older adults could start learning more about the environment, and with the kids' extended childhood, the adults would have enough time to teach them the most efficient and productive technologies. Obviously, an ever-increasing brain size was needed for all these things. But something else was needed, too. The minimum size of a group was going to have to increase beyond the nuclear family for any of these strategies to work. Somehow our ancestors had to acquire the social tolerance of other hominins that our primate relatives conspicuously lack.

Once they could actually stay calm in larger groups, the next step was to form some semblance of organization. To do this, somehow our ancestors needed to break out of the straitjacket of selfishness that natural selection had hitherto imposed. People needed to start cooperating big time. They needed to learn to behave according to norms of core morality. They need to slip the leash of "look out for number one" fitness maximization. And somehow they must have done so or we wouldn't be here to defend scientism. How did it happen?

Darwin tried to deal with this puzzle but failed. He argued that besides operating on lineages of individuals and their traits, natural selection also operated on lineages of groups of people. When these groups competed with megafauna and with one another for territory or prey, the winning groups would have to be the ones whose members worked together, who cooperated with one another to fight off predators, kill prey, and eventually kill off other groups of people. In the long run of competition between groups, those groups composed of people nice to one another, even when unrelated, would have been selected for. Eventually, the only groups left would be those composed of people nice to each other. Thus, according to Darwin, core morality triumphs as fitness enhancing for groups, despite its immediate fitness costs for the individual members of groups.

The trouble with this theory is the arms race. Once a fit enough strategy is in place, Mother Nature will start searching through design space to find new strategies that take advantage of the original one. In this case, the groups composed of nice individuals are always vulnerable to variation in the behavior of new members. A mutation can arise at any time among the offspring of nice people that makes one or more of them start to exploit the niceness of everyone else, to feather their own nests without being nice in return. Through their exploitation of the nice people around them, they will secure disproportionate resources. This improves their survival odds and increases the number of their offspring. After enough generations of such within-group competition, the original group of nice people has become a group of not very nice people. Worse than nihilists, natural selection has produced Thatcherite Republicans. And what is worse, they would subsequently face the original design problem of living too long and having too many demanding kids to survive in small family groups.

If it wasn't group selection, how did blind variation and environmental filtration hit on niceness, on norm following, as a solution to the design problem the ancestors of *Homo sapiens* faced? Mother Nature had one thing to work with that we did share with other primates: big brains and the "social intelligence" that goes with them. Like a few other species, our ancestors had already managed to acquire a fair ability to predict and so to exploit and to protect themselves from the tactics of other animals—predators, prey, other primates. Ethologists who study these species credit this ability to a "theory of mind." We'll adopt their label for it. It's an ability hominins and apes share with whales, dolphins, and elephants—other big-brained creatures.

If our distant ancestors were like present-day chimpanzees, then they engaged in precious little cooperation. Even in the best of circumstances, chimps don't share easily. Food transfer from parent to child is pretty much tolerated theft. Chimps almost never spontaneously help one another and never share information, something even dogs do with their masters. By comparison, contemporary human babies do all these things, and with strangers, well before they can do much more than crawl. They help, they share food, they even convey information before they have language and certainly without knowing anything about norms or niceness. That means that human babies have both an ability conveniently called a theory of mind and an inclination to cooperate; both are hardwired or quickly and easily learned with little experience at a very early age. If these traits are learned early, quickly, and reliably, then they don't have to be innate. But all the cognitive skills we need to acquire them will have to be hard-wired, along with some sort of bias toward learning them. How did humans acquire so much social intelligence and so amiable a disposition to use it?

Here is a theory based on comparative behavioral biology. There is another trait that we share with a few of the species that also have a fair grip on other minds—elephants, some whales, tamarin monkeys, and dogs: cooperative child care. This is a trait absent among chimpanzees and gorillas. The fact that this trait—sharing the care of the offspring of others—arose inde-pendently more than once suggests that it, or whatever triggers it, is a fairly common blind variation. Selection for sharing child care demands improvements in theory-of-mind abilities by spe-cies that already have that ability, such as the primates. Now we have a coevolutionary cycle in which shared child rearing selects for improvements in theory of mind, and improvement in theory of mind enhances the fitness of those practicing cooperative child care, and so on, until you get people almost born to cooperate.

These abilities are being selected for in nuclear families or among very closely related ones. But survival requires larger groups of less closely related people to cooperate. Why suppose that there was strong enough selection for cooperation to trump the short-sighted selfish fitness maximization that threatens to unravel the first stirrings of niceness? After all, the nuclear family is not a group large enough to enable us to move up the food chain.

BEAUTIFUL MINDS: CHARLES DARWIN MEETS JOHN VON NEUMANN

This is where evolutionary biology makes common cause with modern economics to identify the design problem's solution that saved humanity and saves Darwinian theory.

Game theory was invented by Hungarian physicist John von Neumann in the late 1920s. Never heard of him? He designed the first electronic computer, figured out how to build the H-bomb, and invented the U.S. nuclear deterrent strategy during the cold war. How did he manage to remain so anonymous? Mainly because his life was not as dramatic as John Nash's, another of the founders of the field. Nash's path from mathematics through madness to the Nobel Prize was such a good story that it was made into *A Beautiful Mind*, a movie that won four Academy Awards. Von Neumann's mind was at least as beautiful and his contributions to game theory were at least as important. He started the whole enterprise, and without it we wouldn't have the solution to Darwin's puzzle about how core morality is even possible.

The label "game theory" does von Neumann and Nash's branch of economics a profound disservice; it's hard to take seriously a bit of science devoted to understanding games. Despite the name, game theory isn't really about games. It's about all strategic interactions among people, about how people behave when they have to figure out what other people are going to do so that they can scheme together with them or protect themselves from the schemes of others. Notice that to scheme with or against someone else requires that you have a theory of mind. You have to be able to put yourself in the other player's shoes, so to speak, and act as if he or she has a mind that makes choices in order to figure out what you should do. Game theory should have been called the theory of strategic interaction, but it's too late to change names.

Once invented, game theory had rather limited influence outside mathematical economics until it was taken up by evolutionary biologists. Their interest was sparked by the fact that game theory enables us to make explicit the design problem posed by the long-term benefit of cooperation and the immediate cost in individual fitness of doing so.

In economics, game theory assumes that the competitors in the game are rational agents. Of course, evolutionary game theory can't assume that individual animals are rational agents—it doesn't even assume humans are. Nor does evolutionary game theory assume that animals' behavior is genetically hardwired. It requires only that behavior respond to environmental filtration. If hardwired, then natural selection keeps selecting for more and more optimal behavior by filtering the genes that hardwire the behavior.

If the behavior is learned, the learning device is hardwired into the animal's brain. It filters for the fittest strategic behaviors by operant reinforcement, the process B. F. Skinner discovered and named. Operant reinforcement is just natural selection operating over an animal's lifetime. Behavior is randomly, blindly emitted; the environment rewards some of these behaviors and punishes others. In Skinner's lab, the rewards were usually food pellets. In nature, rewards include obvious outcomes like successful feeding foraging, fighting, and reproduction. Punishments are unsuccessful outcomes in these activities. Reinforcement results in the repetition, persistence, or strengthening of the initially randomly emitted behavior. Punishment has the reverse result. Skinner devoted most of his research life to showing how much behavior, including what looks to us to be intended, consciously planned behavior, is the result of this process of blind variation and environmental filtration.

In the case of hardwiring, nature usually has millions of years to fine-tune behavior to its environment; in the case of learning, it often has time only to hit on minimally satisfactory strategies.

Let's set up the problem Darwin tried to solve with group selection in the way that game theorists think about it. Often, they start with a particular model, the famous *prisoner's dilemma* game (PD for short). Suppose you and I set out to rob a bank and we are caught with our safecracking tools before we can break in. We are separated and informed of our rights as criminal suspects and then offered the following "deals." If neither of us confesses, we'll be charged with possession of safecracking tools and imprisoned for one year each. If we both confess to attempted bank robbery, a more serious crime, we'll each receive a five-year sentence. If, however, only one of us confesses and the other remains silent, the confessor will receive a suspended one-year sentence in return for his or her confession, and the other will receive a ten-year sentence for attempted bank robbery. The question each of us faces is whether or not to confess.

As a rational agent, I want to minimize my time in jail. If I think you're going to confess, then to minimize my prison sentence, I had better confess, too. Otherwise, I'll end up with ten years and you'll just get a suspended one-year sentence. But come to think of it, if I confess and you don't, then I'll get the suspended one-year sentence. Now it begins to dawn on me that whatever you do, I had better confess. If you keep quiet and I confess, I'll get the shortest jail sentence possible. If you confess, then I'd be crazy not to confess as well. If I don't confess I might get the worst possible outcome, ten years. So, I conclude that no matter what you do, the only rational thing for me to do is to confess. Game theorists call this the dominant strategy.

Now, how about your reasoning process? Well, it's exactly the same as mine. If I confess, you'd be a fool to do otherwise, and if I don't, you'd still be a fool to do otherwise. You have a dominant strategy—the most rational under the circumstances—and it's the exact same strategy as mine.

The result is that we both confess and both get five years in the slammer. Where's the dilemma? Well, if we had cooperated, we would both have gotten one year. Looking out for our own interests leads us to a "suboptimal" outcome, one less desirable than another that is attainable. Rationality leads to suboptimality; there is an outcome that both rational egoists prefer but can't reach. Hence, the dilemma.

Why should this model of strategic interaction have any bearing on an evolutionary account of social cooperation? Because prisoner's dilemmas are all over the place in social and biological life, and they have been since before there were humans. They must have been especially frequent and important among scavenging hominins on the African savanna a million years ago. Any way you look at it, two hungry human scavengers coming on a recently killed carcass face several distinct prisoner's dilemmas. They know that a fresh kill means that there is a serious predator around, one they can't deal with. They know also that the fresh kill will attract other scavengers they can't deal with either— hyena packs. If they both scavenge, they'll get some food, but the chances of being surprised by predators or more powerful scavengers are high, and the outcome would be fatal. One could watch for predators while the other eats, but chances are the watcher gets nothing while the scavenger feasts. If they each scavenged for a few minutes and then stopped and listened for a few minutes, they'd get some food and avoid a fatal encounter with a predator. But the moment one of them stops to watch, the other will have a clear field to gorge himself at the look-out's expense. What to do?

The dominant strategy is to scavenge like mad and don't bother looking out for threats. If the other guy splits his time between eating and watching, you're better off, and if the other guy doesn't, your watching for predators lets him take the best cuts. One thing they can't do is agree with one another to alternate eating and watching. Even if they are smart enough to figure this out and have enough language to bargain to an agreement, there is no way they can enforce the agreement on one another. That would take time from eating from the carcass and watching for predators. What is more important, neither will be prepared to enforce on the other the promise each makes to alternate eating and watching. That would just take time from eating or watching. Their mutual promises will be cheap talk, empty words. A classic PD.

Of course, watching and eating are not the only strategies available to each scavenger. Another option is to just kill the other guy the moment he turns his back and starts to scavenge. That will leave everything to the killer, at least till a stronger predator arrives. Of course, if they both left the other alone and began to eat, they'd each do better than dying. Neither can afford to risk that. All they can do is warily stalk each other, getting hungrier all the time, while the vultures take all the meat on the carcass.

The PD problem kicks in even before there is a chance to feed. Suppose two scavengers come upon a carcass being eaten by one lone hyena. If they both expose themselves, making noise and throwing rocks, there is a good chance they'll drive the hyena away and have a decent meal. But there is a chance one or both might be injured by the surprised hyena. If one hides while the other tries to scare the hyena away, he'll do better no matter what happens—less risk, more eating time. Each hangs back in the undergrowth, waiting for the other to charge the hyena—that's the dominant strategy. As a result, neither of them gets anything.

But they can't enforce on each other the mutually beneficial strategy of both of them scaring the hyena. Another PD.

In everyday life today, we still find ourselves in PD situations—for example, every time we go shopping. Consider the last time you purchased a soft drink at a convenience store just off the highway in a region of the country you'll never visit again. You have a dollar bill in your hand and want a drink; the salesperson behind the counter has the drink and wants the bill in your hand. He proffers the bottle, with the other hand held out for the money. *His* best strategy is to take your bill and hang on to the drink. If you complain, he'll simply deny you paid him. You won't call the police. You simply don't have time and it's not worth the trouble, in spite of your moral indignation; you're better off just going to the next convenience store on the road. *Your* best strategy is to grab the bottle, pocket your bill, and drive off. Will the salesperson call the police? If he did, would they give chase just for a bottle of Coke? The answer to each of these questions is no. It's not worth their trouble.

Knowing all this, neither of you does the rational thing. Thoughtlessly, irrationally, you both cooperate, exchanging the dollar bill for the drink. There are infinite examples like this. Consider the last time you left a tip, flushed a public toilet, or added some change to a street musician's take. People find themselves in PDs constantly and almost never choose the dominant egoistical strategy. The economists need an explanation for why we are nice when it doesn't look like the rational strategy. The biologist needs an explanation for why we are nice when it doesn't look like the fitness-maximizing strategy.

Here is the evolutionary game theorist's explanation, and it's just what Darwinian theory needs to show that niceness can enhance fitness and thus get selected for. Fortunately for humans, in addition to imposing a small number of single "one-shot" games on our ancestors, nature also imposed on them (and still imposes on us) other quite different strategic choice problems. These problems are made up of a large number of repetitions of the same simple game played over and over with different people. Nowadays, you and a lot of other people go to your local convenience store and purchase something from a number of different people behind the counter. Each transaction is one round in an iterated PD game you and everyone else—shopper and salesperson—is playing. Similarly, in the Pleistocene, scavenging repeatedly presented our ancestors with the same repeated strategic choice problems over and over again. That's what tribal life is all about.

In an iterated PD, there are many possible strategies players can adopt: always defect; always cooperate; cooperate on even-numbered games, defect on odd-numbered games; cooperate five times in a row, then defect five times in a row; cooperate until the other player defects, defect thereafter; defect until the other guy cooperates, then cooperate thereafter. The number of possible strategies is vast. Are there better strategies than always to defect? Is there a best strategy?

Under fairly common circumstances, there are several far better strategies in the iterated PD game than "always defect." In iterated PD, always taking advantage of the other guy is almost never the dominant strategy. In many of these iterated PDs, the best strategy is a slightly more complicated strategy called "tit for tat." Start out cooperating in round 1; then, in round 2, do whatever your opponent did in the previous round. Round 1 you cooperate. If the other player also cooperates, the next time you face that same player, cooperate again. If the other player cooperates in round 2, you know what to do in round 3. If in round 1 the other player defects, trying to free-ride on you, then in round 2 against that player, you have to defect as well. Following this rule after round 1, you will have to continue cooperating until the other guy defects, and vice versa. If you have both been cooperating through 33 rounds and in his 34th game against you the other player suddenly switches to defect, trying to free-ride on your cooperation, then in round 35 against him, you have to defect. If in round 35, your opponent switches back to cooperate, then in round 36, you should go back to cooperation. That's why the strategy is called tit for tat.

Why is tit for tat almost always a better strategy in iterated PD than always defect? In a competition in which tit-for-tat players face each other, they cooperate all the time and so accumulate the second best payoff every time. That's usually a lot better outcome than playing always defect: you get the successful free-rider's top payoff the first time and only the third best payoff all the rest of the time. The more rounds in the iterated PD, and the more chances you have to play with tit-for-tat players and get the second highest payoff every time, the better the outcome for cooperating and the worse for defecting. Provided that the number of individual rounds in the iterated game is large enough, that the chances of playing against the same person more than once are high enough, and that the long-term payoff to cooperating in future games against other cooperators is high enough, it's always best to play tit for tat, especially if you are relentlessly looking out only for number one.

It's easy to set up one of these iterated PD games either among people or in a computer simulation. Give each of two test subjects two cards, one with a D for defect, the other with a C for cooperate. Each subject plays one card at the same time. If both play D, each gets $2; if both play C, both get $5; if one plays D and the other plays C, the D player gets $10 and the C player gets nothing. Now, let a lot of subjects play one another many times. It's also easy to program a computer with a large number of strategies for playing the D card or the C card. Instead of money payoffs, you assign point payoffs to the various outcomes. Play the game or run the simulation 100 or 1,000 times. Add up the payoffs. Among human subjects and computer simulations, tit for tat usually comes out on top.

What's so good about tit for tat? Three things. First, this strategy always starts out being nice—that is, cooperating. Second, a player won't be taken for a sucker; a player retaliates when taken advantage of. Third, a player doesn't have to play against a tit-for-tat player many times to figure out what strategy he or she is using. And it's easy to switch to tit for tat and to start making the same gains.

The message that emerges from human experiments and computer simulations is also clear and also nice. Under a wide variety of conditions in which people face the strategic problem posed by an iterated PD, there will be selection for certain kinds of strategies. The fittest strategies are all variants on tit for tat: they are initially nice—players using them start out cooperating and are quick to forgive and minimally retaliatory; if opponents switch from defecting to cooperating, the tit-for-tat players switch to cooperation; and the strategies are transparent to other players, so it's easy to figure out how to do best when playing other tit-for-tat players—just do what they do.

If many or even just the most crucial interactions in our evolutionary past were such iterated games, then there would have been strong selection for nice strategies. If blind variation could impose tit for tat or some other nice strategy on the members of one or more groups of hominins, then those groups would flourish. Their members would solve the huge design problem imposed on them, and groups of such cooperators would be immune to the sort of subversion from within that undermined Darwin's group selection idea for how niceness could be selected for.

It's a nice story of how niceness could have emerged, but is it

any more than a story? Is there evidence that our hominin ancestors actually faced an iterated prisoner's dilemma often enough
over the time scale needed for cooperative strategies like tit for
tat to be selected for? There is no direct evidence. There was no
currency (natural or otherwise) to measure the payoffs, no way
to measure the frequency and numbers of interactions, and even
if there were, strategic interaction problems don't fossilize well.
On the other hand, when the choice was between extinction or
cooperation, the fact that we are here strongly suggests that cooperative strategies must somehow have been selected for.

Moreover, repeated PD games are not the only ones people
face and are not the only ones that select for niceness. Experiments focusing on other games that people (and computers) play
and that we know our ancestors faced strongly suggest that fitness and niceness really do go together.

Consider this strategic interaction problem, called "cut the
cake": Two players who don't know each other and can't communicate are each asked to bid for some portion of an amount
of money, say, $10. Each is told that if the other player's bid and
theirs total more than $10, neither gets anything, and if the total
of their two bids is equal to or less than $10, each receives what
they bid. In this one-shot game, most people spontaneously bid
an amount somewhere close to $5. In this case, rationality does
not by itself point to any particular strategy. So why should one
be predominant? What is more, the predominance of fair bids is
cross-culturally constant. Across a broad range of Western and
non-Western, agricultural, pastoral, slash-and-burn, nomadic,
and even hunter-gatherer societies, the fair offer is the predominant one.

Consider another game, this one a little more complicated. In
this game, one player gets the first move; call him the proposer.
He proposes how much of the $10 the other player will receive

and how much the proposer will keep. If the player going second, the disposer, agrees, then each party gets what the proposer decided. If the disposer rejects the proposal, neither party gets anything. Since this is a "take it or leave it" game, it's called the ultimatum game. In this game, it would obviously be irrational ever to decline even a very unequal split, since getting something is better than getting nothing. But across the same broad range of cultures, more often than not participants in the ultimatum game offer the other player $4 or more, and often $5. They also reject anything much less than a fair split. And people do this even when a tiny fraction of the total to be divided is a significant amount of money. In a lot of the cultures where this experiment has been run, $1 will keep you alive for a day, yet many people will reject proposals that leave them with less than $4 or so.

When asked to explain their strategies, most people identify a norm of equality as dictating their choice in the first game and a commitment to fairness as doing so in the second. In "cut the cake," people rarely ask for more than 5 units even when they think they can get away with 6. When asked why, they say they do so out of a sense of fairness. They also say that they get angry when the other player makes choices that strike them as unequal. When they play the disposer role in the ultimatum game, people describe their satisfaction at rejecting offers they think are too low. The feeling of satisfaction is evidently worth more to them than accepting a low offer of some amount of money rather than nothing. These games tap into strong feelings that lead people to do things that reflect important parts of core morality—norms of reciprocity, fairness, and equality.

In the experiments, the "cut the cake" and ultimatum games are one-shot games, played just once by people who don't know each other. Consider what happens when you program computers to play these two games over and over using many different strategies over a wide range of payoffs in individual games: demand 9, accept anything; demand 5, accept 4 or more; demand 4, accept 3 or more; and so on. Program a little evolution by natural selection into this simulation: If you start out with a lot of different competing strategies, have the simulation filter out the least rewarded strategies every ten or a hundred or a thousand or a million rounds. Replace each player using an eliminated strategy with a new one using one of the surviving strategies. It doesn't even have to be the best one. Program the computer to make a random choice. What you find is that if you play enough rounds, the strategies that do best overall are very often the ones that are "fair" or "equal." In "cut the cake," asking for half is a winning strategy most of the time. In the ultimatum game, asking for half and refusing anything much less does very well.

What does best in the long run doesn't always do best in the short run, but human evolution was (and is) a long-run process. These computer simulation results, along with similar ones for repeated prisoner's dilemma games, strongly suggest one thing: if we evolved in circumstances that had these kinds of payoffs, there would have been strong selection for core morality. There would have been strong selection for anything that made people adopt norms of fairness, equity, and cooperation.

But how does natural selection get people to adopt such norms? How does it shape such adaptations? What is the quick and dirty solution to the design problems that arise in situations of iterated strategic choice? This problem looks like it's too hard to be solved by genetically based natural selection. Maybe if there were genes for playing tit for tat, they would be selected for. But at least in the human case, if not in animal models, such genes seem unlikely. The solution has to involve some cultural natural selection. It can't, however, help itself to very much culture. After all, we are trying to explain core morality. And to get much culture, you must already have a fair amount of core morality.

IRRATIONAL LOVE, UNCONTROLLABLE JEALOUSY, POINTLESS VENGEFULNESS, AND OTHER HEALTHY EMOTIONS

Mother Nature is ever on the lookout for cheap solutions to design problems. In the rain forest, the design problem was figuring out how to do best, or at least how to avoid doing worst, in a lot of one-shot strategic games. Here selfishness maximized both individual gains and fitness. To this day, chimpanzees won't cooperate to secure food that they then have to share. Real cooperation in the jungle never had a chance. Nice guys finished last. But then hominins found themselves on the savanna, with too many young mouths to feed for too long a time. There they found nothing much to eat except berries, nuts, and what they could scavenge from the megafauna's latest meal, provided they could scare it away and keep other scavengers away.

It's pretty obvious that on the savanna there were new strategic interaction problems in which selfishness and fitness maximization came apart. Under these changed circumstances, nature will start searching through the inevitable variations in behavior for quick and dirty solutions to the new design problem—the iterated strategic game. It will sift through strategies like "be nice only to offspring and mate," "be nice only to close relatives," "be nice to everyone in the tribe all the time," or "be nice to people who were nice to you before." It will filter many other strategies, too.

Until this point in human evolution, the be-nice-to-nonkin strategies were all being remorselessly selected against. But now, on the savanna, the payoffs in strategic interaction began to take on the values of iterated prisoner's dilemma or repeated "cut the cake" or the ultimatum game played again and again. Under these new circumstances, Mother Nature could exploit the ability to read minds that our ancestors shared with the other primates. She could even exploit social intelligence (the theory of mind) and the tendency to share that cooperative child care made mutually adaptive. Hominins already disposed by selection to make cooperative opening moves in a PD encounter would already be acting on a rule that is "nice." Now it only needed to be shaped by operant conditioning—the natural selection in learned behavior Skinner discovered—into one that is retaliatory and clear. A variation in our traits that did those two things would itself strongly select for niceness in others and strongly select against being mean as well.

What kind of a device could nature have hit on in the course of our evolution that could guarantee to others that we will act in accordance with norms of niceness, fairness, equity, and much of the rest of the moral core?

It would have had to be a device that overrides the temptation to cheat, cut corners, free-ride when the opportunity occurs— and temptation can't be resisted, as we all know only too well. Psychologists long ago identified and explained a tendency that humans share with other creatures to prefer the smaller immediate payoffs that free-riding or cheating offers over the larger long-term payoffs that cooperating provides. We tend to have trouble postponing gratifications. From a Darwinian point of view, that used to be a good thing. Nature lacks foresight and can't afford it. It can't select traits whose payoff is very far down the road. By the time it gets down the road, we will probably be dead already. So, for a long time nature selected for immediate gratification over long-term gain. By the time hominins arrived on the scene, this preference for short-term over long-term gain had been firmly hardwired in us. But now all of a sudden, on the African savanna, it became maladaptive. Once payoffs to cooperation became high enough, Mother Nature needed to find a device to get us to resist temptation. Otherwise our posterity wouldn't have been around to secure the benefits of our self-control.

Go back to the reports of people who play the ultimatum game and "cut the cake," and you'll see that Mother Nature already had something in her tool kit that fits this bill very nicely: *emotion.*

Long ago, nature provided mammals with emotions. Darwin was among the first naturalists to study them carefully. One of his last books was titled *The Expression of the Emotions in Man and Animals.* He recorded there the remarkable similarity between human, primate, and canine expressions of emotion. Emotions must go back very far into our evolutionary tree. In humans, natural selection has co-opted emotions to enforce norms. These norms that emotions enforce are often good for our genes but not for us. We honor them in spite of the disservice they do to our interests. Love and jealousy are good examples. Both are strong emotions and are often very high in short-term costs for guys and highly beneficial to the maximization of their (long-term, multi-generational) genetic fitness.

Let's start with love and the design problem it solves for males. A male won't get sexual access to a female unless the male can convince her that he'll be around to share some of his resources with her and the kids he is going to produce. Since females have been selected for not being fooled by mere expressions of fidelity, they demand stronger assurances before they will allow males to have their way with them. As the Hollywood producer Samuel Goldwyn noted, a verbal contract is not worth the paper it is written on. A male's promise is unenforceable. Females can't rely on it because for a male it would be irrational to keep. With millions of sperm, the male's best strategy is to promise, get sexual access, and renege. The mammalian female has only a few hundred eggs and a limited number of ovulatory cycles. She can't afford to guess wrong about a reliable mate. What will reliably guarantee unenforceable promises about the future when it would be irrational for any male to keep them? One thing that would do it is a sign of irrational commitment to the female and to her interests that could not be faked.

Why must the sign signal irrational commitment? Because females recognize that it's irrational of males to commit resources to one female. So the sign the male sends the female really has to be one of irrational commitment. Why must the sign be unfakable? Because a fakable sign of commitment is just that, fakable, and therefore not credible. Love is irrational and unfakable, by males at any rate. In nature's search through design space for a strategy that will secure males' sexual access, the emotion of love looks like it will just do the trick.

Irrational love does not fully solve the male's design problems. After pairing up, the male faces another issue: the uncertainty of paternity. To convey resources to his mate's offspring, he needs assurance that the kids are really his. This is an uncertainty problem females don't have (unless kids get switched after birth). The male needs to reduce the uncertainty as much as possible. One way to do this is to pose a credible threat to anyone suspected of taking advantage of any absence from his partner's bed. To make this threat credible, the male must be motivated to carry it out even when it is crazy to do so. And often it is crazy, since it's the strong, the powerful, and the rich who usually try to take advantage of the weaker. The emotion of uncontrollable jealousy fits the bill perfectly. Revenge must be a credible threat; males must convince everyone that they will take measures to punish cheating wives and/or their lovers no matter how great the cost to themselves.

Overpowering jealousy does the job, though it makes the occasional male actually sacrifice his own short-term and long-term interests. In the overall scheme, the fact that every male is prone to feel such emotions maintains a norm among men and women that effectively reduces the uncertainty of paternity and so enhances most males' fitness. (Of course, female jealousy isn't selected for reducing the uncertainty of maternity. There is little to reduce. But the emotion's unfakable and irrational force deters other females from shifting her partner's resources to their offspring.)

Emotions are hardwired by genes we share and presumably share with other primates and indeed other mammals, as Darwin himself noticed. In us, of course, they get harnessed together with our highly developed theory-of-mind ability and with norms adaptive in our environments. They motivate enforcement of the norms they get paired up with, on others and on ourselves. Some of these norms solve design problems common to humans in all the environments we inhabit. These are parts of the moral core we all share. Others will not be part of core morality but will be locally restricted to the different ecologies that different groups inhabit. Some examples will illustrate how this works.

Anthropologists have uncovered how different ecologies select for differences in local moral norms. For example, there will be quite different norms in pastoral versus agricultural cultures. Shepherds and herders need to solve the problem of asserting ownership over flocks that may spread far beyond their immediate supervision. Among pastoral people, the norm of going to any lengths to punish rustling will be highly adaptive. So there will be strong selection for emotions of anger, revenge, disdain that accompany the norms prohibiting theft of stock animals. Where norms against rustling are not linked with these emotions, the motivation to act on them is reduced. And that lowers the fitness of the pastoralists who endorse the norms but don't have the right emotions. Again, the process is the same as the one that linked sex and pleasure. Nature was selecting among variations for fitness. Of course, in the emotion/norm combination, the linkage is culturally established and transmitted.

By contrast with pastoralists, sedentary farmers can keep an eye on their plows, even when others borrow them without asking. Among cultivators, there will be selection for norms that allow a certain amount of informal borrowing without permission. The emotions that go along with their norms will be different or weaker than among sheep and cattle herders.

The differences in which behaviors are fitness enhancing dictate which norms persist. Variation and selection harness preexisting emotions to enforce them. Not much genetic hardwiring is required for the Darwinian mechanism that finds and enforces moral norms, sometimes globally and sometimes locally. The emotions are bodily feelings and they are hardwired, subject to the usual Darwinian range of variation. But which norms they get harnessed to depends on what is fitness enhancing in an environment. Different environments make different packages of norm and emotion fitness enhancing. Some packages are fitness enhancing in all the environments we have occupied. These are the ones that form our moral core. They are the ones packaged with the same emotions universally, or nearly so. All societies and cultures have words for anger, disdain, shame, and guilt, and in each, they name roughly the same set of bodily feelings. In each culture, they are linked to common norms—the ones in core morality. They are also linked to different norms—ones that reflect local culture and local environmental filtration.

If you think about how, for example, shame and guilt work, you will see that they are emotions practically designed to solve nature's problem of getting us to do the right thing, to be nice, at least for the sake of our genes' futures.

In brief, shame is the unpleasant feeling we get when others catch us not abiding by the norms almost everyone (including us) embraces. Guilt is the unpleasant feeling that overcomes us when we aren't caught. They are both strong enough by themselves to solve the problem nature created for itself when it made us prone to immediate gratification and resistant to long-term benefits.

Long ago in human cultural evolution, parents began drumming tit-for-tat norms into kids already prone to niceness. Shame at being caught free-riding on others' niceness and shame at being taken for a sucker by others' free-riding is easy to instill: "Aren't you ashamed of yourself?" The hard-to-fake tears, red face, and other bodily signs make shame a credible signal that we have learned our lesson and others can start to be nice to us again. Guilt may be even more important, since its unpleasantness, even in anticipation, is often enough to get us to resist the immediate payoff that comes from defecting once in an iterated PD. Those lucky enough to feel guilt when tempted to cheat are fitter than those who don't. Why? Most hominins underestimate the chances of getting caught by others. It's hardwired into us by Mother Nature because that was the fittest strategy before other people as smart as us came on the scene. Once we appeared, the chances of getting caught free-riding increased, but the temptation remained strong. It needed to be counterbalanced by something that would make honesty the best policy. Feelings of guilt fit the bill.

NICE NIHILISM IS ALL WE NEED

Some emotions enforce parts of core morality, and some enforce norms and actions we reject as not being part of core morality or even compatible with it. What do the parts of core morality that emotions enforce have in common with nonmoral or even immoral norms, like honor killing, that emotions also enforce? They are fitness enhancing in their respective local environments.

If we were selected for niceness, how come there are so many SOBs in the world, and still worse, serial killers, moral monsters, and Adolf Hitlers? Biology has the answer. Remember, perhaps the most profound of Darwin's observations was that there is always some variation in most heritable traits in every generation. A distribution of variations—often a normal, bell-curve distribution—is the rule and not the exception. Traits like niceness and packages combining nice norms and emotions that motivate them are the result of the interaction of the long childhood and a large number of different genes that program development. Slight differences in some of them, often together with slight differences in environments, will produce a good deal of variation in every generation. In every generation, there are going to be a few people who are too nice and get walked on and a few people who are not nice at all—saints and sociopaths.

When we add in variations in social skills, intelligence, and other traits, it's inevitable that a certain percentage of any population will turn out to be grifters, thieves, and other victimizers of us nice people. But we'll also have some saints, martyrs, and Samaritans. And of course, in every generation of a population that is large enough, there will be extreme cases—serial murderers like Jeffrey Dahmer or Peter Sutcliffe and worse, charismatic monsters like Hitler and bureaucratic ones like Stalin.

What is the maximum proportion of egoistic free-riders that a society of nice guys can tolerate? Is it 10 percent or one-tenth of 1 percent? It depends on the number of times we end up playing a PD or some other strategic interaction with a free-rider, and it depends on the stakes. When the number of free-riders gets to the point that to protect ourselves from them we stop cooperating with everyone, something has to give. Either society unravels, or we act together to reduce the number of free-riders. Until we reach that point, we nice people will have to tolerate a few sociopaths and psychopaths as inconveniences in our daily lives. What we nice people won't tolerate is Hitlers, Stalins, Mao Zedongs, Pol Pots, and Osama bin Ladens, at least not forever. The trick is to detect them before it's too late.

But wait. Where do we scientistic types get off condemning purdah and suttee, female genital mutilation and honor killing, the Hindu caste system, the Samurai Code of Bushido, the stoning of women who have committed adultery, or the cutting off of thieves' right hands? Isn't the high dudgeon we want to effect in the face of this sort of barbarism flatly inconsistent with nihilism—any kind, nice or not?

Not only do we condemn the blinkered morality of intolerant religions and narrow-minded cultures, nowadays, we condemn some moral norms that we ourselves used to embrace. We think of this change as progress, improvement, and enlightenment in our moral conscience. A good example is the palpable change in the attitude toward homosexuality. The Monty Python crew wouldn't be caught dead making fun of gays in the way they did in the early 1970s, even knowing as they did that one of their number was a homosexual.

Once it's saddled with nihilism, can scientism make room for the moral progress that most of us want the world to make? No problem.

Recall the point made early in this chapter that even most Nazis may have really shared a common moral code with us. The qualification "most" reflects the fact that a lot of them, especially at the top of the SS, were just psychopaths and sociopaths with no core morality. Where most Nazis "went wrong" was in the idiotic beliefs about race and a lot of other things they combined with core morality, resulting in a catastrophe for their victims and for Germany. The same goes for Stalin and his hatchet men, although most of them were motivated simply by fear in addition to having false beliefs. We can equally well find the false factual beliefs behind purdah, suttee, honor killing, and our own now repudiated sexism, racism, and homophobia. Think about how American Christianity managed to reconcile core morality with African-American slavery for over 250 years. All it had to do was combine core morality with lots of false beliefs about African people. Scientism allows for moral "improvement." It's a matter of combining the core morality that evolution has inflicted on us with true beliefs vouched safe for us by science. It's the failure to be scientific and scientistic that leads from core morality to moral mistakes and even moral catastrophe. (More on this in Chapter 12.)

About the only thing that there is to worry about with nihilism is the name. Most people are nice most of time, and that includes nihilists. There is no reason for anyone to worry about our stealing the silver or mistreating children in our care. As for moral monsters like Hitler, protecting ourselves against them is made inevitable by the very same evolutionary forces that make niceness unavoidable for most of us. There is nothing morally right about being nice, but we are stuck with it for the foreseeable future.

Scientism has to be nihilistic, but it turns out to be a nice nihilism after all.

IN WALT DISNEY'S VERSION of *Pinocchio*, the Blue Fairy advises the boy-puppet that when it comes to right and wrong, "always let your conscience be your guide." Then Jiminy Cricket volunteers to be his conscience. If Pinocchio had been human instead of a puppet, he would not have needed the advice or for that matter a grasshopper to help him act on it. Humans have been selected for heeding their consciences—their moral censors. About the only ones who can't do so are the sociopaths and psychopaths who lack them altogether. Scientism shows us that letting our consciences be our guides enhances our fitness, but that doesn't make us morally right, or morally wrong for that matter. Instead it shows that there is no such thing as either morally right or wrong.

In the next chapter, we'll see that when it comes to the conscious, as opposed to the conscience, the situation is quite different. A great deal of what consciousness tells us is just plain false, and provably false. The mistakes that consciousness leads us into are so egregious that the only conclusion scientism can draw is to never let your conscious be your guide. And once we take this moral on board, we'll be ready to really see how radical, how bracing, how breathtakingly revolutionary a worldview scientism really is.

Chapter 7

———— •◆• ————

NEVER LET
YOUR CONSCIOUS
BE YOUR GUIDE

SOME PUZZLES PREOCCUPY PEOPLE EVEN MORE THAN the ones about morality that we settled in Chapter 6. The puzzles are raised by introspection—by watching or listening to ourselves think. Introspection poses the question, *Who is doing the thinking?* And it immediately answers the question: Me, of course. The strident answer sounds very confident as the words form in consciousness. But they obviously don't satisfy. The question keeps coming back, along with others like these:

Who am I, really, and why am I me instead of someone else (usually someone I would rather be)?
What makes me the same person who went to sleep in this body last night, one year ago, ten years ago?
I feel that my choices are really up to me, but do I really have free will? And if I do, why is exercising it such hard work?

*Can my mind, my soul, my person, can I survive the death of
my body? Might my mind, my soul, might I be immortal?*

The last question on this list will concern even the least introspective among us. And introspection—just sort of watching what
we are thinking about from the inside—won't answer it. The other
questions seem like ones that could be settled quickly just by looking into our own streams of consciousness, right? That there is a
"me" in my body, that I remain the same person while everything
in my body changes over the years, that it's really up to me when I
make choices, that right now I am thinking about what I am reading on the page or screen before me: these are all things we just *feel*
we have to be right about. Immediate experience, conscious introspection tells us so. How can we be mistaken about these things?

Alas, we must be. Science provides clear-cut answers to all of
the questions on the list: there is no free will, there is no mind
distinct from the brain, there is no soul, no self, no person that
supposedly inhabits your body, that endures over its life span, and
that might even outlast it. So, introspection must be wrong.

Why trust science more than introspection? We have already
seen that science gives us compelling reasons not to trust our gut
feelings about right and wrong. In this chapter, we'll see that science gives us even more reason to be suspicious of what we think
we know "from the inside" about the mind, the self, the person,
or the will. It will be very hard to give up the wrong answers
about the mind. Introspection has been insisting on them ever
since conscious thought came to have words for its experiences.
Scientism requires that we give up almost everything introspection tells us about the mind.

Science reveals that introspection—thinking about what is
going on in consciousness—is completely untrustworthy as a

source of information about the mind and how it works. Cognitive neuroscience has already established that many of the most obvious things introspection tells you about your mind are illusions. If the most obvious things consciousness tells us are just plain wrong, we can't trust it to tell us anything about ourselves. We certainly can't trust it to answer our unavoidable questions about the mind or the self or what makes us the persons we are.

Scientism can be confident about the right answers to these questions. First, its answers follow immediately and directly from the physical and biological facts. Second, the only arguments against its answers start by taking introspection seriously, something the empirical evidence shows we should never do.

In this chapter, we'll see how conscious awareness tricks us into profound mistakes about how the mind works. In the next chapter, we'll use the diagnosis to show how wrong introspection's answers are to the persistent questions. Then we'll get the right answers that science provides. Introspection is so seductively convincing, however, that it's hard not to be taken in, even when we understand its tricks. That will need explaining, too.

To escape from the snares of consciousness, we won't really need much empirical science about the mind. This is fortunate, since there isn't much yet. The real science of psychology is only just getting started now that we have some tools for figuring out how the brain works. Producing results in psychology is going to be very difficult because it is the hardest science. It is harder than quantum mechanics or superstring theory. This is not because the right theory of how the brain works requires a lot of math we can't make sense of. The full story about the brain will be complicated because it is such a fantastically complicated organ. It's composed of 10^{10} neurons, and each neuron has upward of 1,000 synapses—connections to other neurons. These neural circuits are incredibly sensitive to what happens beyond the brain, within the body and outside it. Just crunching the data about their responses to inputs will be, for a while yet, beyond the tool kit of neuroscience.

Fortunately, when it comes to the persistent questions about our minds, we are not going to have to wait the 200 years or so required to formulate this theory. To rule out introspection's answers, all we need is what cognitive neuroscience can already tell us about neural circuits in the brain, along with the startling results of some pretty interesting experiments. Once we clear the deck of illusions, we can read the right answers to our most urgent questions off from physics and from the neurobiology it ordains.

BLINDSIGHT—THE TRICK
WE CAN ALL PULL OFF

Here is the sort of absolutely obvious thing consciousness tells us has to be true: To tell what color a thing is, you need to look at it, you need to be at least momentarily conscious of its color. If it's yellow, you have to have to the sensation of yellowness, right? Wrong. And if consciousness can be wrong about that, it can be wrong about anything.

The most startling evidence of how unreliable consciousness is comes from the phenomenon of "blindsight," seeing things when you don't have a conscious visual experience of them. This is so weird it's worth repeating: you can *see* stuff without consciously experiencing it, without having the subjective, private, in-your-mind sensation of its shape, color, position, size, texture, and so on. But if you can see stuff without having these experiences, then an idea that has always struck us as dead certain must be completely wrong. This is the idea that to see things you have be conscious of them, you have to have a visual experience of them.

How do we know that there is any such thing as blindsight? Signals from the eye hit the brain at the primary visual cortex. A great deal is known about how this part of the brain processes signals from the retina. It has been clinically established that damage to it causes blindness. But more than a half century ago, experiments on monkeys whose primary visual cortex had been destroyed (probably no longer a permissible experiment) revealed that the monkeys could nevertheless detect shapes and movement. When presented with visual stimuli they should not have been able to "see," they behaved in ways that showed they could respond to the stimuli as if they had seen them.

Though mysterious, no one thought that these experiments had much relevance for human vision. Then a patient (named DB in the subsequent reports) had his right hemisphere's primary visual cortex removed at a London hospital to relieve symptoms caused by a brain tumor. After surgery, DB was subjected to the same experiments the monkeys had been subjected to, with the same startling results. Because DB could talk as well as act, he was able to confirm that, being blind, he had no visual experience of colors. But when asked to reach for something yellow among a set of colored objects, he succeeded in doing so. When asked whether the yellow object was on the left or right, he pointed in the correct direction, though he reported that he could not see anything yellow anywhere in front of him. When asked to point to a square object and ignore a round one, he was able to do that, too, though he had no conscious experience of anything round or square in his visual field. When asked whether a grillwork grating in front of him had horizontal or vertical lines, he gave the right answer, though again, he had no visual experience of (he couldn't "see") the grating itself. When told of the experimental results, DB didn't believe them. He insisted he had just been guessing—that's what the introspective feeling told him he had been doing. DB was the first of many victims of damage in the primary visual cortex who have shown the same abilities. They can discriminate visual stimuli without any conscious visual experience of the stimuli. It's not just simple stimuli they can discriminate. People with blindsight can tell the emotion expressed by faces projected on a screen in front of them even though they can't "see" the faces.

It's not just people with brain damage that manifest these abilities. Normal-sighted subjects show the blindsight ability to discriminate visual stimuli without having the visual experience. This happens when researchers temporarily disturb their primary visual cortex by directing a strong magnetic field at it. Moreover, interfering with other parts of the brain have revealed the existence of hearing without the introspection of acoustical sensations, and touching without the consciousness of any tactile experiences.

The take-home lesson of blindsight is obvious: introspection is highly unreliable as a source of knowledge about the way our minds work. After all, what could have been more introspectively obvious than the notion that you need to have conscious experiences of colors to see colors, conscious shape experiences to see shapes, and so on, for all the five senses? Yet that turns out to be just wrong. If it's wrong, what else that introspection insists on could turn out to be wrong?

WILLPOWER WITHOUT THE WILL?

It's introspectively obvious that deliberate actions are the result of conscious decisions that we make. That couldn't be wrong, could it? Many people who recognize that physics rules out free will have weighed that fact against their introspective feeling that choice is up to them. And they have decided that introspection trumps science, even 500 years of it.

Their line of thinking goes like this: Point your right index finger straight up in front of you. Now ask yourself, "Given the whole history of the universe that led up to the current state of my brain, plus all the laws of nature, known and unknown at work in my brain, is it really still up to me to choose which way to point my finger, to my left or to my right, or neither?" Science answers no. Introspection answers yes. We *just know from the inside* that it's entirely up to us which way we point our index finger. We can feel it. Introspection trumps science.

Too bad for introspection. There is a series of experiments going back about 50 years now that shows conclusively that the conscious decisions to do things never cause the actions we introspectively think they do. The conscious decisions happen too late in the process to even be involved in the choosing. The most famous of these experiments was conducted by Benjamin Libet in the late 1970s (and replicated many times since). The implications of his experiments are obvious. Ever since, defenders of free will have been twisting themselves into knots trying to wriggle out of them.

Libet set up a simple task: Subjects are asked to push a button whenever they wish. They're also asked to note the instant they "decided" to push the button—when they "felt" the conscious act of "willing" their wrist to flex, pushing the finger down on the button. At the same time, the subject's brain is wired up to detect the activity of the part of the brain, the motor cortex, that is responsible for sending the signal to the wrist to flex, pushing the finger down. On average, it takes 200 milliseconds from conscious willing to wrist flexing and finger pressing. But the cortical processes responsible for the wrist flexing start 500 milliseconds before the button is pressed. In other words, wrist flexing is already set in motion, and everything needed to complete it has already taken place 300 milliseconds before the subjects are conscious of "deciding" to flex the wrist and press the button.

The obvious implication: Consciously deciding to do something is not the cause of doing it. It's just a downstream effect, perhaps even a by-product, of some process that has already set the action in motion. A nonconscious event in the brain is the "real" decider. Maybe the real decision to act that takes place unconsciously really is a free choice. Or maybe, since your brain is just a purely physical system, you don't have any free will. No matter which is right, we can't have any confidence that the conscious decision made the button pressing happen—even though we can't get rid of the feeling that it did.

Libet's results have been replicated many times, employing ever greater improvements in the technology for recording what happens in the brain, where it happens, and when it happens. There is greater accuracy in measuring the delay between the start of the button-pressing process and the occurrence of the felt act of willing. And neural measurements have been substituted for asking the subjects to report when they introspected the conscious act of will. The results pull the rug out from under introspection as a source of much knowledge about choice. They completely undercut the evidence introspective experience might give for free choice. The conscious feeling of its being entirely up to me whether I flex my wrist, and when I do so, is just irrelevant to what my body does. By the time I have the introspectively accessible feeling of deciding to move my wrist or finger, the train has already left the station. The brain has already set it in motion. The introspective feeling is too late to have anything to do with it.

The real cause of which way I point my finger (or, in the Libet experiment, the real cause of my pushing the button) is some event in the motor cortex of the brain. That event was first identified by Libet using an old-fashioned electroencephalograph taped to the subject's scalp. Now it can be studied by newer fMRI (functional magnetic resonance imaging) machines. The fMRI machines detect the level of real-time oxygen metabolism in the specific part of the brain where the "decision" to push the button is taking place. None of the events in this part of the brain are experienced at all. They are just the results of other, earlier non-conscious states of the brain (and its environment). These, too, are processes over which the subject has no conscious control. What's more, the neuroscientist can bring about the neural states that cause the wrist to flex and the finger to move just by stimulating this nonconscious region of brain. And sure enough, the unconscious stimulation is followed (2/10ths of a second later) by the introspective feeling of deciding to move it.

Do these results prove that there is no free will? That would be too hasty. It doesn't follow logically from Libet's experiments that there is no free will. But what you certainly can't do after reading about these experiments is trust introspection to tell us whether or not we have free will. We can't trust introspection to tell us *when* we made the decision to push the button. We certainly can't trust introspection to tell us *why* we made the decision we did. Introspection is so unreliable that it would be scientifically irresponsible to ever trust it about anything regarding the will.

Add together the fact that introspection is wrong about the need for a conscious decision to start the body into action and the facts about blindsight—that there is no need for conscious experience to detect sensory features of the world. Between them they show that as a middleman between sensory input and action output, conscious experience is not putting together much of a track record. It gets wrong several things that most people are certain it can't get wrong. How should we treat its other confident pronouncements? What is there left for introspection to be reliable about? Can it be relied on to tell us much about the mind—how the mind thinks, senses, and wills?

Driving through Life with Both Eyes Fixed on the Rearview Mirror

Conscious introspection is wrong about basic facts, like the need for sensations to see things and the role of the conscious will in getting the body to do even simple tasks. It gets worse.

Introspection tells us that human sight is "now-sight." It gives us the absolute conviction that when our eyes are open, we are getting "real-time" access to the way the world is, here and now (minus the lag for the speed of light). But vision is in fact a matter of navigating the highway of life while keeping both eyes relentlessly focused on the rearview mirror. Human sight, which we think gets as close to *foresight* as anything, really just turns out to be *hindsight*. Vision is just another Darwinian process, one that produces the appearance of now-sight by filtering incoming variations for fitness to past environments. This filtering is not done just by our own past environments. The environments of distantly past human, mammalian, and vertebrate ancestors are still at it, filtering our current visual input. Despite appearances, vision is hindsight masquerading as now-sight. Seeing why this is so is both eye opening and fun.

The images in Figure 4 all trick the brain thoroughly. In each case, your brain is fooled into a set of optical illusions. It looks at the images and sees substantial brightness differences, between the squares on the left and right, between the upper and lower faces of the solid, between the centers of the two crosses, and between the light gray shadings on the puzzle piece. But there can't be any brightness differences on the page, just color differences. These illusions illustrate how we can be deceived about things like brightness, color, distance and depth, geometry, and angles.

**FIGURE 4. Brightness/darkness illusions from the
website of Dale Purves (*http://www.purveslab.net/
seeforyourself/*)**

These and other illusions reflect a few of the problems that
the brain continually needs to solve to operate in its environment. The problems are those of figuring out how the local environment is arranged on the basis of completely insufficient data.
Dale Purves, the neuroscientist whose work employs these illusions, calls the problem that the brain has to solve the "inverse
optics" problem. The visual information that hits the retina at
the back of the eye is only two-dimensional. Out of it the brain
has to build a three-dimensional world. So how does the brain
construct the third dimension? These illusions show how the
brain goes about solving the inverse optics problem. They do it by
revealing the ways it can sometimes get the solution wrong.

The illusions work because the same two-dimensional retinal pattern can be produced many different ways. What we see
depends in large measure on three factors about our environment: the source of the light, the object it bounces off, and the
medium it travels through to get to the eye. The *source* of light
might be the sun, a candle, or a light bulb. It shines on an *object*—
a building, a dice cube, a glass of water, the page you are looking
at in this book—which reflects the light to our retinas through a
medium—clear air or smoke, a dirty windowpane, or maybe sun-
glasses. Variations in sources produce differences in illumination,
or *luminance*. Changes in objects' surfaces (dusting it, cleaning
it, polishing it) produce differences in *reflectance*. The condition

of the space between the object and the eye produces differences in *transmittance*. The very same electrochemical reactions on the retina can be produced by different packages of these three variables. That's why the illusions in Figure 4 work. The images trick you because they are each combinations of source, object, and medium that we rarely experience. These unusual packages produce the same retinal patterns as the quite different and much more frequent packages of source, object, and medium that normal life produces.

Let's focus on the sensation of the bright square in the middle of the left cross in Figure 5. Once you see how this illusion works, it's not hard to apply the lesson to explaining the others. In normal life, this sensation is usually the result of a strong light source behind a cross with an open middle square. In Figure 5, obviously, there is no strong light behind the cross illuminating its center from the back. The luminance of the white in the middle of the two crosses is the same. In Figure 5, an unusual package of source, object, and medium produces *the same sensation* that we usually experience from a bright source behind the cross. The illusion reveals a problem that the brain has to deal with and mostly gets right: there almost always is a bright source behind the square. How does the brain figure that out? How does it get

FIGURE 5.

from an ambiguous two-dimensional retinal image to the right three-dimensional situation out there in the world? The image produced by the package of luminance, reflectance, and transmittance is not enough. This is the inverse optics problem: the brain has to work back from the retinal image to its source in the local environment.

The brain can't get the right answer about what's out there from the incoming data by some fancy formula that extracts the package of luminance, reflectance, and transmittance from the retinal image. There are too many packages of light source, object, and atmosphere that give the same result, that produce the same retinal image. The way the brain solves this problem is by (continually) guessing. It treats incoming retinal data as the same package of source, object, and medium that was selected for in the brain's past (and in the evolutionary past of the human brain when similar retinal stimuli were produced). It just assumes that what's out there now is what was out there the last time it had that kind of retinal data.

Beginning at birth, each brain experiences and stores a whole set of retinal images and their associated packages of guesses about source, object, and medium. The brain just picks out of those stored packages the package that was best adapted in the past for meeting the brain's needs—for avoiding injury, getting nourishment, getting pleasure, and so on. In other words, the visual cortex of the brain "looks" out at the world and just sees what it was reinforced for thinking was out there in its past. And the reinforcement is not just for success in the individual brain's past—what the brain has experienced in its own lifetime. Our optical systems have been tuned through millions of years of dealing with packages of source, object, and medium. Long-past packages shaped the optical systems of our evolutionary ancestors and through them shaped our current visual experiences. We don't "see" the way the world around us is now, we "see" the way it was most frequently in the past, including the evolutionary past.

This past trajectory—both personal and evolutionary—explains why illusions like the bright square in the cross of Figure 5 work so well. In the evolution of eyes on our planet, and in our own experiences since birth, we and our ancestors had to deal with things and their surroundings that didn't usually differ hugely in luminance.

When something's luminance is much greater than its surroundings, that is almost always the result of a bright light source. The cross on the left in Figure 5 is a rare case. There is a great luminance difference between the inside of the cross and its arms, even though there is no light source behind it. The white square on the left cross has exactly the same luminance as the white square on the right; it's their surroundings that differ. The inside margins of the left cross are low in luminance; the inside margins (and the whole squares) on the right cross are high. In our experience, high luminance difference without a light source behind the object is rare. That's why your brain gets it wrong—why it fails to solve the inverse optics problem correctly.

When high-luminance targets and low-luminance surroundings hit the retina, the brain responds in ways appropriate to a source of brightness. Our brain was selected for doing this, hardwiring the illusion in the last geological epoch. In our evolutionary past, the source of brightness was usually fire, and there was selection (genetic in the species, operant conditioning in the individual) for brightness sensations to trigger burn-avoiding behavior. Natural selection has operated on the genes that build the visual system of mammals, programming them to build neural equipment that can learn burn avoidance in just a few trials, or none. And there was also selection in the individual lives of mammals for engaging in burn avoidance behavior

FIGURE 6.

when sensations of brightness occurred. Now when it detects brightness, the visual circuitry of the brain generates processes elsewhere in the brain appropriate to the presence of a warm or hot object in the vicinity, whether there is one there on not.

Nature has found a quick and dirty solution to the inverse optics problem for the brain: Use past luminance value differences between targets and their surroundings to generate a guess about brightness that can guide behavior. This solution very occasionally produces illusions, but most of the time it produces crucially adaptive behavior.

When we look at Figure 6, the brain produces sensations of different brightnesses of the three target diamonds on each cube, even though the actual luminance values of all the diamonds is exactly the same. Because of the past history of how shadows have shaped the neural networks in the optical system from retina to brain, each of the three diamonds on each cube elicit a different sensation of brightness (even though they are all the same color).

Treating different packages of source, object, and medium as "the same" in luminance—by responding in the same way to them—is crucial to tracking things in the environment over time. It's what enables us and other mammals to see a fire or the surface of a pond or a cliff edge as "the same," even when clouds obscure the sun, when the flames or the waves change their reflective properties, or when smoke or mist obscures the fire or pond's surface or the cliff's drop-off.

The inverse optics problem is just one of many inverse sensory problems. There is an inverse acoustical problem, an inverse tactile problem, an inverse olfactory problem. They are all solved in similar ways. Humans and other animals navigate the world using a "rearview mirror." It was created by a Darwinian process of natural selection operating in Earth's environment over the last billion years or so. This hardwired rearview mirror gets a bit of fine-tuning in each of us, from birth onward. The fine-tuning results from operant conditioning, another Darwinian process of blind variation and environmental filtration for guesses that successfully navigate the demands of current environments. In your particular visual system and in mine, no amount of fine-tuning can overcome the evolutionary past. That is why the illusions in Figures 4, 5, and 6 continue to work, even when you know that they are illusions and you know how they trick us.

This research shows that conscious introspection persistently foists illusions on us. The visual system works so fast and so smoothly that we think of it as a continually updated "motion-picture record" of our surroundings. But this is an illusion. The visual system is continually producing the illusion of matching a target—the outside world—by processing variations—in luminance differences, for example—through the filter of stored guesses from previous environments. With luck, of course, there will be enough similarity between past and present environment for the inputs to produce behavior that is still adaptive. The illusions, of course, show that this is not always the case.

In a world where physics fixes all the facts, where there are no future purposes or past designs, where the second law drives all adaptation, Mother Nature had no alternative. She could only have built sensory systems that track the past, not the instantaneous present, still less the future, near or far. The surprise is that ongoing vision—"now sight"—tracks the distant past of our species along with our own childhood pasts. But the rearview mirror through which we watch the landscape go by is entirely hidden from introspection. Natural selection has produced in us the confident feeling that along with a little foresight, we have a lot of now sight, when all we ever really have is hindsight.

WE HAVE SEEN that consciousness can't be trusted to be right about the most basic things: the alleged need for visual experiences to see colors and shapes, the supposed role of conscious decisions in bringing about our actions, even the idea that we have now sight instead of hindsight. If it can be wrong about these things, it can be wrong about almost everything it tells us about ourselves and our minds.

The discoveries reported in this chapter can't fully prepare you for how wrong introspection is. Nothing really can. Ultimately, science and scientism are going to make us give up as illusory the very thing conscious experience screams out at us loudest and longest: the notion that when we think, our thoughts are about *anything at all*, inside or outside of our minds. I know this sounds absurd, but we'll see why this must be so in the next chapter. The physical facts fix all the facts. It's because they do that thinking about stuff is impossible. What is more, neuroscience has already made it plain how the brain thinks without its thoughts being about anything at all. Thinking about things is an overwhelmingly powerful illusion. Once we learn how this profound illusion is produced, we'll understand why it's hard to cast the illusions of consciousness aside for the real answers to the relentless questions about self, mind, soul, free will, and the meaning of life. But we will also see why we must do so.

Chapter 8

———— ◆ ————

THE BRAIN
DOES EVERYTHING
WITHOUT THINKING
ABOUT ANYTHING
AT ALL

NOW WE ARE MORE THAN HALFWAY THROUGH this tour of how science answers the persistent questions. So far, science's challenges to common sense and to ordinary beliefs have not been difficult to accept. But the going is going to get much harder. In this chapter and the next two, we will see that several of the most fundamental things that ordinary experience teaches us about ourselves are completely illusory. Some of these illusions are useful for creatures like us, or at least they have been selected for by the environmental filters that our ancestors passed through. But other illusions have just been carried along piggyback on the locally adaptive traits that conferred increased fitness on our ancestors in the Pleistocene. These fellow travelers are the ones we need to stop taking seriously because they prevent us from recognizing the right answers to our unavoidable questions. What is more, in the environment we humans are creating that will filter our own future evolution, they may turn out to be maladaptive traits. As nihilists, we can't condemn maladaptive traits as morally bad ones. But we certainly can figure out whether or not these maladaptations are ones that we or our successors would want.

Some of the conclusions to which science commits us sound so bizarre that many people, including scientists and philosophers, have gone to great lengths to avoid them, deny them, or search for a way of taking the sting out of them. Among the seemingly unquestionable truths science makes us deny is the idea that we have any purposes at all, that we ever make plans—for today, tomorrow, or next year. Science must even deny the basic notion that we ever really think about the past and the future or even that our conscious thoughts ever give any meaning to the actions that express them. I don't expect you to accept these outrageous claims without compelling arguments for them. Moreover, once you are convinced to accept them, you won't have to deny that we think accurately and act intelligently in the world. You will just have to deny that we do it in anything like the way almost everyone thinks we do. Your answers to the relentless questions keeping us and other people up nights will have to be definitively different from most people's answers. What's more, your views about the importance of history and the social sciences, literature and the humanities, will have to be decidedly deflationary. I am not going to ask you to take my word for all this quite yet.

You can see why many who seek to make science accepted by everyone would be unhappy with these counterintuitive conclusions. These unwelcome conclusions have not escaped the notice of scientists and philosophers, and they have sought to avoid or mitigate them. Ever since science became central to our culture, there has been a veritable industry devoted to harmonizing science's findings with the prescientific worldview. A great many deep thinkers have devoted themselves to this project for half a century now, under the banner of "naturalism," without much success. Scientism stands on the shoulders of giants: all those great naturalistic philosophers who have tried to make peace between science and ordinary beliefs and have failed.

Since we are going to move further and further away from common sense and ordinary beliefs about the most basic things—the things it's hard to imagine we could be wrong about—it's worth working out exactly why science trumps common sense. The only route to theoretical science starts with everyday experience and employs reasoning that is certified by common sense to be iron-clad. At the point we have reached in our tour, science tells us that what everyday experience teaches is quite mistaken and that conscious introspection is unreliable. Since we needed both of them to get to this point, it looks like there is some sort of contradiction lurking in scientism. Looks are deceiving.

WHY SCIENCE TRUMPS COMMON SENSE, EVEN WHEN ITS CONCLUSIONS ARE BIZARRE

Why trust science over everything else, including the human experiences we needed to build science? The usual way to answer this question begins with the technological success of science and then reflects on the general reliability of its experimental methods, as well as the self-correcting character of its institutions. That was the approach Chapter 2 employed to underwrite physics as our metaphysics, our fundamental theory of the nature of reality. This approach is right but doesn't work very well with people who need stories and resist learning much science to begin with. There is, however, a much more convincing argument that needs to be put on the table before we really begin turning common sense upside down. It is the overwhelming reason to prefer science to ordinary beliefs, common sense, and direct experience. Science is just common sense continually improving itself, rebuilding itself, correcting itself, until it is no longer recognizable as common sense. It's easy to miss this fact about science without studying a lot of history of science—and not the stories about science, but the succession of actual scientific theories and how common sense was both their mother and their midwife.

The history of science is in some respects like Plutarch's story of the ship of Theseus. In the story, as each plank of the ship rotted away or mast broke or rope parted, a duplicate plank or mast or rope was made and substituted. After a certain point, the entire ship was composed of replacement parts. The philosophical question this raises is whether, after all the original parts are replaced with duplicates, Theseus's ship is still numerically the same one he started out with. Now, imagine that instead of perfect replacements, the sailors had used their ingenuity to substitute new, improved parts on the ship. Starting with a Greek trireme galley and carried on long enough, the result could well have been a nuclear attack submarine. Whether the ship at the end of the process is the same ship as the one at the beginning we can leave to philosophers. But whether it reflects an advance in knowledge of nautical reality is not debatable. And this is the way to understand how common sense and ordinary experience become science.

Physics started with "folk physics," a whole load of partly or mainly false beliefs about how things move. Regrettably, many of these beliefs are still with us in common sense. Yet all it takes is common sense to see that common sense about motion has to be wrong.

Most people think that to keep a ball in motion, you need to continually apply some force to it. To keep it going, you have to push it from time to time, not just on Earth but in the vacuum of space. Physics was built on this common sense. From Aristotle's' physics onward for 1,900 years, nonzero velocity was held to require the continual application of a force on the object in motion. It took a simple commonsense thought experiment by Galileo to refute common sense: Set a ball in motion down an indefinitely long inclined plain, and it speeds up as it rolls. Set a ball in motion up an inclined plane, and it slows down as it rolls. Now, set a ball in motion on a perfectly level surface. What does common sense say will happen? It continues to roll without speeding up or slowing down, right? Stands to reason. It can't do what it does in either of the other two cases when it's rolling down or up. "Gee, I never thought about it that way," says common sense. "I better revise my beliefs about motion." It only took 2 millennia to come up with that thought experiment, but its impact on history can't be minimized. We now know Galileo's conclusion as Newton's first law of motion. Too bad we were not taught it that way.

Galileo's little thought experiment led to a revision of common sense. The revision required the physicists to scrap Aristotle's formalization of common sense in favor of a radically different conception of reality, one that tied forces to accelerations instead of velocities and led right to Newton's second law of motion. The steps are just as easy and obvious, just as commonsensical as the ones we ran through in the last paragraph. After Galileo, it became physicists' common sense that a ball moving in a straight line at constant velocity doesn't have any forces acting on it. So, by common sense, if the ball is moving in a straight line but changing velocity, or moving on a curved path (jut another way to change its velocity), there must be a force acting on it. *Voilà!* Newton's second law. Common sense.

It would be easy to go on and on until we have built the whole of physics. Starting from physics, the same process results in chemistry and biology.

Science begins as common sense. Each step in the development of science is taken by common sense. The accumulation of those commonsense steps, each of them small, from a commonsense starting place over a 400-year period since Galileo, has produced a body of science that no one any longer recognizes as common sense. But that's what it is. The real common sense is relativity and quantum mechanics, atomic chemistry and natural selection. That's why we should believe it in preference to what ordinary experience suggests.

No matter how bizarre the conclusions that science commits us to, they are the latest steps on a long path, one traversed by a methodical, careful process using highly reliable equipment. It's a path found literally by detecting the mistakes of common sense, one at a time, and avoiding them. It's too bad there isn't enough time to teach everyone science as common sense correcting itself.

In what follows, our progress is increasingly going to involve identifying the mistakes that common sense is still making and the dead ends they lead to. That's because once we get past biology and into the sciences of the mind and human society, we don't yet have all the theory we need to understand what is going on. At this point, however, we do have a good idea of the kinds of mistakes common sense keeps making. Knowing them is almost enough to answer the yes or no questions we started with in Chapter 1.

Here is some commonsense wisdom: One thing consciousness does is retrieve information from the brain. Someone asks for your birth date or social security number, and up it comes into awareness. Then you read it off your introspection and answer the question. You can't find your keys, so you concentrate. Suddenly the location pops up into consciousness. Sometimes you have a "senior moment" and forget your boss's name. Then all of a sudden (when it's too late) it's shouting itself out to you inside your head.

Blindsight, the Libet experiments, and the rearview mirror of experience should make us deeply suspicious of this apparently obvious matter. Why shouldn't your conscious thought about your birth date just be a by-product, a side effect, of whatever is going on nonconsciously in your brain when it makes you answer someone's question with your date of birth? Why couldn't the brain's nonconscious storage of where your keys are produce the conscious thought about where they are after it has figured out their location and started heading that way? Can introspection be completely wrong even about its role in accessing the information stored in the brain? It has to be.

Introspection must be wrong when it credits consciousness with thoughts about birthdays, keys, and bosses' names. But the mistake introspection makes is so deep and so persuasive, it's almost impossible to shake, even when you understand it. At first you won't even be able to conceive how it could be a mistake. But it has to be. *The mistake is the notion that when we think, or rather when our brain thinks, it thinks about anything at all.*

I know. Your immediate reaction is that this couldn't be a mistake. You may even go back and reread that last, italicized sentence of the last paragraph. It couldn't have meant what you thought it said. The sentence seemed to say that when we think, we are not thinking *about* what we are thinking *about*, and that's just a plain contradiction. So you conclude that you must have misread the sentence. You did. What the sentence said is that thinking is not a matter of thinking *about* things. Of course we think. No one denies that. It's just that thinking is nothing like what conscious introspection tells us it is. Introspection's mistake is the source of most of the mistaken answers that have been given to the persistent questions. It is also the source of most of the religious ideas people have as well. That's because of the role of this one illusion in the emergence of our fixation with stories, as we'll see. It's such a deep mistake that it won't be easy to recognize. Even after it is recognized, like the visual illusions in the last chapter, it sticks with us.

We have to see very clearly that introspection tricks us into the illusion that our thoughts are *about* anything at all. That's what the rest of this chapter does. Then, in Chapter 9, we will see how the trick is done. Once science shows us the trick and how it's done, we will be able to apply the understanding to correctly answer the most unavoidable questions raised by the mind and the self. But what follows here is the hardest part of this book. We will walk through the science we need to expose the illusion three different ways. Even after we do so, however, it will be impossible to avoid the illusion entirely. The best we can do is watch out for its insidious attempts to subvert scientism and keep them at bay.

THINKING ABOUT (IS) THE UNTHINKABLE

In 1950, Herman Kahn, a game theorist at Rand Corporation in Santa Monica, California, wrote a book about when the United States should launch a nuclear attack on the Soviet Union. Kahn may have been the model for the eponymous character in Stanley Kubrick's film *Dr. Strangelove, or: How I Learned to Stop Worrying and Love the Bomb*. Kahn's book was disturbing enough even to its author, who gave it the title *Thinking about the Unthinkable*. He and his frightened readers need not have worried. As we'll see, it can't be done. You can't think *about* the unthinkable, because you can't think *about* anything at all.

Suppose someone asks you, "What is the capital of France?" Into consciousness comes the thought that Paris is the capital of France. Consciousness tells you in no uncertain terms what the content of your thought is, what your thought is *about*. It's about the statement that Paris is the capital of France. That's the thought you are thinking. It just can't be denied. You can't be wrong about the content of your thought. You may be wrong about whether Paris is really the capital of France. The French assembly could have moved the capital to Bordeaux this morning (they did it one morning in June 1940). You might even be wrong about whether you are thinking about Paris, confusing it momentarily with London. What you absolutely cannot be wrong about is that your conscious thought was about something. Even having a wildly wrong thought about something requires that the thought be about something.

It's this last notion that introspection conveys that science has to deny. Thinking about things can't happen at all. The brain can't have thoughts about Paris, or about France, or about capitals, or about anything else for that matter. When consciousness convinces you that you, or your mind, or your brain has thoughts about things, it is wrong.

Don't misunderstand, no one denies that the brain receives, stores, and transmits information. But it can't do these things in anything remotely like the way introspection tells us it does— by having thoughts about things. The way the brain deals with information is totally different from the way introspection tells us it does. Seeing why and understanding how the brain does the work that consciousness gets so wrong is the key to answering all the rest of the questions that keep us awake at night worrying over the mind, the self, the soul, the person.

We believe that Paris is the capital of France. So, somewhere in our brain is stored the proposition, the statement, the sentence, idea, notion, thought, or whatever, that Paris is the capital of France. It has to be inscribed, represented, recorded, registered, somehow encoded in neural connections, right? Somewhere in my brain there have to be dozens or hundreds or thousands or millions of neurons wired together to store the thought that Paris is the capital of France. Let's call this wired-up network of neurons inside my head the "Paris neurons," since they are *about* Paris, among other things. They are also *about* France, *about* being a capital city, and *about* the fact that Paris is the capital of France. But for simplicity's sake let's just focus on the fact that the thought is *about* Paris.

Now, here is the question we'll try to answer: What makes the Paris neurons a set of neurons that is *about* Paris; what make them refer to Paris, to denote, name, point to, pick out Paris? To make it really clear what question is being asked here, let's lay it out with mind-numbing explicitness: I am thinking about Paris right now, and I am in Sydney, Australia. So there are some neurons located at latitude 33.87 degrees south and longitude 151.21 degrees east (Sydney's coordinates), and they are about a city on the other side of the globe, located at latitude 48.50 degrees north and 2.20 degrees east (Paris's coordinates). Let's put it even more plainly: Here in Sydney there is a chunk or a clump of organic matter—a bit of wet stuff, gray porridge, brain cells, neurons wired together inside my skull. And there is another much bigger chunk of stuff 10,533 miles, or 16,951 kilometers, away from the first chunk of matter. This second chunk of stuff includes the Eiffel Tower, the Arc de Triomphe, Notre Dame, the Louvre Museum, and all the streets, parks, buildings, sewers, and metros around them. The first clump of matter, the bit of wet stuff in my brain, the Paris neurons, is *about* the second chunk of matter, the much greater quantity of diverse kinds of stuff that make up Paris. How can the first clump—the Paris neurons in my brain— be about, denote, refer to, name, represent, or otherwise point to the second clump—the agglomeration of Paris? (Take a look at Figure 7.) A more general version of this question is this: How

How can this:

be about this:

**FIGURE 7. The Paris neurons are supposed to be *about*
Paris. How do they accomplish this trick?**

can one clump of stuff anywhere in the universe be *about* some
other clump of stuff anywhere else in the universe—right next to
it or 100 million light-years away?

There are several answers to this question we have to rule out.
The Paris neurons aren't *about* Paris in the same way, for example, that a picture postcard or a diorama or pop-up book's three-

dimensional layout is *about* Paris. They don't in any way look like the Arc de Triomphe or the Eiffel Tower or the Place de la Concorde. They don't have the same shape, two-dimensionally like the postcard or three-dimensionally like an architect's model, of some part of Paris. The Paris neurons aren't shaped like Paris or any part of it. They won't look like Paris from any angle.

So what? The Paris neurons don't have to share anything in common with what they are about in order to be about Paris. Consider the stop and yield signs in Figure 8. Do they have to look like stopping or yielding to be about stopping or yielding? Of course not.

Well, why are red octagons *about* stopping and yellow triangles *about* yielding? In every country in the world, the red octagon means "Stop!" It communicates a whole imperative sentence expressible in different languages by "Halt!," "Fermata!," "Arrêter!," and so on. Red octagons don't look like any of these one-word sentences. They don't look like the action of stopping or the command to stop. Red octagons don't have to look like the action or the command in order to be *about* stopping. Same goes for the Paris neurons. They don't have to look like Paris to be *about* Paris. Right?

FIGURE 8. Stop sign and yield sign

Could the Paris neurons be about Paris the way red octagons are about stopping? This is the theory impressed on us by introspection of our own thoughts about Paris—and about stop signs for that matter. In fact, the more consciousness thinks about it, the more certain we are that the shapes and squiggles outside our head are *about* stuff because of the way the thoughts in our head are *about* them.

This can't be correct, not if thoughts about stuff are sets of neurons wired together (and they can't be anything else). It's not hard to show why, although it will take several steps. We'll take it slowly, step by step, using common sense, and come to a deeply uncommonsense but utterly compelling conclusion.

Red octagons are about stopping because someone (in fact, a committee in the state of Michigan in 1915) decided that thereafter, in Michigan at any rate, they would mean "Stop!" There is nothing that is intrinsically "Stop!"-ish about red octagons. Downward pointing yellow triangles—yield signs—could have been chosen as stop signs instead. Red octagons are about stopping because we interpret them that way. We treat them as symbols for the imperative variously expressed in English as "Stop!," in Greek as "σταματάω!," and in Chinese pictograms as "停止." The Greek and Chinese inscriptions don't mean "Stop!" to us non-Greek and non-Chinese readers because we don't interpret them as being about stopping. The point is that a red octagon or any other clump of matter—ink marks on paper or pixels on a screen—is about something else only because it has been interpreted by someone to be about it.

Let's suppose that the Paris neurons are *about* Paris the same way red octagons are *about* stopping. This is the first step down a slippery slope, a regress into total confusion.

If the Paris neurons are about Paris the same way a red octagon is about stopping, then there has to be something in the brain that interprets the Paris neurons as being about Paris. After all, that's how the stop sign is about stopping. It gets interpreted by us in a certain way. The difference is that in the case of the Paris neurons, the interpreter can only be another part of the brain.

Let's see exactly why. Call that part of the brain the neural interpreter. It's supposed to interpret the Paris neurons as being about Paris the way we interpret the red octagons as being about stopping. How can the neural interpreter interpret the Paris neurons as being about Paris? The interpreter neurons would have to have different parts that are about two different things, about Paris and about the Paris neurons. Already we can see trouble coming. We started out trying to explain one case of neurons being about something—Paris. Now we have two cases of neurons being about things—about Paris and about the Paris neurons.

Why does the neural interpreter have to be both about Paris and about the Paris neurons? Because somewhere inside the neural interpreter there have got to be neurons that are *about* the fact that the Paris neurons are about Paris.

Let's consider the simpler case first. The neural interpreter is supposed to interpret the Paris neurons as being about Paris. It can't interpret the Paris neurons just by reproducing them, copying them, by hooking up some of its neurons in the same way the original Paris neurons were hooked up (or in any other way for that matter). That wouldn't be enough. Here are two ways to see why that is not enough. First, show the red octagon in Figure 8 to someone who has never seen or heard of a stop sign (assuming there's any such person left in the world). Just seeing the picture or committing it to memory won't be enough for that person to interpret the shape as being about stopping or about anything else for that matter. Remember those strange squiggles from Greek and Chinese? Even if you memorized them so you could reproduce the squiggles, that wouldn't be enough for you to interpret them as being about stopping. You'd have to add something to your memory, or image, of the squiggles to interpret them.

Similarly, the neural interpreter has to add something to the Paris neurons (or maybe to its copy of them) to interpret them as being about Paris. What can it add? Only more neurons, wired up in some way or other that makes the Paris neurons be about Paris. And now we see why what the neural interpreter has to add is going to have to be about Paris, too. It can't interpret the Paris neurons as being about Paris unless some other part of it is, separately and independently, about Paris. These will be the neurons that "say" that the Paris neurons are about Paris; they will be about the Paris neurons the way the Paris neurons are about Paris.

Now the problem is clear. We see why the Paris neurons can't be about Paris the way that red octagons are about stopping. It's because that way lies a regress that will prevent us from ever understanding what we wanted to figure out in the first place: how one chunk of stuff—the Paris neurons—can be about another chunk of stuff—Paris. We started out trying to figure out how the Paris neurons could be about Paris, and our tentative answer is that they are about Paris because some other part of the brain—the neural interpreter—is both about the Paris neurons and about Paris. We set out to explain how one set of neurons is about something out there in the world. We find ourselves adopting the theory that it's because another set of neurons is about the first bunch of neurons and about the thing in the world, too. This won't do.

What we need to get off the regress is some set of neurons that is about some stuff outside the brain without being interpreted—by anyone or anything else (including any other part of the brain)—as being about that stuff outside the brain. What we need is a clump of matter, in this case the Paris neurons, that by the very arrangement of its synapses points at, indicates, singles out, picks out, identifies (and here we just start piling up more and more synonyms for "being about") another clump of matter outside the brain. But there is no such physical stuff.

Physics has ruled out the existence of clumps of matter of the required sort. There are just fermions and bosons and combinations of them. None of that stuff is just, all by itself, *about* any other stuff. There is nothing in the whole universe—including, of course, all the neurons in your brain—that just by its nature or composition can do this job of being about some other clump of matter. So, when consciousness assures us that we have thoughts *about* stuff, it has to be wrong. The brain nonconsciously stores information in thoughts. But the thoughts are not *about* stuff. Therefore, consciousness cannot retrieve thoughts *about* stuff. There are none to retrieve. So it can't have thoughts *about* stuff either.

Remember, the original problem was how the Paris neurons can be about the fact that Paris is the capital of France. We simplified the problem to how they can be about Paris. The answer to that question appears to be that the Paris neurons *cannot* be about Paris. But we could have used the same strategy to show that they can't be about France or about the relationship of "being the capital of" that is supposed to hold between Paris and France. In other words, the Paris neurons that carry the information that Paris is the capital of France can't be about the fact that Paris is the capital of France. When we think that Paris is the capital of France, our thought can't be about the fact that Paris is the capital of France. It can't be *about* anything.

Feeling a bit baffled? Read on.

Sea Slugs, Rats, and Humans—
It's All the Same to Neuroscience

Swell. Then how does the brain store information if not in thoughts about stuff? Where are all those beliefs that enable us to get around the world to be found in the brain? And what about the wants, desires, hopes, and fears we have that team up with our beliefs to drive our behavior? How does the brain store them? Neuroscience is beginning to answer these questions. We can sketch some of the answer in the work that won Eric Kandel the Nobel Prize in Physiology or Medicine. The answer shows how completely wrong consciousness is when it comes to how the brain works. Indeed, it shows how wrong consciousness is when it comes to how consciousness works.

Kandel started out by discovering how the sea slug learns things. The sea slug is a pretty big snail without a shell. It can grow to more than 50 centimeters, or a couple of feet, in length. More important, it has a small number of rather large neurons that are easy to identify and easy to monitor right down to the molecular processes that go on inside these neurons and in between them.

Like Pavlov's dogs, only more easily, the sea slug can be subjected to conditioning experiments. Recall Pavlov's famous experiment: by presenting a dish of meat (the unconditioned stimulus) to dogs and ringing a bell at the same time over and over again, he was able to get them to salivate at the sound of the bell without the meat. The sound of the bell was the "conditioned" stimulus. Similarly, the sea slug can learn to withdraw its gills and its siphon from a conditioned stimulus. For example, combine a harmless electrical stimulus (the conditioned stimulus) on one nerve with a painful stimulus (the unconditioned stimulus) on another nearby nerve. The sea slug will soon respond to the painless electrical stimulus alone the way it originally responds to the combined painful and painless stimuli. It will withdraw its gill and siphon. *Voilà!* Learning by classical conditioning.

The real beauty of sea slug training is that Kandel was then able to see how the conditioning changed the neurons.

The changes are broadly of two types, depending on the conditioning experiments. Pair the unconditioned stimulus (the painful shock) and the conditioned stimulus (the harmless one) a few times. Then the sea slug will respond to the harmless stimulation alone once or twice, but will soon cease to respond to it. Pair the unconditioned and the conditioned stimulus several times, and the sea slug will continue to respond to the unconditioned stimulus—the harmless one—for a long time. Kandel discovered the source of the difference. A little training releases proteins that open up the channels, the synapses, between the neurons, so it is easier for molecules of calcium, potassium, sodium, and chloride to move through their gaps, carrying electrical charges between the neurons. This produces short-term memory in the sea slug. Training over a longer period does the same thing, but also stimulates genes in the neurons' nuclei to build new synapses that last for some time. The more synapses, the longer the conditioning lasts. The result is long-term memory in the sea slug.

The genes in the nuclei of each cell that control its activities are called somatic genes, in contrast with the germ-line genes in sperm and eggs, which transmit hereditary information. Both kinds of genes contain the same information, since the order of DNA molecules in each of them is the same. Somatic genes are copied from germ-line genes during embryonic development.

Now, the sea slug does not actually learn and store any information that could be expressed in thoughts *about* stimuli. It doesn't have the thought, "Uh oh, painless electrical stimulation in neuron 1. That means painful stimuli is coming in neuron 2, so it's time to pull back the gill." What the sea slug has learned is not some new fact *about* the world. It has acquired a new habit to do something under certain conditions. It did this because its neurons were rewired into a new input/output circuit, creating the new habit. The sea slug has learned to respond to a particular stimulus and retains that response pattern for a long while. It's learned to do something; it hasn't acquired a thought *about* something.

Twenty years after he figured out learning and habit formation in the sea slug and won the Nobel Prize for it, Kandel turned his attention to how the mammalian brain learns and stores information. His model was the rat. In his new experiments, the rat had to learn where the life raft was in a deep-water tank. Kandel showed that the rat acquires and stores the location of the raft in the tank via the same changes in the neurons of its brain as those by which the sea slug learns and remembers its new habit. Of course, in the sea slug, the changes take place in a few neurons, and in the rat they take place in thousands. But in each animal, what happens is pretty much the same. The process involves the same neurotransmitters; the same calcium, sodium, chloride, and potassium molecules; and the same genes switching on and off in the neuron's nucleus to build synapses of the same structure and composition. Just many more of them.

Sea slugs learn to do something and rats learn the location of the life raft. What they learn and how they learn it differ only by degree. One involves changing a few neural connections; the other involves changing many neural connections. But the neurons all change in the same way. What may look like the rat's learning some fact *about* the world—where the life raft is in the tank—turns out to be just the rat's acquiring a new set of neural circuits. The part of its brain that first stores information—the hippocampus—does so by rearranging input/output circuits that now respond to input stimuli in a new way.

The next step in the research program that started with sea slug learning was to figure out what happens to the neurons in the human hippocampus. This is the part of the brain that, as in the rat's brain, first stores information that usually gets expressed as thoughts *about* stuff—like where and when you were born, what your mom looks like, and what the capital of France is. Surprise, surprise! What goes on in the human hippocampus is the same as what goes on, neuron by neuron, between the neurons in the rat's hippocampus when it stores the location of the life raft in the tank. It's also the same as what goes on among the sea slug's neurons when they store its response to a mild electrical stimulus. All three involve the same changes in existing synapses and the same somatic gene expression to build new synapses. The big difference is one of degree, the number of neurons involved. In the human hippocampus (and the rest of the cortex, too), there are vastly more neurons to be changed, even more than in the rat hippocampus. But the basic process is the same.

Neuroscientists have already begun to discover how information is distributed within large sets of neuron circuits in our brain. The large sets are composed of vast numbers of small sets of neurons with extremely specialized abilities. These small sets of neural circuits have specific response patterns because they are very highly tuned input/output circuits. Here is a typical example of such a circuit: By the time your brain has fully developed, there are actually a set of neurons whose synapses have been wired together so that the only thing they do is respond to the visual input of your mother's face, with some neural output that leads to mother-recognizing behavior like your saying "Hi, Mom" when you see her face.

How can neuroscientists know this? Simply because they can knock out those neurons temporarily with strong but localized magnetic fields, and the only thing that will change is that you won't recognize your mother's face. You will recognize her voice on the phone, her smell, her handwriting. But when she comes into the room, you won't know who she is; when she speaks, you will accuse the stranger before you of being an impostor imitating your mother's voice. When she tells you her name and that she is your mother, it won't help; you won't recognize her. Otherwise, your responses to various stimulations will be perfectly normal. Once the neuroscientist turns off the magnetic field and thus reactivates the specialized neurons encoding the normal response to your mother's face, you won't have any trouble putting a name to it.

These neurons are just a clump of matter. They are not intrinsically *about* your mom. They don't look like your mom. They are not like a picture of her. They can't be interpreted or decoded by some other part of your brain into a picture or description of your mom. There is nothing that distinguishes them from any other reinforced synaptically connected neurons in your brain, except their history of being wired up as a result of early-childhood development and firing regularly under the same circumstances throughout your life.

None of these sets of circuits are *about* anything. And the combination of them can't be either. The small sets of specialized input/output circuits that respond to your mom's face, as well as the large set that responds to your mom, are no different from millions of other such sets in your brain, except in one way: they respond to a distinct electrical input with a distinct electrical output. That's all packages of neural circuits do in the rat and the sea slug. That's why they are not *about* anything. Piling up a lot of neural circuits that are not about anything at all can't turn them into a thought about stuff out there in the world.

That was one lesson already learned by working through the Paris neurons: piling up more neurons, in the form of neural interpreters, for example, won't turn any number of neurons already wired together into a circuit that is *about* anything else at all.

Go back to what's going on in the sea slug neurons, whose molecular biology is just like our own neurons' molecular biology. Sea slugs learn to do something when their neurons arrange themselves into a new input/output circuit. There's no reason to suppose that once they learn to withdraw their siphons after they receive a mild shock, the sea slugs' neurons start to constitute thoughts *about* mild electrical shocks or *about* siphon withdrawal or *about* anything at all. They have acquired some new circuit wiring, that's all. There is no *about*ness being produced in the sea slug neurons. When the rat acquires and stores information "about" the location of the life raft in the tank, that's just the neurons in its hippocampus being reorganized into new input/output circuits. They have changed in the same way that the neurons in the sea slug have changed. Similarly, knowing what your mother looks like or that Paris is the capital of France is just having a set of neurons wired up into an input/output circuit.

The molecular biology of the sea slug conditioning, the rat hippocampus, and the human hippocampus are exactly the same—give or take a few amino acids and polynucleotides. When a human has learned something that introspection insists is a thought *about* something—like what your mother looks like—what's really going on is something quite different. What's really been "learned" is the exquisite coordination of so many packages of neural connections that the behavior it produces looks like it's the result of thoughts *about* things in the world. That is especially how it looks to introspection. But looks are deceiving, as we so clearly saw in the last chapter.

Nevertheless, introspection is screaming at you that you do have thoughts *about* your mother. Scientism calmly insists that we will have to try to ignore this tantrum until the next chapter, when we have the tools to deal with it directly. Meanwhile, there is a third way of seeing that the brain can't contain anything that is a thought *about* stuff. This way combines the first two reasons, the one from physics and the one from neuroscience.

Question to the *Jeopardy!* Answer "The Same Way a Computer Stores Information"

Physics and neuroscience both tell us, for different reasons, that one clump of matter can't be *about* another clump of matter. Computer science combines both to show that human brain states can't really be about stuff for exactly the same reason that the internal workings of your laptop can't really be about anything at all.

Suppose you are reading this book on a Kindle or an iPad, or even on an old-fashioned computer screen. On the screen there are pixels spelling out the sentence

Never let your conscious be your guide.

Why is this arrangement of dark and light squares on the screen—this clump of matter—*about* consciousness, or *about* guiding you, or *about* never letting the former be the latter, or *about* anything at all? Obviously, because you have interpreted the pixels as being *about* consciousness and *about* guiding and *about* never letting something happen. Computer hardware designers and computer software engineers designed the pixel configurations to represent letters and words and sentences— that is, to be *about* letters and words and sentences. You look at the pattern of pixels and interpret it to be *about* the subject of the sentence formed by the pixels.

Going back even further in the design process, electrical engineers interpreted the CPU's (central processing unit's) semiconductor circuits as "logic gates"—that is, as being about "and" and "or" and "not." Without interpretation by someone, neither the pixels nor the electrical charges in the computer's motherboard nor the distribution of magnetic charges on the hard drive can be about anything, right? They are just like red octagons. They get interpreted by us as letters spelling English words. That's how they come to be *about* the things that the pixels are about. So, no *about*ness anywhere in the computer without interpretation by us—by our mind, our brain.

When a computer gets programmed, the only changes in it are physical ones: mainly the distribution of high and low currents or north and south magnetic charges to its circuits or magnetic media. These changes in voltage or magnetic pole store both programs and data. Together, they determine output, usually the pixels on the screen.

After building a computer that beat the world chess champion several times, the computer scientists at IBM began seeking a greater challenge. They sought to program a computer, named Watson (after the founder of the company), to play the American quiz show *Jeopardy!*. They built a computer that not only stored as much (or more) information as a human brain, but could deploy that information appropriately—that is, produce pixels that humans interpret as questions to *Jeopardy!* answers. The achievement was far more impressive than merely beating Garry Kasparov. But the computer scientists were just arranging Watson's circuits to respond to voltage-pattern inputs with voltage-pattern outputs. When they scanned vast quantities of data into its memory circuits, they were endowing its circuits with information, but not with thoughts (or anything else) that are *about* stuff.

It's remarkable that Watson is pretty good at *Jeopardy!*. Yet its electronic circuits don't need to be about anything, including about how to play Jeopardy, for it to be pretty good at the game, good enough to beat most people.

How does Watson manage to do it without having any thoughts about stuff? How does it search through its data for the right response when its data consist of nothing but vast assemblages of high- and low-voltage currents in microchips and distributions of magnetic charges on hard drives? How does it even understand the quizmaster's question—or rather the answer, since this is *Jeopardy!*—without having thoughts about anything at all, without even thoughts about the language the question is asked in? Computer scientists know how Watson does it. How vast is the information stored? Roughly as vast as an educated adult human stores for *Jeopardy!*-type uses. How intelligently does Watson deploy it? Approximately as intelligently as an educated adult human deploys it for constructing questions to answers. If Watson can store and employ all that information without having a single thought *about* anything, then so can we. After all, your brain is a computer, too.

What Kandel's work and a lot of neuroscience going back a hundred years has shown is that, among other things, the brain is at least in part a computer. It's composed of an unimaginably large number of electronic input/output circuits, each one a set of neurons electrically connected to others through their synapses. The circuits transmit electrical outputs in different ways, depending on their electrical inputs and on how their parts—individual neurons—are wired up together. That's how the brain works. It's more powerful and more efficient than any computer we'll ever be able to build and program. Maybe the brain is a lot of separate computers, wired together in parallel along with other peripheral "devices"—the eye, the tongue, the ear, the nose, the skin. But that it is at least a computer is obvious from its anatomy and physiology right down to the individual neurons and their electrochemical on/off connections to one another.

The brain is a computer whose "microprocessors"—its initial assemblies of neural circuits—are hardwired by a developmental process that starts before birth and goes on after it. Long before that process is over, the brain has already started to modify its hardwired operating system and acquire data fed in through its sensory apparatus. What happens to it doesn't differ in any significant way from what happens to Watson. Our brain inputs data via changes in air pressure on the eardrum (sounds, noises, words), the irradiation of light photons on the retina (gestures, images, inscriptions), and similar input from the other sense organs, instead of through magnetic or voltage changes that Watson uses. But they are all just physical processes. Just as Watson stores enough information and processes it to win at Jeopardy without any of its states being *about* anything at all, our brain accomplishes the same trick. Beliefs, desires, wants, hopes, and fears are complex information storage states, vast packages of input/output circuits in the brain ready to deliver appropriate and sometimes inappropriate behavior when stimulated.

The brain's neural states, like the states of the semiconductor circuits in a Mac or PC (or in Watson for that matter), are not by themselves intrinsically *about* anything at all. What you have got is a lot of neural architecture geared up to respond with exquisite appropriateness to external and internal stimuli. Its responses produce characteristically human behavior—for example, making noise with your throat, tongue, teeth, and breath (that is, speaking). In addition to the many other effects inside the body that these neural activities produce, they also produce the illusion that the thoughts in there, in the brain, are really *about* the world. This is such a powerful illusion that it has been with us forever, or at least for a couple of hundred thousand years.

Here's an analogy that may help illustrate just what sort of an illusion we're dealing with. Remember, it's just an analogy, imperfect at best.

A single still photograph doesn't convey movement the way a motion picture does. Watching a sequence of slightly different photos one photo per hour, or per minute, or even one every 6 seconds won't do it either. But looking at the right sequence of still pictures succeeding each other every one-twentieth of a second produces the illusion that the images in each still photo are moving. Increasing the rate enhances the illusion, though beyond a certain rate the illusion gets no better for creatures like us. But it's still an illusion. There is nothing to it but the succession of still pictures. That's how movies perpetrate their illusion. The large set of still pictures is organized together in a way that produces in creatures like us the illusion that the images are moving. In creatures with different brains and eyes, ones that work faster, the trick might not work. In ones that work slower, changing the still pictures at the rate of one every hour (as in time-lapse photography) could work. But there is no movement of any of the images in any of the pictures, nor does anything move from one photo onto the next. Of course, the projector is moving, and the photons are moving, and the actors were moving. But all the movement that the movie watcher detects is in the eye of the beholder. That is why the movement is illusory.

The notion that thoughts are about stuff is illusory in roughly the same way. Think of each input/output neural circuit as a single still photo. Now, put together a huge number of input/output circuits in the right way. None of them is about anything; each is just an input/output circuit firing or not. But when they act together, they "project" the illusion that there are thoughts about stuff. They do that through the behavior and the conscious experience (if any) that they together produce.

The neural circuits in the brain are much more exquisitely organized than the still photos on a 35 mm filmstrip. They are related to one another in ways that produce many outputs, behaviors of all sorts, that are beautifully adapted to their local and global environments. It's because of the appropriateness of these outputs to specific circumstances that we credit their causes—the neural circuits—with being *about* those circumstances. That is the illusion: somehow neural circuits must literally be *about* those circumstances, carrying descriptions of them, statements about them that make the outputs appropriate to the circumstances. The cumulative output that all these millions of simple input/output circuits produce is so appropriate to the brain's environment that we are tempted to identify a statement expressed in some language we happen to speak as what all those neurons working together must be thinking. And the subject of that statement must be what they are *about*. There is no such statement. It's an illusion, a trick, like a lot of still pictures conveying the illusion of motion.

But our analogy needs a little fine-tuning. Still pictures don't show movement. Putting them together into movies projects the illusion that there is movement by the images in them. But in the real world there *is* movement, and the illusion of movement in movies tracks the reality of movement in the world. However, the illusion of *about*ness projected by the neurons in our brain does *not* match any *about*ness in the world. There isn't any. Maybe we could improve the force of the analogy if we focused on Disney movies or kids' cartoons or *Avatar*. There are no Na'vi in reality. There is no *about*ness in reality.

But introspection is making you respond, "It can't be an illusion." It may grant that the brain is so fantastically complex that it can navigate the world even while looking through the rearview mirror. And for all it knows, maybe conscious acts of will are not what cause the body to move. Maybe the brain stores information in neural circuits that aren't really *about* stuff. But surely, the thoughts I am conscious of right now have to be *about* something. These conscious thoughts aren't just input/output circuits, empty of content. I can be tricked by the movies into the illusion of motion. But introspection can't be tricked into the illusion that its thoughts are about stuff, even if the thoughts are illusory. Right now, I am thinking about the problem of how conscious thought can be about stuff. Introspection is telling me, firsthand, exactly what I am thinking about. How can anyone deny that?

No matter how hard it is to deny, we have to do so. Appearances to the contrary, it's no easier a trick for conscious thoughts to be about stuff than for nonconscious thoughts—brain circuits—to be about stuff. Let's quickly run through why this is.

You're consciously thinking that Paris is the capital of France. So your thought is about Paris, about capitals, and about France, right? Whatever it is in your brain that the conscious thought consists of, there will have to be 3 or 20 or 100 or 100 million neurons that together make up the conscious markers (silent sounds, shapes, words, images) for "Paris," for "is the capital of," and for "France." These markers somehow get put together into the conscious thought, right?

These neural markers in consciousness will have all the same problems being about Paris, about capitals, or about France that any nonconscious neurons in the brain have. The basic neural processes going on in conscious thought have to be just the same as the basic neural processes going on when the brain nonconsciously thinks. These processes are the only things neurons and sets of neurons do. Consciousness is just another physical process. So, it has as much trouble producing *about*ness as any other physical process. Introspection certainly produces the illusion of *about*ness. But it's got to be an illusion, since nothing physical can be *about* anything. That goes for your conscious thoughts as well. The markers, the physical stuff, the clumps of matter that constitute your conscious thoughts can't be *about* stuff either. The real problem is to explain away this illusion. Doing so is going to dispose of a lot of other illusions as well.

In the next couple of chapters, we'll see how deeply wrong consciousness is when it comes to the self, free will, human purpose, and the meanings of our actions, our lives, and our creations. It's all because of the illusion that thought is *about* stuff. And we'll explain why introspection keeps screaming at us that thoughts, whether conscious or not, really are about anything at all.

Introspection is screaming that thought has to be about stuff, and philosophers are muttering, "Denying it is crazy, worse than self-contradictory. It's incoherent. According to you, neither spoken sentences nor silent ones in thought express statements. They aren't about anything. That goes for every sentence in this book. It's not about anything. Why are we bothering to read it?"

Look, if I am going to get scientism into your skull I have to use the only tools we've got for moving information from one head to another: noises, ink-marks, pixels. Treat the illusion that goes with them like the optical illusions in Chapter 7. This book isn't conveying statements. It's rearranging neural circuits, removing inaccurate disinformation and replacing it with accurate information. Treat it as correcting maps instead of erasing sentences.

Chapter 9

◀ ◆ ▶

FAREWELL TO THE
PURPOSE-DRIVEN LIFE™

FOR SOLID EVOLUTIONARY REASONS, WE'VE BEEN tricked into looking at life from the inside. Without scientism, we look at life from the inside, from the first-person POV (OMG, you don't know what a POV is?—a "point of view"). The first person is the subject, the audience, the viewer of subjective experience, the self in the mind.

Scientism shows that the first-person POV is an illusion. Even after scientism convinces us, we'll continue to stick with the first person. But at least we'll know that it's another illusion of introspection and we'll stop taking it seriously. We'll give up all the answers to the persistent questions about free will, the self, the soul, and the meaning of life that the illusion generates.

The physical facts fix all the facts. The mind is the brain. It has to be physical and it can't be anything else, since thinking, feeling, and perceiving are physical process—in particular, input/output processes—going on in the brain. We can be sure of a great deal about how the brain works because the physical facts fix all the facts about the brain. The fact that the mind is the brain guarantees that there is no free will. It rules out any purposes or designs organizing our actions or our lives. It excludes the very possibility of enduring persons, selves, or souls that exist after death or for that matter while we live. Not that there was ever much doubt about mortality anyway.

This chapter uses the science of Chapter 8 to provide scientism's answers to the persistent questions about us and the mind. The fact that these answers are so different from what life's illusions tell us from the inside of consciousness is just more reason not to take introspection seriously.

THE GRAND ILLUSION DOWN THE AGES AND UP FROM BIRTH

The neural circuits in our brain manage the beautifully coordinated and smoothly appropriate behavior of our body. They also produce the entrancing introspective illusion that thoughts really are about stuff in the world. This powerful illusion has been with humanity since language kicked in, as we'll see. It is the source of at least two other profound myths: that we have purposes that give our actions and lives meaning and that there is a person "in there" steering the body, so to speak. To see why we make these mistakes and why it's so hard to avoid them, we need to understand the source of the illusion that thoughts are about stuff.

In Chapter 8 we saw that the "thoughts" in the brain can't be about anything at all, either things inside or outside the brain. The brain doesn't store information that way. Rather, it stores information about the world in vast sets of input/output circuits that respond appropriately to one another and to their environment. These responses are so appropriate that it looks to us from the outside that other people's brains are full of thoughts about the environment. From the inside, the illusion is even more powerful. So, where exactly does it come from?

To explain where the illusion that thoughts are about stuff comes from, we start with a simple case of the exquisite appropriateness of the input/output circuits to their environment. A fly passes in front of a frog's visual field. The frog's tongue flicks at the fly and brings it into its mouth. We watch this display and marvel at the frog's ability, something we can't do. We marvel at the fact that the frog knew that the little black thing in front of it was a source of food, knew exactly where it was headed, and knew where to flick its tongue in order to capture and eat it. Where did it store the information it needed to do this neat trick? In its neural circuitry, of course. But how did its neural circuits attain the ability to store this information?

The answer: natural selection. In the evolutionary past, there was strong selection for genes that build nerve circuits in the visual system that are stimulated to fire just by little black moving dots in the frog's visual field. Big dots won't do it, nor will motionless little ones. The advantage of such circuits is obvious. The only moving little black dots in the frog's environment are insects it can eat. There was also selection for (genes that build) other circuits wired to take as inputs the visual system's output and send their own output to other neural circuits that ultimately trigger tongue flicking. The process was just blind variation and environmental filtration. Over the evolutionary history of frogs, variation resulted in a few neural circuits connected to the eyes and the tongue in ways that happened to result in eating; most didn't. The ones that did were selected for. There is nothing special about these neural circuits or different from other neural circuits that can do this job, other than their fortuitously connecting circuits from the eye to circuits for the tongue. Theses neurons aren't any more about the fly than others that could do the same job but don't because they are hooked up to other circuits. Frogs aren't smart enough to learn how to flick flies by operant conditioning. Their survival is testimony to how finely Mother Nature (aka genetic natural selection) can tune the appropriateness of responses to the environment.

We are, of course, amazed at the environmental appropriateness of the frog's tongue flicking. We say, "The frog knows where the fly is. There must be neurons in its brain that contain information about the fly's speed and direction." It's perfectly natural for us to say this, but it's an illusion that results solely from the environmental appropriateness of the dot-detection to tongue-flicking chain of neural inputs and outputs. The frog's neural circuitry can't be about the fly; they can't be about anything. So, when we say that there are neural circuits in the frog that acquire information about flies, store this information, and make use of it to stimulate, direct, or control tongue flicking, we are either speaking metaphorically or we have succumbed to an illusion.

Now let's turn to the human case. Here the behavior is even more exquisitely appropriate to the environment. Our behavior is not limited to anything as simple as flicking our tongue at edible insects. We engage in conversation. What could be more exquisitely appropriate to our environments? The appropriateness is, however, only different in degree from the appropriateness of the frog's tongue flicking. And the neural circuits that produce the behavior differ only in number and in circuit wiring from the neurons in the frog. If the only differences are differences of degree, then whatever information our brain stores, we don't store it in a way that is different from the way frogs store information; we just store much more information and much different information. The notion that we store it in propositions, statements, thoughts, or ideas about stuff is still just as illusory.

The illusion that a frog's neural circuitry is about stuff has only one source: the phylogenetic selection of hard wiring that produces the behavior when appropriate. The illusion in the human case has two sources. One source is phylogenetic, the evolutionary biology of our species. The other part is ontogenetic—infant and childhood development and lots of learning. In the human case, each source has another component, absent in the case of other animals. The human illusion that thought is about stuff is also powered by an internal, introspectively driven process that matches up with a process externally driven by other people's (operant) shaping of our behavior.

The phylogenetic process started with whatever it was that distinguished *Homo sapiens'* evolutionary ancestors from other primates—chimpanzees and gorillas. There was one trait we shared in roughly equal measure with other primates: a preexisting hard-wired "theory of mind," the ability to predict at least some of the purposeful-looking behavior of other animals. There was, however, another trait that other primates lacked, but which for some reason we share with other animals like elephants, dolphins, dogs and tamarin monkeys: an incipient inclination to share and help. Among hominins, this inclination started to be selected for on the savanna for reasons we discussed in Chapter 6 (longevity, too many kids too close together, long childhood dependence, and the need for teamwork in scavenging).

Without some really neat adaptations, hominins would not have prospered; we might not have even survived. At least once, if not several times, our ancestors found themselves in an evolutionary bottleneck, with populations driven down to levels that made us an endangered species. We are not very strong or fast or tough compared to the other primates or compared to the megafauna we had to protect ourselves from and eventually hunt. All that megafauna selection pressure made natural selection grab onto the first solution that came along for solving the problems we faced. There had to have been strong selection for cooperation and collaboration to scavenge in larger groups, to hunt, to make and use tools, and to establish divisions of labor that dealt with a large number of offspring and their extended childhood dependence.

Solving these problems resulted in repeated cycles of selection between better solutions and the enhancement of the two traits—theory of mind and inclination to help—over and over again for a million years or so. Between them, a better and better theory of mind and a willingness to share, especially information, produced first the level of collaboration and coordination required for survival, then improvements that eventually produced dominance of the environment and finally made language possible. Just getting minimal coordination on which grunts go with which actions or tools or predators or prey requires a highly developed willingness to collaborate, a well-refined theory of mind, and a prodigious capacity to learn from experience.

One tip-off to the importance of helping and sharing for the emergence of language is in the differences between humans and chimps that have learned to use languages. Neurogenomics—the study of which genes are switched on in our brain cells—has not yet uncovered the details of exactly what differences in size and structure distinguish our brain from those of other primates and enable us to speak. But one clue to the difference is how chimps use the languages that experimenters have taught them. Chimps have learned to use sign language or move plastic markers on a board to communicate. They have even been known to create sentences conveying novel ideas. But their creative use of language is almost exclusively to express imperatives such as "Give Washoe [the chimp's name] grape." Chimps don't help each other or people much, and they only share things grudgingly (they tolerate theft by their younger kin). Unlike even very young human speakers, when chimps do have some language, they don't use it to share information, that is, to cooperate and collaborate. If they did, debates about whether they can "speak" would end.

Among humans, the coordination of grunts, gestures, and shrieks with other behavior and with the behavior of others got more and more complicated over evolutionary time. And in a new feedback loop, it began to enhance the very coordination and collaboration that was necessary for it to get started. The process probably took a million years of genetic and cultural evolution. Speech itself probably couldn't have even started earlier than 400,000 years ago. That's when the human larynx evolved into a position that makes well articulated noises possible. But helping others figure out what you were going to do by grunts, gestures, howls, and shrieks got started long before. Of course, grunts, gestures, shrieks, and marks on the ground, for that matter, can't themselves be about other chunks of matter any more than neural synapses can. We haven't gotten to the illusion of *about*ness yet. But we are getting closer.

Natural selection turned grunts, shrieks, and gestures into coordination devices between people. That required shared memory of which grunts go with which actions. These stored memories didn't have to come into consciousness to work. But of course hominins are conscious, and pretty soon introspection began to be filled with a silent version of the noises and gestures humans were producing along with the actions. The silent noises and gestures imagined in the mind were our species' original sources of the illusion that conscious thoughts are about stuff.

What people had begun doing, however, was just silently talking or writing or otherwise moving markers around in consciousness. Conscious thinking, then and now, is almost always the silent subvocal succession of word-sounds. Just try counting in your head; it's the same noises that you make when you count out loud, but the noises are in your mind. As we saw at the end of Chapter 8, those markers that your consciousness runs over as you silently count are no more capable of being about something outside of themselves—in this case numbers—than any other clump of matter. Conscious thought is this stringing together in the mind of "tokens"—silent sounds, shapes, sensations—somewhere in the brain, in just the way that gesturing or shrieking or talking or writing is the stringing together of noises or hand gestures or facial movements or marks on paper outside of the brain. None of them is about anything.

Of course, there's lots of cognition without silent speech. In fact, most thinking is nonconscious. For example, when you speak, you are completely unaware of the thoughts you need to go through to produce what you say. Similarly, as you read these ink marks, you are not conscious of the thinking required to produce the silent "noises" you are now experiencing, the silent noises that trick you into thinking that the marks on the page or screen you are looking at are about stuff. But we are dead sure that the markers in conscious thought are ones about stuff. And the process that produced that illusion piggybacks on the one that first coordinated vocal sounds and actions among hominins predisposed to use their theory of mind to cooperate.

Back to the evolutionary process. The environment persistently filtered for variations that fine-tuned coordination of noises and actions into proto-language, pidgins, and eventually full-fledged language. In each individual, the process carried along conscious markers that silently reproduced the grunts and shrieks that hominins made when collaborating. When the behaviors and the noises and their silent copies in consciousness became finely tuned enough to their environment, the result was the illusion that the grunts and the thoughts were about stuff.

Let's consider how the illusion of *about*ness emerges onto-genetically, in the infant and child. Here there is already a fair amount of experimental evidence that sheds light on the process. Just after birth, babies can discriminate about 600 sounds. There are hardwired neural connections in the newborn brain that respond distinctively to that many sounds. No *about*ness there, just different hardwired input/output circuits. Exposure to English noises from its parents pares down the number of sounds the baby can discriminate to about 45. The winnowing from 600 noises to 45 can't have produced any *about*ness either. But now appropriate responses to these 45 sound stimuli have become adaptive—they pay off in milk, comfort, attention. Still no *about*ness in the baby's consciousness, but already the illusion has kicked in for the parents: they start treating the baby's thoughts as being about stuff—food, warmth, companionship.

Experiments comparing children under 2 and adult chimps show that both have about the same factual understanding about space and time, objects and causation. But unlike chimps, the kids are already spontaneously collaborating with others. Unlike chimps, and without training or reward, they are willing to coordinate their behavior to mesh with different behavior by other people. The differences between humans and chimps in this regard is a window on the evolutionary history of language and on its emergence in the individual.

The proclivity to collaborate spontaneously, recognizably, and without reward powerfully strengthens other peoples' illusion that the baby has thoughts about stuff. Meanwhile, the illusion of *about*ness in the child's introspection emerges during the very same period when the baby finds itself consciously running through the noises it has heard and made. It is a gradual process that begins when the silent sound markers in consciousness—

"ma" or "milk"—begin repeatedly to match events in the baby's immediate environment. The introspective illusion builds as the child's brain becomes sophisticated enough to respond to other people's pointing gestures, sometimes paired with sounds. The process of illusion-building finishes off when the neural circuits in the child's brain have been trained by operant conditioning to respond appropriately to noises other people make that coordinates their behavior with the child's. At this point, the neural circuits are also generating silent versions of these speech markers in consciousness. The child is well on the way to absorbing the illusion that conscious markers like "ma" and "milk" are about specific features of their circumstances.

The cognitive capacities that create both illusions—the observer's illusion that the baby's thoughts are about stuff and the baby's introspective illusion that its thoughts are about stuff—have been selected for over evolutionary time. Elemental versions of the same process must have occurred among our hominin ancestors at all ages. Throughout life, not just in early childhood, packages of noises and coordinated actions were shaped by processes of selection operating on behaviors. At the same time, there was very strong selection for neural capacities that preserve, extend, and speed up the development of more of these packages. After all, cooperation was a matter of life or death. That is why humans, unlike other primates, are equipped with several hardwired cognitive resources needed for learning to share information early and quickly.

These cognitive resources made possible early and accurate learning of any human language at all by any normal human infant at all. Ever since the earliest work of Noam Chomsky, there has been a research program in cognitive linguistics that aims to identify these distinct human capacities and even to locate them in the human brain. There is no doubt that they were being shaped and selected for by the factors that selected for the theory of mind and the proclivity to cooperation that our ancestors needed to survive. The hardwired capacities were needed to learn language early and accurately. But they weren't enough. As most cognitive linguists will acknowledge, the innate brain structures can't do much more than detect something like grammar or syntax. They had little role in determining which shrieks and grunts would go with which behaviors. Otherwise we would not all be able to learn every language from birth equally well.

Since every component of the conscious and unconscious states of the brain involved in all these processes—both the evolutionary ones and the ontogenetic ones—are just clumps of matter, there can't be any *about*ness anywhere in the process, just the overpowering illusion of it.

The complex behavior of people is beautifully suited to their circumstances, even more beautifully suited than a frog's flicking at a fly. That's why humans think their brains just have to be carrying around thoughts about those circumstances, thoughts about their own wants and needs, and thoughts about how to exploit those circumstances to meeting their wants and needs. Introspection of our own consciousness strengthens this conviction even more. We assume that other people are like us, that they have minds that carry around thoughts about their circumstances and their needs. Combined, introspection of ourselves and observation of others drive us to the inescapable conclusion that we and everyone else have thoughts about other people's minds. Our thoughts about their thoughts plus the theory of mind lead us to conclude that many of their thoughts take the form of purposes, plans, designs, aims, and objectives. These purposes and designs, aims and objectives drive behavior in the appropriate direction—the future, right?

Once it emerged in human evolutionary history, the illusion that thought is about stuff took hold firmly. Why? Because we began talking "about" it, especially in the context of plans, purposes, and designs. Plans, purposes, and designs are illusions, too. But they enabled us to begin telling stories to ourselves and others. The stories were just by-products of the solution to the number one design problem that faced *Homo sapiens* in the Pleistocene: ganging up on the megafauna.

Having thoughts about the future is necessary for having plans, purposes, or designs. In fact, all you need to have a plan is to think about something you want in the future and about how to go about getting it. That much is obvious. But if your brain can't think about anything, it can't have thoughts about the future. To have a design for how you want things to be arranged, you have to have thoughts about how to arrange them. To act on your plans, your designs for how things should be in the future, you have to have thoughts now about how to bring about your plans, some thoughts about what tools and resources you will need. Purposes, plans, recipes, and designs in the head have to be thoughts about stuff in the world—thoughts about how you want it to be arranged in the future and thoughts about how it's arranged now. All this is obvious. Less obvious is the fact that the brain has no trouble taking steps that will be rewarded (or punished), depending on how things turn out in the future. But it doesn't do this by having thoughts about the future or anything else for that matter.

Since there are no thoughts about things, notions of purpose, plan, or design in the mind are illusory. Farewell to the purpose-driven life. Whatever is in our brain driving our lives from cradle to grave, it is not purposes. But it does produce the powerful illusion of purposes, just like all the other purposeless adaptations in the biological realm.

Scientism could have reached the conclusion that there are no purposes or designs in the brain without any help from neurolinguistics, behavioral biology, or evolutionary anthropology. There are no purposes or designs in nature. Newtonian physics banished them from reality. Darwinian biology explained away their appearance everywhere. That has to go for our brain as much as for any other physical thing in the universe. Scientism is already committed to a purpose-free mind. It's the job of the neurosciences to explain how the brain works without purposes and how the brain produces such a beautiful appearance of purpose without its reality.

Neuroscience has already started on this task in its demonstration of how neurons deliver the behavior that looks overwhelmingly like it's purpose driven. Neuroscience has not yet done much to explain why some of this neural activity is conscious introspection or how consciousness works to help produce the illusion of *about*ness.

Purpose and its parent, *about*ness, are illusions created by introspection. The noises and the marks we "address" to one another were long ago hit on by Mother Nature as quick and dirty solutions to survival problems. These noises and marks were jumped on by natural selection to solve the problem humans faced coming out of the rain forest into the savanna. During this process, the illusions emerged that these noises and marks are about stuff, have meanings, and that the meanings and *about*ness are in our heads, in our conscious minds. All there really was and is are these markers, ones that come out of our mouths and are heard by others, and silent ones that move around in introspection. The noises, and eventually writing, along with the silent markers in conscious thought, are what eventually produced the beginnings of culture—storytelling. Then rudimentary culture selected for further elaboration of these markers in

speech, in introspection, and in writing. It also fostered, reinforced, and elaborated the illusion that they meant stuff. So
deeply did the illusion become embedded that no one noticed
it until science had been underway for several hundred years.
With a pedigree that stretches back into the Pleistocene, no
wonder the illusions that thoughts and words are about stuff
are the hardest ones to give up.

Scientism enables us to stop worrying about these meanings
along with meanings of our lives—and the meaning of human
life in general. As we'll see, it helps us see through the snake oil
sold to those of us who seek meaning, and science shows why
none of their nostrums really work for most people. It's because
the nostrums are built on illusion—usually self-inflicted illusion.
Do we need a substitute, a replacement, an alternative to meaning
to make us go on living? The short answer is no, and the details
are given in Chapter 12.

MOTHER NATURE MADE US CRUDE
CONSPIRACY THEORISTS

Natural selection made us crude conspiracy theorists, using
the introspective markers we mistake for our own plans and
designs to cause behavior, and using other people's noises and
inscriptions to figure out their behavior. This sort of conspiracy
theorizing to predict other people's behavior has limited but
long-standing adaptive value. That's why Mother Nature found a
way of addicting us to it. We use other people's behavior, including the noises they make (their talk) and the inscriptions they
scratch out (their writing), along with our own silent markers
and mental images, to guide our expectations about other people's behavior. When we get it right, there's the relief from curiosity and the psychological satisfaction that makes us keep doing

it. Do enough of that sort of thing and you get stories with plots: biographies, histories, and of course, historical novels, psychologically satisfying even when they are sketchy or fictional (think of the *Iliad* and the Bible).

For all its headiness, conspiracy theorizing using mental markers and spoken or written ones brings with it the illusion that the markers are thoughts about stuff. The theorizing plus the illusion is the folk psychology we all embrace. It's imperfect because it is a quick and dirty solution to the pressing design problem nature needed to solve to get us past the African bottleneck. Because the markers that move around our introspectable minds only crudely indicate what is really going on in each person's brain, folk psychology doesn't do a very good job. It breaks down badly once you use it to predict a lot of people's actions. It's not very good when it is used to explain or predict someone's actions with any precision or over a long period of time. Folk psychology is almost never able to predict exactly what people will do or explain what they did beyond the relatively low level of precision of a good yarn.

The notion that thought is about stuff doesn't even approximate what is going on in the brain. That's why the folk psychology that rests on it can't be improved, even when we rein in conspiracy theorizing and try to make it more "scientific."

When you consciously think about your own plans, purposes, motives, all you are doing is stringing together silent "sounds" or other markers into silent "sentences" (or fragments of them) in your head. These sentences in your conscious thought are not even rough approximations of what is going on in your brain. They are simply indicators of the brain states doing the actual work in cognition and behavior. What is going on in consciousness when it introspectively "thinks about stuff" is just a crude indicator or symptom, similar to the way a fever is just a symptom of any one of a hundred different illnesses. The often incomplete, ungrammatical, ambiguous sentences and sentence fragments in conscious thought are in fact only rough moment-to-moment symptoms of ever-shifting packages of millions of connections in the brain. These vast packages of input/output circuits drive behaviors appropriate to the circumstances. Recall how Kandel showed that the brain stores information as abilities. Everything we do consciously, including talking out loud to others or silently to ourselves, is just the brain manifesting some of those abilities. That's why the conscious sequence of markers that pass for thoughts about stuff can't be rough approximations of the information the neurons store. Neural circuits are input/output devices. They have the ability to respond to inputs with outputs. Images and sentences can't approximate abilities.

To see the problem, try the following thought experiment: You can ride a bicycle or drive a car or scramble an egg. Try expressing any of those abilities in a set of diagrams or a set of sentences "about" bicycle riding or driving or frying an egg. You would run through a huge number of photos or sentences and you still would not have communicated the ability. The sentences won't ever describe much of your know-how, and they will include information that really isn't required. That's because you can't express the relevant information in sentences or pictures. No one can adequately convey or display any complex ability in terms of statements you have to know or believe in order to have the ability. And no diagram or even a movie can do it either. Try writing down the ability to ride a bike—not the instructions about how to learn, but the ability that is learned. Can't be done.

There is a more obvious reason why conscious thoughts about stuff can't approximate neural circuitry. Introspection can't let us in on conscious thoughts about stuff to begin with. There aren't any such thoughts in consciousness. There is just the play of silent noises or other markers across consciousness. And those markers aren't about anything either. Combining the markers with a lot of other physical processes in the brain and the body, or indeed behavior by other bodies, couldn't make the markers have *about-ness* either.

Our conscious thoughts are very crude indicators of what is going on in our brain. We fool ourselves into treating these conscious markers as thoughts about what we want and about how to achieve it, about plans and purposes. We are even tricked into thinking they somehow bring about behavior. We are mistaken about all of these things. Meanwhile, our brain's input/output circuits are working, behind the curtain so to speak, creating these illusions by playing markers out in a (quasi-)grammatical or syntactical order though consciousness. Whatever neural arrangements these conscious markers consist of, they are almost certainly not sufficient in number or organization by themselves to drive the behavior that is supposed to result from conscious thoughts about stuff. When it comes to causing and guiding our actions, the stream of consciousness is pretty much just along for the ride, like the conscious feeling of choosing in Libet's experiments. This is just another reason to treat conscious thoughts as crude indicators, not rough approximations of anything the brain is actually doing.

This is not to deny that consciousness does some important things in our psychology. It's probably too big a deal not to have been organized by natural selection to solve some design problem or other, perhaps several. Exactly what its functions are, what design problem it solves, neuroscience has not yet figured out. It's tempting to suspect that among its functions—one of the adaptations it confers—is the illusion that thought is about stuff. After all, that illusion is one that Mother Nature seems to have pounced on to ensure our survival.

If propounding the illusion that thought is about stuff were really one of the adaptations consciousness conferred on us, it was a very dirty solution. Because our conscious thoughts are poor indicators of the neural causes of our behavior, the predictions we make in ordinary life, based on them, about our own behavior are pretty weak. Our predictions of other people's behavior, based on guesses that they, too, have thoughts about stuff, are even worse.

Given how bad folk psychology is at predicting and explaining our own and other people's actions, it's a wonder that it was good enough to provide a quick and dirty solution to the design problem our species faced when it left the rain forest for the savanna and its megafaunal predators. If Mother Nature had had world enough and time enough, she might have crafted a more elegant solution to the problem of getting us to cooperate, coordinate, and collaborate well enough to survive on the savanna. A more elegant solution might have limited our assignment of purposes or thoughts to animals more complicated than frogs. It certainly would not have gone in for the panpsychism that treats everything as if it were the manifestation of some mind's purposes. But the only way it could make the love of stories innate was by overshooting and projecting our thoughts onto the rest of nature, seeing conspiracies everywhere. It's natural selection overshooting that produces religion. Perhaps scientism is an incipient response to strong natural selection for improvements to our ability to predict human behavior. Such an improvement will be needed if our species is to survive in the environment we have created for ourselves since the Holocene began 10,000 years ago.

Nature exploited the folk psychology theory that introspection imposed on our ancestors. It made use of the fiction to produce enough cooperation, coordination, and collaboration to get us to the top of the African food chain and then through a couple of ice ages to the top of the food chain everywhere. Once we got into the Holocene, the obstacles to a scientific understanding created by introspection's illusions began to really make their mark on human culture. They generated our partiality to stories and our resistance to science. They will probably continue to do so for most people, even after neuroscience succeeds in accurately predicting and explaining behavior and our attachment to the illusions of introspection.

History, biography, the "interpretative" social sciences, all the literary arts and humanities are the result of conscious introspection's commitment to explaining human affairs in terms of purposes, plans, designs—thoughts about the way the world is and the way it might be. We love Homer's *Iliad*, Murasaki Shikibu's *The Tale of Genji*, Styron's *Sophie's Choice*, Thucydides's *History of the Peloponnesian War*, Churchill's *History of the Second World War*, Boswell's *Life of Johnson*, and Shakespeare's *Henry V*. We love them because they are so good at exploiting the brain's taste for stories with plots. We mistakenly think—or rather feel—that only plots can convey understanding of human affairs. Our literature, too—from epic poems to stream of consciousness—is the search for motives and meanings in thoughts about things. Once it becomes evident that such thoughts are poor guides to the neural causes of what we do, much of the mystification and frustration of the humanities becomes clear.

The thoughts about human actions that are supposed to give them meaning and purpose have no reality in the brain. Our own apparent thoughts about things are crude indicators of the real causes of our own behavior. We guess at the thoughts of others from their behavior, their actions, their statements and speeches, their letters and diaries. But the results of our guessing are equally unreliable indicators of what actually moves people. How people behave, including what they say and write, does place some constraints on how we perceive their thoughts. Behavior limits what thoughts about the world we put in people's heads. But the constraints aren't strong enough ever to narrow down our guesses to just one set of sentences that fits all the physical facts about anyone's behavior and circumstances. Even if the constraints did permit us to narrow down our guesses about which markers are currently playing across a subject's consciousness, the result still would not improve our understanding, our explanations, our predictions of behavior, for those same markers could be the results of any number of quite different packages of neural circuits, and each package would have a different effect on behavior.

Once you recognize that there is no way to take seriously both what neuroscience tells us about the springs of human action in the brain and what introspection tells us about it, you have to choose. Take one fork and seek interpretation of human affairs in the plans, purposes, designs, ideologies, myths, or meanings that consciousness claims actually move us. Take the other fork, the one that scientism signposts, and you must treat all the humanities as the endlessly entertaining elaborations of an illusion. They are all enterprises with no right answers, not even coming closer to approximating our understanding of anything. You cannot treat the interpretation of behavior in terms of purposes and meaning as conveying real understanding. It often allays the intermittent feeling of curiosity, of course. The ability stories have to allay that feeling is what natural selection exploited to solve the design problem of getting us from the Pleistocene to the present.

It's obvious why most people have chosen the interpretative culture of the humanities, the path of embroidering on illusion, even after science hit its stride. To begin with, there was selection for the theory-of-mind ability, which carried along conscious thoughts that seem to be about the conspiracies behind people's behavior. The ability still works, up to limits that social and behavioral science has discovered. Like any by-product of a local adaptation, interpreting people's behavior in terms of motives is hard to shake, even when the brain's predictions go wrong, sometimes catastrophically wrong. We won't give up relying on interpretation until long after the ability that carries it along has ceased to be adaptive. Why? Because interpreting other people's lives by figuring out what their thoughts might be about is fun, entertaining, and sometimes even great art. That's how interpretation fools us into thinking it's doing the work instead of the neural circuits.

It's a lot harder to do science than it is to spin out stories about why people do things in terms of their possible or plausible thoughts about stuff. Experimental science and abstract mathematical theorizing are difficult—boring drudgery for most people. But both are required to produce a neuroscientific explanation of human behavior. So, even many of us who endorse scientism will continue to read and watch and listen to the histories, biographies, memories, novels, films, plays, and broadcasts that employ the illusory approach of finding meaning and purpose in human affairs. It's easier to follow and much more entertaining than science because it comes packaged as stories, and science never does. Fortunately for us, being scientistic doesn't require we become scientists.

Now we know what's wrong with stories. We know how we got saddled with a love of them. And alas, we also know why it's so difficult for science to displace stories.

WHATEVER CONSCIOUSNESS DOES NOW, IT WASN'T SELECTED FOR ITS POWER TO PLAN AHEAD

Conscious introspection is still screaming that what it says goes: thought has to be about stuff. And how can anyone deny the obvious fact that our lives are full of projects—long-term and short-term? People bake cakes following recipes, they plan their vacations and then go on them, they organize their studies to fulfill all the requirements to graduate from university, they spend years writing books, and they join together in multigenerational projects like building cathedrals or fighting a Thirty Years' War (for religion, of course). How can anyone in their right mind deny this?

Of course people build cathedrals, write books, graduate from university, go on vacations, and bake cakes. That's not in question. The question is what role conscious thought about the future plays in all this. Science tells us that introspection's picture of how all this happens and the role thought about stuff plays in it can't be right.

Why take science's word for it? We've already answered that question. Nevertheless, it's worth reminding ourselves how far introspection overreaches when it insists that no one could do anything like these things, alone or with others, unless conscious thought has most of the ideas, gives a lot of the orders, and crowns the achievement with the verbal expression of its approval.

One very obvious way to shake this conviction is to think about all the great achievements of beavers working together to build dams and lodges, wordlessly and without even training by their parents. If anyone thinks beavers do it by conscious thought and planning, consider the lowly insect. Within their highly structured, long-lasting, increasingly complex colonies, ants and wasps engage in division of labor and provide themselves and one another with the necessities of life. Some ants herd, cultivate, and feed other insects, aphids, while protecting them from predators and securing from them nourishment for themselves and their ant offspring. The farmer ants make the aphids secrete nourishment by milking them. The aphids release their honeydew when the ants stroke them with their antennae. Aphids don't survive over cold winters, but the ants store the eggs. In fact, queen ants, the ones that reproduce to form new colonies, will carry an aphid egg along with them and start a new farm in the colony they create. Some species of aphid-cultivating ants have branched out into caterpillar cultivation; they allow a species of butterfly to lay its eggs among their aphids. The resulting caterpillar feeds on aphids. But at a certain point in caterpillar development, a couple of ants will move the caterpillar to their nest, where the caterpillar will produce honeydew in the nest. Thus, the ants are saved the trouble of carrying the honeydew into the nest from the aphids outside. Eventually, butterflies emerge and lay their eggs back in the aphid farm.

The phenomena revealed in the colonies of cultivator ants cry out for the language of purpose, planning, and design. In writing the preceding paragraph, I had to guard myself from employing terms like "in order to," "for the sake of," "so that." I didn't entirely succeed. The complexity and coordination of the social insects would justify giving a role to consciously formulated thoughts in each individual ant about how to do their job if it were not ruled out by their simple neural circuitry. The resulting social institutions of herding, protecting, farming, milking, and cultivating that the colony organizes demand a teleological, goal-directed view of nature. Or, rather, they would demand it if not for the fact that they were all the result of blind variation and environmental filtration. Indeed, molecular biologists are on the verge of identifying the genes and tracing the sequence of mutations that brought about the social insects.

In the ant colony, each and all engage in different activities of greater and lesser degrees of complex organization. Their individual behaviors are coordinated, and they produce adapted outcomes that improve and increase in size and complexity over at least as many generations as in humans would be required to build a cathedral. And they do it all with somewhere on the order of 25,000 neurons total and no consciousness whatever. That's about 10 million times fewer neurons than the average human is stuck with, though genetic and anatomical data strongly suggests that what goes on in each of the ant's neurons is not much different from what goes on in each of ours.

Are the achievements of humans 10 million times more impressive than what ants can do? Is building a cathedral 10 million times more complicated than building an ant colony? The question is silly. The point is not. Common sense's assertion that conscious planning is the only way that complex human creations emerge is belied by a great deal of scientific evidence about how this happens among other animals.

Having 10 million times more neurons than an ant probably has something to do with the fact that we are conscious and self-conscious. But it's sheer bluster for common sense to assert that it knows anything much of what consciousness does, or how it does it, from introspection alone.

Science doesn't deny that most of what we do requires thinking. It has not even ruled out the possibility that the conscious brain states are required for behavior of the sort that results in complex human achievements, works of art, artifacts, buildings, social institutions, even vacations to Paris. It denies only introspection's take on what that role is. To repeat, neuroscience has yet to identify the function or functions of consciousness. As noted, it is probably too prominent in our mental lives merely to be an unavoidable by-product with nothing to contribute to survival and reproduction. Nevertheless, there is one thing consciousness can't contribute: It cannot contribute thoughts about the future or thoughts about how to arrange the future to match up with current thoughts about how we want things to be. For that reason, it cannot contribute purposes, plans, or projects. All that is an illusion foisted on us by a process that this chapter has sketched. The illusion, like others, rides piggyback on a complex ability—the theory-of-mind ability—that has been improved on by selection about as far as it can go. That ability had a payoff in the Pleistocene. It continues to pay dividends in ordinary life. The illusion that we actually have thoughts about the mind—ours and everyone else's—is carried along for the ride. Because it's so hard to surrender, it will obstruct neuroscience's opportunities to identify the ability, explain how it works, and treat its pathologies.

WE BEGAN THIS CHAPTER asking where science gets off pulling rank on common sense, telling it where it goes wrong. The answer is so compelling that its result is scientism, as defined in Chapter 1. Now we see that the real question is where common sense comes off making claims about how things really work on the basis of a very unreliable guide—conscious thought and introspective access to it.

It's hard to give up the insistent assertions of introspection that common sense endorses. Even those who are prepared to let science trump common sense when the two conflict would rather find some acceptable compromise between them. In particular, scientists and philosophers have sought a way to reconcile science to the *about*ness of thoughts and the feeling of purposefulness that fill up our lives. Among philosophers, this quest has come to be known as naturalism: the late-twentieth- and early-twenty-first-century attempt by philosophers to reconcile natural science with as many of common sense's answers to the persistent questions as possible. It's not for lack of trying that none of them have succeeded (by their own standards) in their effort to naturalize the self, the will, the purposes, projects, and plans that seem to guide people's lives, along with their moral, aesthetic, and other values. By now it is clear why naturalism has not worked out for human affairs.

As we'll see, the last nail in the coffin of naturalism is hammered in not by scientism, but by those who oppose both scientism and naturalism. In the next chapter, we explore their demonstration that science can never capture the subjective point of view of the self, the thinker and spectator, the person inside the human body. The conclusion that scientism comes to is that objections to naturalism are correct. If there were a subjective point of view that belongs to the self, then this would indeed be a fact not fixed by the physical facts. Since the physical facts do fix all the facts, there is no such point of view, no self, no person, no soul. That is the last illusion of introspection.

Chapter 10

◆

You've Got
to Stop
Taking Yourself
So Seriously

The illusion that there is someone inside that has thoughts about stuff is certainly as old as the illusion that there *are* thoughts about stuff. They almost certainly evolved together as a package deal. But if the physical facts fix all the facts, there can't be a me or you inside our bodies with a special point of view. When it fixed the facts, physics ruled out the existence of selves, souls, persons, or nonphysical minds inhabiting our bodies. It's easy to see how it ruled them out, much easier than it is to see the illusion of *about*ness that fostered them. Seeing the illusion of self helps loosen the hold of the illusion of purpose, plan, and design. If there is no one to cook up and carry out plans, purposes, and designs, then they couldn't be real, could they? As for free will, it's also hard to see its point without a self to have free will.

COULD ANY DAY BE "FREAKY FRIDAY"?

The simplest way to see why scientism makes us give up the self is by reflecting on a couple of silly movies that show how totally incompatible with science a self or person in the body really has to be. *Freaky Friday* and *Vice Versa* are movies that have been remade at least seven times between them. A teenager and her mother (or a father and his son) exchange bodies, and mayhem ensues. The audience watching the movie, including little kids, thinks it understands the story perfectly well: we have no trouble with people switching bodies because we have no trouble with people not being their bodies (or their brains for that matter). They are the very same individual people, despite the fact that each has exchanged bodies, including brains, too. If this exchange were even slightly hard for children to understand, Disney would not have filmed the story so many times.

But this scenario only works if the self, the person, the mind, that moves from one body to the other in this story is not a physical thing at all. Notice that mom and daughter don't trade anything physical at all, not the tiniest fermion or boson, when they make the body switches. So, the self has to be completely non-physical. Of course, it always has a location in space and time. One of the two selves in the switch is first somewhere vaguely behind the eyes of the mom or dad and then behind the eyes of the daughter or son, and vice versa. That's how we think of their selves. That's how we think of our own selves.

Why do we all think of the location of this "I," this self, this person as somewhere behind the eyes? A nice thought experiment (of philosopher Daniel Dennett's) shows why. Imagine that your brain is removed from your body and placed in a vat, with wireless transmitters implanted at all the ends of all the nerves leading out of the brain. Wireless receivers are implanted in your now empty skull at the nerve endings from your body. So, your brain is still able to completely control your body. Now, your body is standing in front of the vat that contains your brain. Your eyes are open and you are looking at your brain in the vat with the antennae protruding from it.

First question: Where is your point of view? Introspection answers: It remains where it was before the brain was removed from your body, somewhere behind your eyes (even though that location is in the hollow skull). You just can't force yourself to relocate your point of view into the vat. Second question: Are you in your brain being looked at from your point of view? That feels totally wrong, and it shows that introspection doesn't locate us where our brain is. It locates us—our selves, souls, minds, persons—at our POV, somewhere behind the eyes.

This self is supposed to continue to exist through all the changes in our body over the course of our lives. If all those switches envisioned in movies, literature (Kafka's *The Metamorphosis*, for example), and myth make sense, then the self can't be a material thing. It can't be a lot of fermions and bosons or anything composed of them. In fact, it can't be anything but a geometrical point (no length, no height, no depth, no parts, no mass, no charge) perpetually located somewhere in the middle of our head. That, at any rate, is what introspection tells us forcefully and persistently about the self, soul, mind, person.

Mainly because it's so hard to shake introspection, people have accepted the existence of the self distinct from the body practically forever and in every culture. The existence of the self was so certain that neither philosophy nor psychology, when it got going as a science, was challenged to explain how such a nonphysical self could control the physical body. This problem only gets serious once it begins to look like physics fixes all the facts, including the facts about the mind.

Meanwhile, there is a big payoff to leaving unchallenged introspection's confidence in a nonphysical self or person: it gets us life everlasting. If introspection is right about the self, then it's easy to show that it must be immortal and can outlive our body. This is the conclusion almost everyone has always wanted. The argument goes like this: not spatial, therefore no parts; no parts, therefore can't be taken apart, can't be divided into parts, splintered, crushed, melted away, evaporated, changed, harmed, nuked, or destroyed by any physical process. It's immortal, or at least not threatened by anything physical.

Of course, this conception of the self as a nonphysical object leaves completely unexplainable how it controls, directs, or moves the body. Having no parts to rearrange makes it impossible to explain how over time each of our selves changes in moods, character, personality, wants, and values, not to mention beliefs. Change requires some rearrangement, in parts or of parts or by parts. But there are no parts to rearrange in a geometrical point.

Most advocates of the nonphysical self have been happy enough with the immortality payoff not to obsess about the incoherence it carries with it. They are not troubled by the problem of how there could be a particular thing that has neither parts nor mass nor charge, that doesn't take up space at all, but that can change itself in the way the mind, person, or soul is supposed to change minute to minute, day by day, year by year.

Scientism tells us that all this nonspatial, nonphysical self, person, soul is just so much wishful thinking. The self whose existence introspection is so sure of is not physical. None of the alleged facts about it are fixed by physics. Ergo, the alleged facts about the self are not facts at all. They are mistakes. There is no self, soul, person. Scientism must firmly deny its existence. The self, as conveyed to us by introspection, is a fiction. It doesn't exist.

Before psychological experiments began to make us realize

how unreliable introspection is, few were prepared to challenge its insistence that there is a single enduring self that exists continuously throughout each life. Those who saw the problems of a nonphysical, nonmaterial self tried in vain to show that the self was part of the body. Almost always the favored part was the brain. No luck. To begin to see why, just think about Dennett's brain in the vat or the *Freaky Friday* movies, where no brains are exchanged while selves are. The movies don't make sense if the self is physical, because the mom's body and the daughter's body don't trade anything physical at all when they trade selves. When your brain is moved to a vat, introspection tells you that your self stays in your empty head, where its point of view is. Physical things don't behave like that.

There is no self in, around, or as part of anyone's body. There can't be. So there really isn't any enduring self that ever could wake up morning after morning worrying about why it should bother getting out of bed. The self is just another illusion, like the illusion that thought is about stuff or that we carry around plans and purposes that give meaning to what our body does. Every morning's introspectively fantasized self is a new one, remarkably similar to the one that consciousness ceased fantasizing when we fell sleep sometime the night before. Whatever purpose yesterday's self thought it contrived to set the alarm last night, today's newly fictionalized self is not identical to yesterday's. It's on its own, having to deal with the whole problem of why to bother getting out of bed all over again.

The notion of an enduring self is another part of the mistake that introspection makes when it thinks consciousness is making plans that guide behavior. Thinking about things seems to require a thinker; planning for things seems to require a planner. Humans, like other animals, have been selected for taking steps over time that preserve and protect them and that exploit their environments in ways that enhance their fitness. They even make use of their naturally selected capacities to do things that may harm their fitness or that have no effects on fitness either way, like inventing calculus or building a cathedral. These activities give the appearance of purpose and planning. Insofar as introspection rationalizes these activities as the result of the reality of planning—real thoughts about futures need a real planner, one that lives long enough to carry out the plans no matter how long it may take. So, the fiction of the enduring self is almost certainly a side effect of a highly effective way of keeping the human body out of harm's way. It is a by-product of whatever selected for bodies—human and nonhuman—to take pains now that make things better for themselves later. For a long time now, Mother Nature has been filtering for bodies to postpone consumption in the present as investment for the body's future. It looks a lot like planning. Even squirrels do it, storing nuts for the winter. Does this require each squirrel to have a single real enduring self through time? No. If not, then why take introspection's word for it when it has a track record of being wrong about things like this, when the self just looks like part of the same illusions and is supposed to have features that physics tells us nothing real can have.

For all we know, consciousness may have some function in organizing the body to do things that look like they are the results of purposes and plans. Neuroscience just doesn't know enough about the brain yet to rule that out. But it can already rule out common sense's theory of what consciousness is contributing to individual action and to human affairs.

IT'S ALL DESCARTES'S FAULT

Introspection and folk psychology are not going to allow scientism to get away with its denial that there is a self, person, or soul in the body. And they seem to hold a trump card in their hand: the I, the self, the soul that has a POV inside the skull is just the mind. Scientism can't deny that we each have a mind. In fact, it insists that we have one and that it's the brain. That's where introspection, folk psychology, and a couple of thousand of years of philosophy counterattack. First they try to undermine the notion that the mind is the brain, and then they use that to refute scientism's claim that the physical facts fix all the facts.

No one can deny the mind's existence, certainly not scientism. Now, there is an army of philosophers from René Descartes in the seventeenth century to Jean-Paul Sartre in the twentieth only too happy to prove to you that the mind can't be the brain. In fact, Descartes provided an argument for its separate existence that looks absolutely airtight. But if the mind isn't the brain, then there exists at least one nonphysical kind of thing; at least one set of facts won't, after all, be fixed by physics. These will be the facts about the mind, the self, the person, and maybe even the immortal soul. It's enough to roll back at least three chapters' worth of scientism and its answers to the persistent questions.

Descartes's argument went like this: *Cogito, ergo sum.* I think, therefore I am. Even if everything I think is completely wrong, there still needs to be an "I" having the wrong thoughts, having all those false beliefs. So, there is at least one belief that can't be wrong, the belief that I exist. How does this make trouble for the notion that the mind is the brain? Easy. The existence of my brain can be doubted. In fact, many people (especially theists) have done so. I can easily imagine what it would be like to find out I didn't have one—say, by looking at an ultrasound of my skull and discovering that it's empty. That's all Descartes needed. Look, I can doubt my brain's existence. I can't doubt my mind's existence. Therefore, there is something true about my mind that is not true about my brain: My mind has the property that its existence can't (logically can't) be doubted by me. My brain lacks that feature. So, my brain can't be my mind!

Think Descartes has pulled a fast one here? You are not alone. Scientism may be excused from not taking this line of thought too seriously. But it gets more serious. I also can't doubt that I am having experiences. Introspection may be all wrong about whether my experiences tell me anything about reality, about the physical chunks of matter outside my mind that cause my experiences. But I can't deny that there are experiences "in my mind." Scientism admits their existence when it insists that these experiences should not be taken too seriously as a guide to how the mind works. So a serious argument that experience can't be physical would make things very sticky for scientism.

Since scientism admits that experiences exist, they will have to be physical for scientism to be true. If the facts about experience can't be fixed by physics, scientism will be false. More specifically, if the facts about my experiences can't be fixed, explained, accounted for by neuroscience, then scientism will be false.

Ever since Descartes, clever people have been trying to show one way or another that neuroscience can't explain obvious facts about experience. They have been devising problems, conundrums, dilemmas, and paradoxes to disprove scientism's assertion that the mind is just the brain. Most are just variations on Descartes's ploy. Those skeptical of science and credulous about religion have been grasping at these straws for centuries.

Does scientism actually have to take Descartes's argument and others like it seriously? Does it actually have to diagnose each of their mistakes, or any of them? No. Even before you hear them, science provides a compelling reason that they must all be wrong. One has only to weigh the evidence for scientism—500 years of scientific progress—and the evidence against it—including those cute conundrums. It's clear which side has the weightier evidence.

Scientism isn't required to figure out what is wrong with these proofs that experience can't be physical, so minds can't be brains. That's the job of science—neuroscience in particular. Scientism can ignore the conundrums, dilemmas, and paradoxes that the arguments generate. Science cannot. These problems are signposts in the research program of the science of the brain. Unraveling them will be some of its marks of progress. Meanwhile, scientism can already be confident that they will be unraveled.

Nevertheless, there are a few reasons to sketch the most entertaining of these arguments, even though scientism already knows they have to be wrong. First, they are wonderful, entertaining, thought-provoking riddles. Second, it's important for scientism to see how these arguments cheat. Third, the arguments are among the last serious challenges to scientism. Science has managed to dispose of all the other arguments that have been advanced to show its limits, ever since the fifth century BC.

It was then that an Athenian named Zeno provided a knockdown argument that motion through space was impossible. The argument seemed to show that it was logically contradictory for things to move even the smallest amount through space. For something to move an inch, it will have to cover ½ inch. To do that, it will have to go ¼ inch, and so on, through an infinite series of smaller and smaller distances. Since an infinite series of events can't ever be finished, the thing's motion can't even get started. Everyone knows that things do move. There must be a paradox, a problem here that physics has to solve. It took science about 2,000 years to figure out what was the matter with the "paradoxes" of motion that Zeno devised. It required Newton's invention of calculus and 100 years of further development in mathematics to solve Zeno's paradox. Zeno may have been a smart-ass, but he did physics a big favor. Unraveling the paradox was important for the advancement of math and physics. There is a lesson here for the conundrums facing neuroscience.

It will probably take less than 2,000 years for science to show what type of a neurological phenomenon consciousness is and thus to unravel the arguments against the mind's being the brain. At any rate, let's hope so. But it won't be easy, because the arguments against the mind's being the brain cheat. They stack the deck against neuroscience so that it cannot succeed in meeting their challenge. The arguments demand that neuroscience take conscious introspection seriously. But they subtly deny it the use of any tools to do so. Naturally, if science cannot apply any of its methods to understand introspection, scientism won't be able to show what is wrong with the arguments.

Most of these arguments were cooked up by philosophers. The first one that we will explore starts with the fact that each person's introspective experience is subjective and qualitative. It gives an example of subjectivity that everyone can grasp, then tries to show that the subjectivity of experience everyone can grasp can't be described by any amount of correct neuroscience. If experience can't be described by neuroscience, then experiencing is something neurons can't do, at least not by themselves. Whatever it is that does have the experiences, it just can't be the brain. Something or someone has them, and it must be the self with its subjective point of view. So, the mind, where the experiences occur, can't be the brain at all.

The argument gets its neatest force from an example dreamed up by a contemporary philosopher, Thomas Nagel. Ask yourself, "What is it like to be a bat?" Remember, bats detect their surroundings by echolocation. Nagel could have used a dog or a whale or any animal. But because bats echolocate instead of using their eyes, asking what it would be like to be a bat brings Nagel's idea home with a bang. Suppose we say, "Well, it's like being

Jonesy, the sonar guy on the U.S. submarine in *The Hunt for Red October*, head down, looking for blips on the sonar screen and listening for pings." Wrong. That's what it would be like to be a human inside the head of a bat, using sonar screens to convert the acoustical data the bat receives into human visual experiences. That's not the way the bat does it. Other suggestions meet with the same objection. We can't tell what it is like to be a bat. We know only what it's like to be us, we know only the nature of our subjective experiences. Other organisms have their own kinds of subjective experiences, and even the most extensive neurological study we could make of them and of their brains won't capture what it's like to have those experiences. Neuroscience can only show what goes on in the bat's brain when it's having its echolocating experiences. It cannot tell us what having those experiences is like.

Once Nagel has you convinced that no amount of neuroscience can tell you what it's like to be a bat, it's a small step to the conclusion that no amount of neuroscience can tell me what it's like to be you—or tell you what it's like to be me. Can neuroscience tell you what my experience of red is like? No. The only thing neuroscience can tell you about my experience of red is how the neurons are arranged and how they fire when I look at a stop sign. It can tell you a lot, and someday it will tell you everything about the causes and effects of my experience. What it can't tell you anything about is what my experience of red *is like*.

The closest anyone can get to telling what my experience of red is like is to look at the same stop sign. If you do, you will conclude, "His experience of red must be like the experience I am now having." Neuroscience can't improve on this method. It can't tell you what it's like to have someone's experience, your own or someone else's. A Martian reading the complete textbook of finished human neuroscience wouldn't be clued in to what it's like to experience red or indeed what it's like to be one of us. Something about reality—that there is a fact about *what it's like* to have experiences like ours—will be missing forever from science. This fact about reality will not be one fixed by physics. Scientism refuted.

Nagel drew a more modest conclusion from the bat problem. He didn't deny that the mind is the brain. He just concluded that we don't have the slightest idea of how it could be the brain. Other philosophers have gone much further than Nagel. The German philosopher (and sometime Nazi) Martin Heidegger built a whole metaphysics out of the conviction that physics and the rest of science can't ever explain the subjectivity of experience. Nagel's example gets at what Heidegger thought was missing from science. Heidegger went further, however. He argued that subjectivity is the most important fact about us, that science can't explain it, and that we therefore have to reject science as the correct description of reality. We need to build our picture of reality up from the nature of subjective experience. Heidegger is scientism turned upside down.

So, should scientism worry? Certainly not about Heidegger's version. Almost everything he wrote is just laughably wrong when it's intelligible at all. In fact, the blindsight results are enough to give us pause not just about Heidegger, but about the magnitude of the problem that subjective experience presents to scientism. It should also help us see the trick in the argument that science will never be able to explain subjective experience.

Blindsight experiments show that knowing what it's like to see red, what it's like to have the subjective experience of red, may be unnecessary for understanding vision. In these experiments, blind subjects and even sighted ones whose visual cortex is disturbed can tell what color something is even when they are not conscious of its color. The experiments show that you can do what vision is supposed to do without subjective experiences. That means we can do a lot of the neuroscience of perception without ever dealing with subjective experience. Studying how the neural circuits of the visual cortex process inputs when we have the sensation of red and when we don't should also enable us to identify the neural circuits that constitute *what it's like* to have the sensation. More important, even if our lab equipment can't do that job, it may be able to come up with a complete explanation of all human behavior while ignoring subjective experience. Pretty good.

The possibility of such an explanation shows why the argument from *what it's like* to have a red experience cheats science of any chance to explain what it's like. The argument demands that neuroscience tell us what it's like to experience red or to experience the smell of garlic or to experience the feeling of being tickled. But it insists that to answer this question, it won't help a bit to know all the effects, in the brain or the rest of the body, of experiencing red or garlic or the sensation of being tickled. Telling us everything about what else happens just because you have these experiences won't help us understand the experiences themselves. The same goes for telling us what causes the experiences. Suppose we know everything about what events, processes, or changes in the body or the brain bring about these experiences. That won't help us know what they are like either. Furthermore, figuring out what experiences are composed of, what they are made of, what their parts, components, constituents are, doesn't help answer the question of what it's like to have them either.

But then what will enable anyone to answer the question of what having subjective experience is like? Nothing. We have already ruled out all the possibilities for answering this question. The demand is that science explain what it's like to experience red, but not tell us anything about its causes and effects or what it is made up of in the brain or anywhere else. This, in effect, ties the hands of science. The method that science uses to tell us about things—fermions, gravity, genes, neural circuits—is to identify their causes, their effects, and their composition—how they work. The challenge to neuroscience of explaining what it's like to be a bat turns out to be the demand that it solve that mystery with its hands tied behind its back. It's no surprise that science can't solve a problem posed this way. After all, science isn't magic (of course, magic isn't magic either).

So, why suppose there is a problem lurking in Nagel's question about what it's like to be a bat? Pretty clearly, the problem is the result of taking introspection seriously. It's the feeling introspection gives us that even after everything about the brain is known, there will still be something left unexplained. Why? Because introspection can't conceive how causes, effects, and composition explain what experience is like. But there is no reason to allow introspection to guide us.

Nevertheless, Nagel's argument is really cool. It's the sort of puzzle any philosopher would give his soul to have invented, if he had a soul. There is another thought experiment that makes the same point as Nagel's. But it shows much more clearly how these arguments cheat. This one goes back a long way, to the eighteenth-century physicist, mathematician, and philosopher Gottfried Leibniz. His theological beliefs made him particularly eager to find arguments against scientism just when it was beginning to pick up speed with Newton's work.

In his most famous work, *The Monadology*, Leibniz tried to prove that "perception can't be explained by mechanical principles, that is by shapes and motions, and thus that nothing that depends on perception can be explained in that way either." Leibniz knew nothing of neuroscience, still less of the molecular biology of the synapse. But his argument was meant to work no matter what post-1700 science might tell us about physical processes on any scale. He says, "Imagine there were a machine whose *structure* produced thought, feeling, and perception." Of course, we don't have to imagine this. The brain is such a machine. It was made by Mother Nature through natural selection, a process no different in kind from the trial-and-error tinkering of a slow and dim-witted inventor with endless time and lots of resources. Here Leibniz introduces an idea that science-fiction writers have been employing off and on since he invented it: "We can conceive of the brain's being enlarged while maintaining the same relative proportions among its parts, so that we could walk into it as we can walk into a mill." Or alternatively, as Isaac Asimov supposed in *Fantastic Voyage*, we can shrink ourselves to a size that would enable us to walk around the fantastically complicated machine that is a human brain.

Leibniz wrote: "Suppose we do walk into it; all we would find there are cogs and levers and so on pushing one another, and never anything to account for a perception." Or, updating a bit, all we would ever find are sodium and potassium molecules moving one way or the other, complex neurotransmitter molecules changing molecular shape as other molecules come into contact with them. We would never find anything that introspection identifies as an experience, a sensation, a feeling, even a thought about stuff. We would never find anything that reveals what it's like to have a sensation of yellow, an experience of pain, a smell or sound, or any other experience.

Leibniz's thought experiment leads straight to Nagel's conclusion—that it's inconceivable that matter in motion, regardless of how complicated, could turn out to be experiences with qualitative feels to them, like colors, sounds, pains, smells, touches. But Leibniz took matters one step further. He concluded, "Perception must be sought in simple substances, not in composite things like machines." A simple substance is one with no pieces, no moving parts, no components. It can't be broken down into whatever might turn out to be the basic building blocks of physical reality, what we now think to be fermions and bosons. And if the mind is what has perceptions, then it has to be one of these simple non-physical substances. Scientism refuted, QED.

How should scientism respond to such an argument? Well, we know that there are no spiritual substances—simple or complex. One or more of the premises of Leibniz's argument must be wrong. And we know we can't rely on introspection to check on any of the premises of his argument. Nor can we give weight to introspection's feeling that there will still be something left to explain—what it's like to have experiences—once we understand completely how the brain works. So, when it comes to the persistent question of what the mind is, scientism can disregard objections that are based on Leibniz's thought experiment or Nagel's. It can disregard the argument that subjectivity is not physical, so there must be a nonphysical mind, person, self, soul that has the subjective experience. It can disregard denials that the mind is the brain.

Is this intellectually responsible? Yes. Our evidence for the truth of physics as the complete theory of reality is much stronger than our evidence for the truth of the conclusion of any thought experiment that relies on introspection. Plus, introspection is wrong about so much, it can't carry any weight against science. Scientism is safe to conclude that there are flaws in Nagel's argument and Leibniz's. We don't know where the slips occur. But we know that their conclusions are false.

To repeat, it would be intellectually irresponsible for neuroscience to disregard these arguments. They present in a wonderfully effective way some of the great scientific challenges that face neuroscience. It's a challenge scientistic non-neuroscientists are confident neuroscience will eventually resolve. The challenges of neuroscience are not problems for scientism.

Free Will? Are You Kidding?

Even before it gets around to denying that there is a self, a soul, or a person to have free will, science has already disposed of the possibility that it might have any. The denial that there is any self, soul, or person to have the free will is just icing on the cake.

Science's argument against the possibility of free will is disarmingly direct, and it doesn't even need Libet's discovery that feelings of willing come too late in the process to play any role in our actions.

The mind is the brain, and the brain is a physical system, fantastically complex, but still operating according to all the laws of physics—quantum or otherwise. Every state of my brain is fixed by physical facts. In fact, it is a physical state. Previous states of my brain and the physical input from the world together brought about its current state. They were themselves the result of even earlier brain states and inputs from outside the brain. All these states were determined by the operation of the laws of physics and chemistry. These laws operated on previous states of my brain and on states of the world going back to before my brain was formed in embryogenesis. They go back through a chain of prior events not just to before anyone with a mind existed, but back to a time after life began on this planet.

When I make choices—trivial or momentous—it's just another event in my brain locked into this network of processes going back to the beginning of the universe, long before I had the slightest "choice." Nothing was up to me. Everything—including my choice and my feeling that I can choose freely—was fixed by earlier states of the universe plus the laws of physics. End of story.

No free will, just the feeling, the illusion in introspection, that my actions are decided by my conscious will.

Wait, isn't the world really indeterministic at the basement level? Recall from Chapter 2 that there are plenty of events occurring every day at the subatomic level, among the fermions and bosons, that are random, the result of shear probabilities and nothing else. Such events have been occurring right back to the big bang and before it. This is quantum indeterminism. Could subatomic indeterminism obtaining among the fermions and bosons in my brain somehow free my choices from determinism? This is a wishful thought that has occurred to some people. It can't. Sensing, feeling, and thinking are all processes that take place through the interaction of many large macromolecules in the neurons. These molecules are all much too big and there are too many of them milling around for the occasional quantum irregularity to have an effect even on a single neuron, let alone on lots of them or any other part of the brain.

Suppose, nevertheless, that such an event did occur. What if somewhere in my brain, there is a spontaneous quantum event, completely undetermined by the state of the rest of the universe. What if it starts the chain of events that sooner or later produces my choice, complete with the feeling of free will. Could that undetermined quantum event give me even a little free will? Hardly. That sort of start to the process of choice means not just that my choices are not up to me, but that they are not up to anybody or anything in the universe. I can't bring about such spontaneous quantum events. Neither can anyone else. Such a random event would control me—switching on a process that leads to my actions the way Dr. Frankenstein turns on his monster with a jolt of electricity. Except in this story there is no Dr. Frankenstein. Quantum mechanics couldn't give us free will even if it produced real indeterminism at the levels of organization that mattered to my brain.

In fact, very few people understand quantum physics and the molecular biology of the brain well enough even to pretend to argue from quantum mechanics to free will or to anything else about the mind. All the real resistance to science's denial of free will comes from introspection, from "looking into ourselves." Introspectively, it just feels like you choose; it feels like it's completely up to you whether you raise your hand or stick out your tongue. That feeling is so compelling that for most people it tips the scales against determinism. They just know "from inside" that their will is free. We'll never shake the feeling, but we can recognize and avoid the mistakes it leads to, as well as the mistakes that lead to it. Besides taking conscious experience seriously, the notion of free will helps itself to a self to do the willing. Now that we see that the self is an illusion, it should be easier to give up the notion that the self is free.

There is a more fundamental idea of free will than the conscious feeling that it's up to me which way I will decide. It's the idea that we humans are autonomous agents who act on plans and projects that we give to ourselves, as opposed to having forced upon us by others. This notion of free will or freedom as autonomy—self-rule—has a long pedigree in European philosophy that runs back through Kant, the philosopher who could not see Darwin coming. It's not going to take scientism any longer to dispose of this theory than the others. Since the brain can't have thoughts about stuff, it cannot make, have, or act on plans, projects, or purposes that it gives itself. Nor, for that matter, can it act on plans that anyone else favors it with. There are no plans. That's just more of the illusion Mother Nature exploited for our survival.

THE LAST FOUR CHAPTERS have given us a lot to think about. Perhaps too much to swallow? Conscious introspection is wrong about the very things it is supposed to know best. Our brain navigates us through life very nicely, thank you, without ever thinking about anything at all. The meanings we think are carried by our thoughts, our words, and our actions are just sand castles we build in the air. The same goes for the plans, designs, hopes, fears, and expectations by which we delude ourselves into thinking we organize our lives. The last step, denying the self and free will, that's not even hard compared to the first three things scientism makes us take on board.

How could we have gotten things so wrong? Besides, if all this is true, why haven't we heard about it from the neuroscientists? A lot of people will argue that since these conclusions are unthinkable by us, they have to be wrong. And there are others—mainly philosophers—who have worked hard for decades trying to show that science has a way of accommodating all the things the last four chapters have jettisoned.

Scientism needs to respond to these objections and questions, and the doubts they raise. First, think back to the arguments of the first six chapters of this book. Everything in the last four chapters was already ordained by the fact that physics fixes all the facts and excludes purpose or design from our world. If you are going to allow that real purposes and designs can somehow pop up out of nowhere in a world where physics had hitherto fixed all the facts, you might as well have put God into the universe at the outset.

In the second half of the twentieth century, three generations of the smartest philosophers who ever took science seriously tried to reconcile it with the idea that we have thoughts about stuff. Solving the problem was crucial to dealing with the deepest problems about logic, about language, even about ethics and values. It was a central part of the philosophical program of naturalism. Anyone who had succeeded would have secured the glory of Kant. No one came close, as even their most sympathetic colleagues were quick to tell them. When scientism says that the brain can't have thoughts about stuff, it stands on the shoulders of these philosophical giants who tried to show otherwise and failed.

Second, these illusions about the mind were for a long time absolutely crucial to our species' survival. Mother Nature had every incentive to really hardwire them into our brain, or come as close to it as possible. What would really be surprising is if the illusions were easy to dispel.

But dispelling the illusions about the mind is crucial to scientism and to science and technology. At the end of Chapter 4, we noted that the illusion of purpose was the second deepest illusion scientism needs to dispel. The deepest illusion is that thought is about stuff. We have seen that this latter illusion brings the illusion of biological design along with it, when natural selection overshot and made us conspiracy theorists about everything.

Dispelling the illusion of purpose in nature has been crucial to all of the scientific and technological advances of the biological sciences. In fact, it is what made them sciences. The same is true for neuroscience and its future. You can't work with an illusion. If you want to make real progress, you have to give it up, no matter how deeply you are taken in by it.

Neuroscientists are like other scientists. They specialize narrowly. They are not given to speculation outside their subdisciplines. Still less do they want to attract hostile attention or lose grant funding by publically undermining cherished illusions. They are not going to take sides on scientism for love or money.

Success in neuroscience doesn't require them to do so. Like every other science, neuroscience begins with data, not with deductions from scientism's axiom that physics fixes all the facts. But reputations are made and progress is achieved in neuroscience, like the other biological sciences, by theories that show how physical—especially electrochemical—facts fix neural facts and create the illusions that introspection reports.

We have dealt with a lot of the unavoidable questions by now. The answers science gives are all short, unambiguous, and deeply contrary to so much that mystery mongering, everyday life, and deep philosophy suggest. You might think that we have now finished scientism's self-appointed task. But there remains one more set of questions that often gives people sleepless nights. These are the questions about the meaning of our lives, our human past and future—the questions of history.

Chapter II

◄●►

HISTORY DEBUNKED

SOME PEOPLE ARE NOT JUST ABSORBED BY THE PER-
sistent questions about their own nature and fate. They are
also concerned with everybody's past and future. This does not
make them busybodies; it makes some of them history buffs
and in some cases historians. There are also a lot of other people
with the same interests—understanding the human past and
future—who look to economics, sociology, social psychology,
anthropology, the scientific study of politics, or some combination of all of these sciences, to answer our persistent questions
about humanity.

Most of the persistent questions they seek to answer are variations on the following ones. Scientism's answer to each of them is
provided:

What is the meaning of history? Does it have a point? No
meaning, no purpose, no point.

Does the past have lessons for the future? Fewer and fewer, if
  it ever had any to begin with.
Where is civilization headed? Nowhere in particular; there is
  no long-term or even medium-term trajectory to its path.
Is there progress, improvement, enlightenment, in history?
  Not much, and what there is can only be local and
  temporary.
Can we or anyone control the direction of human history?
  Not a chance.

Perhaps you're thinking that scientism should be more upbeat
about these matters. After all, science is acquiring more and more
knowledge about the past and present, along with a scientific grasp
on human affairs. There has been undeniable scientific progress in
the understanding of nature (including human nature).

We should be able to parlay all that science into a real understanding of our future. If it turns out that old-fashioned history
can't answer these persistent questions, perhaps newfangled social
science can. The most scientistic, the most prolific, and the most
influential of all science and science-fiction writers, Isaac Asimov,
must have thought that eventually science would get around to
doing for human history and human affairs what it had done
to make the rest of nature subject to prediction and control. At
any rate, he wrote a lot of science fiction (mainly the *Foundation*
series) that assumed science would do so.

Alas, scientism realizes that Asimov's aspirations were overly
optimistic. Scientism recognizes that history is blind, and the
empirical sciences of human behavior are myopic at best. The
blindness of history and the nearsightedness of social science
both stem from the same factors that shape scientism's answers
to the other persistent questions about reality, biology, morality,
and the mind.

By fixing all the facts, physics excludes purpose from physical reality. Since physical reality is the only kind of reality there is, it has also excluded purpose from the biological domain. Darwin made good physics' claim to banish purpose from nature. The process he discovered underlies the appearance of purpose wherever it emerges, even in the human mind.

Not only are the individual acts of human beings unguided by purpose; so are their thoughts. Combine the purposeless but well-adapted thoughts and behavior of a lot of people over a long time, and the result is history. Could history have purpose, meaning, or a direction even when people lack them? Sure, it could, if there were any purposes. But physics has already ruled them out. Science excludes God's designs, or some purpose operating in the universe to navigate events into some safe harbor hidden in the future. There is no alternative to blind variation and environmental filtration in human history, so there is no source for meaning or purpose in our history.

As we shall see, science can do more than just deduce the purposelessness of the past and future from physics. It can provide detailed diagnosis. But it is important to remember why scientism can be so confident about science's answers to the persistent questions about history.

Philosophers of history—Christian ones, Hegelian ones, Marxian ones—have all claimed to make sense out of history by disclosing its end point: judgment day for the first, the triumph of reason for the second, the withering away of the state for the third. Physics tells us those hopes are all in vain. Most historians are less ambitious. Many seek only to explain events or epochs by making sense of the actions of people—either groups of them or individuals like Napoleon or Martin Luther. At its best, what they produce often has as much entertainment value as a good historical novel. But it is not much more likely to produce useful information than what we got from the teleological philosophers of history.

To see why, consider biography—history one life at a time. Once it's realized how crude our best guesses are about the meaning of anything that individual people do, the problem of biography becomes manifest. We'll never know the meaning of any individual human action—the particular motives expressed in thoughts about ends and about the means that led to the action. That's not because we can't get inside people's heads to mind-read their thoughts. The reason is much more profound. It's because the human brain is not organized into thoughts about anything at all. Our best guesses are not even approximations. They are at best rough indicators. This makes biography a blunt explanatory instrument at best and mostly just storytelling.

Add together enough biographies to produce a history, and the result may be an increasingly accurate description of what happened: who did what to whom. But as you pile on the biographies, the explanation of what happened—the historical event—becomes much blunter by several orders of magnitude. The more people involved in the event, the more inaccurate the explanation is bound to be. This wouldn't much matter if history were judged on the same standards as historical fiction—as stories. But it's supposed to tell us why things really happened the way they did. For all we know, this is something that historical explanation never provides. The reason starts with its reliance on folk psychology. But the problems facing history don't end there.

Those Who Learn the Lessons of History Are in Danger of Following Them

Historians are fond of quoting the American philosopher George Santayana, who admonished us thus: "Those who do not learn the lessons of history are suffered to repeat them." In a similar vein, Winston Churchill justified his own obsession with history: "The farther back you can look, the farther forward you can see." There was also Marx's joke: "History repeats itself, first as tragedy, then as farce."

The track record of historians has not vindicated these claims. So far, at any rate, the study of the past hasn't told us much about the future. Historians, generals, and especially politicians have much more frequently drawn the wrong lessons from history than the right one (that there are no lessons).

Nevertheless, many historians insist that their work be judged on the foresight it is supposed to confer. This goes double for the historians who wish to shape a country's diplomacy or its economic and social policies. Henry Kissinger became a power broker because he convinced people that knowing what happened at the Congress of Vienna in 1815 was going to help Nixon deal with the Soviet Union's leadership.

Scientism shares with these historians the insistence that to provide knowledge, their discipline has to show improvement in predictive success. The alternative is to treat the discipline of history as a source, not of knowledge, but of entertainment. As a source of enjoyable stories or polemics written to move readers to action, to tears, or to nostalgia, history is unbeatable. But few historians are prepared to treat their discipline as merely literary art. Yet that is inevitable, unless history can be put to successful predictive use.

Unfortunately for historians, history—the actual events of

the human past—shows no pattern, cycle, or regularity that can provide predictive knowledge about the human future. Scientism has strong proof that it can't. That is why, when it comes to providing the foresight required to certify something as knowledge, history is bunk. The past is not just bereft of meaning. The only patterns it may have had in the past cannot be exploited to provide foreknowledge.

Scientism's reason for pessimism about history as useful knowledge, like so much else in its understanding of human affairs, starts with an insight from Darwinian evolutionary biology. Evolution results when generation after generation of blind variations on adaptive themes are passively filtered by the environment. Passive filtering permits all those variants that are minimally good enough to hang around to make more copies of themselves. The result is cumulative *local* adaptation. Adaptation is local because it's relative to the environment. What is adaptive in one environment—say, white fur in the snowy Arctic—becomes maladaptive in a new one. That's what will happen when global warming moves the Arctic snow line north of the polar bear's habitat. Geological and climatological environments change slowly and mostly remain constant for epochs. This allows for the gradual accumulation of small changes eventually to produce adaptations of "extreme perfection" (Darwin's words). As species proliferate in the evolutionary history of Earth, their members begin to have effects on one another and on members of other species. Animals and plants become part of one another's environments, their ecosystems. We are familiar with many cases of this phenomenon: predators and their prey, symbiosis, mutualism, mimicry, parasitism. Most of these relationships arise between animals and plants of two different species. But sometimes they occur between animals and even plants in the same species.

When this happens, among animals especially, the evolution

248 • The Atheist's Guide to Reality

of adaptations can speed up wildly. Each animal's environment includes other animals. So its environment changes as fast as variations arise in the traits of the other animals. The polar bear coat remains thick for scores of millions of years because the Arctic remains cold all that time. Meanwhile, the seal's ability to detect polar bears by smell, instead of sight, gets better and better. That strengthens selection for polar bears with a tendency to hunt seals from downwind. That in turn puts pressure on seals to switch to some other predator detection system, and so on, until one species or the other (or both) go extinct. For obvious reasons, biologists call these patterns "arms races," invoking the image of how each move in the technology of warfare has evoked a countermove, all the way from the stirrup and the lance to the SAM missile and the stealth bomber. Arms races occur at many different levels of the biological domain all the way down to the DNA. We have come across them before in this book. There are whole research programs devoted to the evolutionary arms races between copies of selfish genes that live together on the same chromosomes for millions of years and struggle constantly to exploit one another.

As arms races speed up, they increasingly limit the biologist's ability to predict the future course of evolution, for biologists cannot tell how individual groups or species temporarily locked in competition or cooperation with each other will break out of the pattern. This is because variation is constant and blind. The "space of alternative variations" through which mutation and gene shuffling can "search" for new and improved adaptations is huge. It cannot be charted by any biologist. And even if biologists could do so, exactly which variations actually emerge is an equally insolvable problem. Whenever members of groups find themselves competing (or for that matter temporarily cooperating against some third gene), small variations in the traits of each will continually emerge. The variations are random and can't be foreseen by anyone. Eventually, one variation or other will provide one of the animals with an advantage over a competitor. Or it will provide an opportunity to take advantage of another animal's temporary cooperation. In biology, nothing is forever; no matter how long a pattern or a regularity holds, it will eventually be overthrown, and overthrown in a way that biologists can't predict. This is the problem faced in agricultural and medical technology. Eventually, every breakthrough in antibiotic or pesticide research is overtaken by an unforeseen new random variant in its target population.

Natural selection is the process Darwin discovered operating in natural history. Human history is just the recent natural history of *Homo sapiens*. So the study of human history can't be any more predicatively useful than the study of natural history. In fact, it has to be much less useful. Soon after the Darwinian process passed through 13.6998 billion years of evolution and arrived at us, the arms races became fast, furious, and pervasive. Nothing in human culture remains constant long enough to be relied on to forecast the future.

Once humans appeared on the scene and began competing, first with the megafauna, then with *Homo erectus* and the Neanderthals, and finally with one another, the arms races ceased to be conducted only between genetically inherited traits. Now they began also to be fought between variant behaviors, tools, strategies, moves, and countermoves that were and continue to be culturally transmitted and selected.

The design space of biological variation is huge. It's all the genetically possible ways in which traits can change. The design space of human cultural variation is many, many, many orders of magnitude larger. It's all the behaviorally possible ways in which human traits can change. And the environments—the cultures that filter the behavioral variants—are themselves changing continually as well. The combination of unaccountable variation filtered by continually changing environments makes the future of human evolutionary trajectories totally unpredictable, no matter how much we know about their past trajectories. That's why history is bunk.

Human history is a thoroughly Darwinian process. Like all other Darwinian processes, it can't repeat itself, not even as farce. It is always and unpredictably producing novelty, which historical study can't anticipate. The lesson of history—both natural and human—is that there are no lessons to extract from it.

SCIENTISM HAS TO BE DARWINIAN ABOUT HUMAN AFFAIRS

If human affairs really are Darwinian, then like biological processes, they will have no meaning, and they will be driven by arms races. Knowing human history will be useless for anything but telling diverting stories. But are we really committed to a Darwinian view of human history? Yes. In fact, science and scientism commit us to a Darwinian view of all of human culture. So we'd better be able to convince ourselves that such a view is correct.

Showing that human affairs are thoroughly Darwinian is easier than it looks, however. Just for starters, remember the moral of Chapter 6. Back in the Pleistocene, Darwinian processes shaped us to be mostly nice. Ten thousand years of culture is too short a time to beat it out of us. Moreover, Darwinism doesn't require treating culture as "red in tooth and claw." It's not always a Darwinian competition in which the weak go to the wall and devil take the hindmost. There is also no need to view everything human as genetically hardwired. Darwinian processes can work perfectly well without being hardwired. Whenever and wherever, in nature or culture, we find the appearance of purpose Darwin assures us that the reality has to be blind variation and natural selection. Now, human affairs show the appearance of purpose all over the place. Since most aspects of human affairs look like they have been designed and have functions, they have to be Darwinian adaptations.

There is a simple argument for this conclusion, whose premises scientism is already committed to. It shows that Darwinian processes rule culture as thoroughly as they do biology:

First, almost all significant features of human affairs—historical actions, events, processes, norms, organizations, institutions—have functions and therefore are adaptations.

Second, the only source of functions or adaptations in nature—including human affairs—is the Darwinian process of blind variation and environmental filtration.

Science and scientism are committed to the second premise. As we'll see, most historians and social scientists are committed to the first premise, no matter how dubious it sounds at first blush.

How could almost everything in human affairs be an adaptation? That sounds like an idea worthy of Pollyanna or Voltaire's Dr. Pangloss, who thought everything was for the best in this best of all possible worlds. Even in biology, not everything turns out to be an adaptation. Much of evolution is a matter of drift—the play of chance on small and sometimes even large populations. Why do African elephants have large ears when Indian elephants have small ones? Why do African rhinoceroses have two horns when Indian rhinos have only one? The answer may be that it's just a matter of chance—drift. At some point or other in the evolution of elephants and rhinos, separate herds almost certainly went through some extinction-threatening bottlenecks. If all that was left of a previous mixed herd of each were small-eared male elephants and double-horned rhinos and they were permanently cut off from the other sort of elephant and rhino by, say, the rising Red Sea, that would produce the difference between elephants and rhinos in Africa and India today—by drift alone and without any adaptation. Recall from Chapter 4 that there was a similar situation for the original populations of *Homo sapiens*.

Almost nothing of real interest in human affairs is the result of random drift alone. Even more than in biology, the significant features of social life are largely or even wholly adaptations for someone or some group or some human practice. Human social life consists largely of adaptations constructed by individuals and groups to cope with their environments. These environments consist mostly of the behavior of other individuals and groups—the effects of their adaptations. We are all parts of many environments constantly filtering adaptation variations blindly produced by each of us.

Some adaptations are ones that people think they designed—institutions like the U.S. Constitution or artifacts like the Eiffel Tower. Of course, as Chapter 9 revealed, people are wrong about whether anything is consciously designed. The process in the brains of innovators, inventors, members of groups that negotiate and bargain to create enduring organizations, and people who build cathedrals is nothing like what they think. It's almost always just another case of blind variation and environmental filtering—where the variations are neural and the filtering is also neural. Alas, we don't yet know enough about how thinking works to say more. We do know enough about Thomas Edison and Alexander Graham Bell to see plainly that most inventing really is trial and error—blind variation and filtering out failures till the result is good enough. But it's even blinder and less the result of intentional design than we realize.

Along with the human institutions people mistakenly think were the result of intentional design, important adaptations emerged from history without anyone intending, designing, or even recognizing them. This is especially true of long-standing, pervasive, and significant ones. Think of the British constitution, feudalism, or the Roman Catholic Church, three adaptations that were around for a long time without anyone supposing that they were designed.

Besides human adaptations, there are certain features of human life that are best thought of as symbionts or parasites, living on human life and changing it for the better or for the worse, but always adapting to ensure their own survival. For example, it's difficult to think of tobacco smoking or heroin addiction as adaptations, because they are so harmful to humans. But they are practices that have persisted and spread throughout human history. They persisted and spread until their environments changed and their effects started to be selected against. Tobacco smoking and heroin addiction are not human adaptations; they are practices with adaptations of their own that enable them to exploit humans. They spread and persist for long periods while making people worse off and lowering their fitness. But it's still a Darwinian process that carries them along.

Chinese foot binding is a clear example of how it works. Foot binding persisted for about 1,000 years in China. How it got started is unclear. But it caught on because women with bound feet were more attractive as wives. Bound feet were a signal of wealth, since only rich families could afford the luxury of preventing daughters from working. Girls with bound feet were also easier to keep track of and so likelier to be virgins. Thus, when the practice first arose, foot-bound girls had more suitors. Their fathers could get away with paying smaller dowries and would have more grandchildren. Pretty soon, every family that could afford it was binding their daughters' feet to ensure they'd get married. In fact, everyone *had* to bind their daughters' feet just to compete in the marriage market. The result? When every girl's feet were bound, foot binding no longer provided an advantage to anyone in the marriage market. Moreover, all girls were worse off, less fit than their unbound ancestors because they couldn't walk and suffered other health effects.

Foot binding started out as a new move in an arms race, a transitory adaptation for some girls and for some families. By the time it became really widespread and fixed, it was actually a physical maladaptation, reducing every foot-bound girl's fitness. Once everyone was doing it, no one could get off the foot-binding merry-go-round. Not binding one's daughters' feet condemned them to spinsterhood. Here we have a tradition, a norm—"Bind daughters' feet!" As a result of its widespread adoption, it ceased to be an adaptation for the people whose behavior it governed. Why did it persist despite its maladaptive effects on foot-bound girls? For whom or for what were its features adaptations? For itself, for the practice, for the norm, for the institution of foot binding. More exactly, foot binding had features that gave its early adopters advantages over others. Thus, it took hold. It's early adoption made it more attractive (indeed exigent) for others. Thus, it spread. It's wide adoption made it impossible for the adopters to stop. Thus, it persisted. Like any parasite, the practice persisted because its own features were adapted to exploit the "weaknesses" of humans and their institutions—marriage, the desire for virgin brides and smaller dowries, the desire to control women before and after marriage. Environments change: foot binding went extinct in the twentieth century. The same thing is happening to tobacco smoking now.

Once we widen our focus, the claim that almost everything significant in human affairs and its history has or had a function, is or was an adaptation, becomes much more obvious.

The second premise treads familiar ground: only Darwinian processes can produce adaptations, whether biological or social. The only apparent alternative to Darwinian processes producing adaptations is intentional human design. But Chapter 10 showed that there is no such thing, just the illusion of planning and intentional creation. What individuals do, alone or together, over a moment or a month or a lifetime, is really just the product of the process of blind variation and environmental filtration operating on neural circuits in their heads.

People overestimate the scope or effectiveness of what they think is intentional planning in human affairs. They underestimate the degree to which human life requires the emergence of adaptations that no one could ever have designed. The best example of how adaptations arise that no one ever designed, or even could have designed, is the price system that springs up wherever markets are established. It was the (ersatz) Nobel Prize–winning realization of Friedrich Hayek that the price system is a vast information storage and distribution device—a virtual computer. It runs a program that forces buyers and sellers to reveal the prices they are really willing to sell for and buy for. It sends each buyer and seller only the information the individual needs to make decisions about what to buy and what to sell. It's even self-repairing. Sometimes it breaks down. But no individual or group can *permanently* hijack or otherwise exploit the market price system to enrich themselves, although people are always trying. No individual agent dreamed up this wonderful institution. No individual or group could do the job as well (that is the reason the centrally planned economies of the former Soviet empire collapsed). That makes it the prime example of a social organ "of extreme perfection" that can only result from a Darwinian process.

The two premises—everything significant in human affairs is an adaptation and Darwinian processes are the only ones that can produce and maintain adaptations—ensure the blindness of history because they ensure the ubiquity of arms races everywhere and always in human history. These arms races get faster and faster as time goes by. When and where an arms race breaks out cannot be foretold, since it is always the unforeseeable outcome of adaptive variations. Nor can the outcome of an arm's race be anticipated, since the environment filtering for outcomes in arms races is human culture, something that is itself moving too rapidly to be the target of prediction.

How can we be certain that both cultural variations and cultural environments are unpredictable? It's not enough that they could not have been predicted in the past. Lots of things science couldn't predict with accuracy in even the recent past it now does a great job at predicting. If you live where it snows, when was the last time you were surprised by a snowstorm? In fact, better weather prediction is a good example of why the future of human culture really is becoming increasingly unpredictable, more and more unpredictable than it was in the past. Increasingly over the last 500 years, and now predominantly, the source of the most significant variations and environmental filters in human culture has been science and technology. That's how weather prediction got to be so much better in our lifetime. For predictions about human affairs to be at all accurate, they must be based on expectations of where the next moves will be made at the frontiers of the sciences and at their points of technical application. History is no more capable of providing us with such information than is a patent clerk. Even the greatest and most famous patent clerk of them all, Albert Einstein, couldn't have done what needs doing for us to know the future pace and direction of scientific change. And that is what we need to make history useful.

That's why when it comes to predicting the future, history is bunk with a capital B.

Human Progress? Not Much, Pretty Local, and Likely to Be Threatened

Is there such a thing as human progress? Does history reveal the long march of civilization to what Winston Churchill called the broad sunlit uplands? Is there anything to the hope of Martin Luther King that Barack Obama is so fond of quoting: "The arc of the moral universe is long but it bends toward justice." Almost certainly not. On the other hand, we are probably not going to hell in a handbasket either.

In natural history and in human history, all progress is local. When one geological epoch gives way to another, yesteryear's or yesterday's advantage can become today's handicap. That's how the dinosaurs became dinosaurs. The same goes for our history, especially once human culture began to be the most important environmental filter in our own evolution.

Read a book like Barbara Tuchman's *The Distant Mirror* or William Manchester's *A World Lit Only by Fire*, and it will be hard to deny that since the Black Death there has been some real progress in human history. But if there has been, it is local progress in two senses. First, almost all of it has resulted from technological progress driven by Darwinian processes operating in science. This is what has enabled us literally to enhance our adaptive fitness by adapting the local environment to human needs and wants. It's clear that we may succumb, like the dinosaurs, to some exogenous shock, like an asteroid, or an endogenous one, like global warming. Even if we don't make ourselves extinct by our impact on the environment filtering us for fitness, we will inevitably change it to make today's adaptations tomorrow's maladaptations. If we are lucky, we'll last as long as the dinosaurs—225 million years. Don't bet on it. In a 100 million years or so, supersmart rats or loquacious cockroaches may be at the top of the food chain worldwide. With any luck, by the time that happens at least some of our descendants will be living around other stars.

Humanity has survived many environmental vicissitudes on the way from its first emergence to the present. Fortunately, the environment changed enough or we fortuitously hit upon some variation in our traits—language or technology, perhaps—that made survival and expansion possible. The gravest environmental challenge we faced in recorded history was the Black Death of the fourteenth century. Gene sequencing now tells us that the plague killed more like 50 percent of the Western world's population instead of the merely 30 percent long supposed. Why has the bubonic plague not revisited humankind on a worldwide scale? Because the ones who survived it were just the ones with genetically encoded variant traits making them and their descendants—us—resistant to the plague. Darwinism in action. What this bodes for our own future is minimally optimistic. However much we bugger up the planet, probably lurking within the range of our current genetic variation is a suite of traits that will enable some of our descendants to survive almost any environmental challenge—climate change, pollution, toxic chemicals, radiation waste.

Scientism gives us confidence that humankind will survive, but almost certainly not unchanged, genetically as well as culturally. You can call this local adaptation of successive generations "progress." But that is not really what anyone was hoping for.

In fact, human cultural evolution is going to show much less local progress than even the local progress of biological evolution. The cultural environment that filters variations for increased adaptiveness changes too quickly for significant local progress. Think about personal computer data storage: we went from 5½-inch floppy disk drives to minidisk drives to compact disk drives to no disk drives at all in a matter of 15 years. Given enough time, engineers could have improved the floppy, the mini, the compact disk. They never had the time. The culture was moving too fast to make much local technical progress in each format. The Austrian economist Joseph Schumpeter is famous for one big idea: that capitalism is creative destruction. It's not just capitalism that moves the goal posts, changes the rules, makes us all move twice as fast just to stay in place. It's the unpredictably changing culture always tearing down yesterday's environmental filters and replacing them with new ones, making long-term movement in any one direction—local progress—rare. That's why the trajectory of human culture is more a matter of fashion than progress.

How about moral progress? Until the twentieth century, one might have been pardoned for thinking that the world was slowly but surely progressing. It might have been moving in the direction of greater fit between human economic and social institutions, on the one hand, and core morality on the other. But the events of the twentieth century suggest that those worried about the survival and expansion of core morality should not count on humanity's having a self-civilizing trajectory. Core morality, as Chapter 5 explained, emerged as an adaptation long ago and far away in human evolution. It did so under circumstances apparently very different from our current environment. Are the environmental features of the early human evolution that selected for core morality still in force? If so, we can expect core morality to persist as an adaptation; if not, then almost no matter what we do, it will be subject to the vagaries of drift as an adaptively neutral trait—like small ears on the African elephant. Or perhaps core morality will start to be selected against as a maladaptive trait, like the ivory tusks on the same elephants. The bigger they are, the more likely the elephant is to be killed for them by the top predator on the African savanna—*Homo sapiens*.

As noted in Chapter 6, there is always variation in the degree to which individuals accept and act on core morality. The variation produces at least a few moral monsters in every generation. And local environmental changes, especially in science and technology, seem to have given such monsters more scope to be monstrous than they had in the past. So much for local progress.

The worst of it is that even knowing all this is hardly any help.

The Darwinian character of human cultural change means that there is little likelihood that a scientific understanding of human affairs can ameliorate the human condition long-term. It may even be unable to avoid the worst-case scenarios of the human future. For humanity as a whole, even a little bit of local progress will be mostly dumb luck. Let's see why.

WHY THE HUMAN SCIENCES (EVEN ECONOMICS) CAN'T DO MUCH BETTER THAN HISTORY

Is this pessimism about progress shortsighted? Maybe history can't help us foresee the future or help us forestall its worst outcomes. But what about science? Surely, scientism has to be optimistic about the prospect that properly conducted, the behavioral and social sciences will have the payoffs that the natural sciences have had. The methods that have worked in physics, chemistry, and biology should work in psychology, sociology, economics, and political science, too, shouldn't they?

The scientific study of humanity has been taking this thought to heart for a hundred years or so. The same agenda has been set for each of the human sciences. As in natural sciences, the aim is to uncover reliable regularities, generalizations, laws, models, theories. Together with data about the present, these discoveries will enable us to predict, control, and improve the future. At least they will provide the available means to adapt ourselves to futures we may be unable to control. Of course, there will be the problem of keeping the power that social science confers on us away from those who don't share core morality. But perhaps science will enable us to predict who those people are and help us create institutions that prevent them from exploiting other humans.

Alas, none of this is in the cards. When it comes to foresight, unlike the natural sciences, the social sciences (including economics) can't help being myopic. They can never see far enough ahead to provide even much local progress in human affairs. Supposing otherwise is just not taking scientism seriously. It is not difficult to see why this is so.

The empirical, experimental, data-collecting social and behavioral sciences are all in the business of discovering patterns in behavior—social and individual. Then they aim to explain these patterns by constructing models and theories that will also enable us to predict new instances of them, and to do so with increasing precision and reliability. So far so good. This is taking scientism seriously. We should applaud it and encourage it.

The trouble is, we already know from Darwinian biology that all the patterns to be discovered about human affairs are temporary. They are "local equilibria," periods of calm or stasis between arms races, when competing strategies exactly balance each other. Some equilibria last longer than others, but all are destined to be overtaken by events.

What is a local equilibrium, and why must it always be unraveled? As we have already seen, biology provides clear examples. Here's another one: For millions of years, there has been a pattern of cuckoos parasitizing finches—laying their eggs in finch nests and leaving the work of hatching and feeding their offspring to the finches. This is a local equilibrium in cuckoo/finch relations. The cuckoos lay just enough eggs in finch nests to survive as a species, but not so many as to threaten finch extinction or finch countermeasures. It can't last forever. Either finch genes will hit upon a fortuitous variation that enables them to escape from this parasitism, or they will go extinct. That will threaten the cuckoos, of course. Given enough time, finch populations will produce a random genetic variation that enables finches to distinguish cuckoo eggs or cuckoo young and kick them out of the nests. Or maybe some finch gene will mutate into one that produces a cuckoo toxin that will eventually rid finches of this parasite. A gene for anticuckoo toxin will spread in finch populations. The more serious the parasitism of cuckoos, the faster it will spread. Once it has spread widely enough, it will start an arms race, in which cuckoo genes will be selected for making an antidote to the new toxin, if such a move is available in the design space of cuckoos. As a result, cuckoos and finches will struggle until they find some new temporary modus vivendi, a different pattern, a new local equilibrium in cuckoo/finch relations. Or it will result in the eventual disappearance of one or both species.

Now, speed up the arms races and the weaponry from the slow pace of the genes and their limited gene products to the ever-accelerating pace of cultural evolution. The local equilibrium between *Homo* and lions may have lasted a million years. But the local equilibrium between lord, vassal, and serf in European feudalism (a label invented long after the period's end) lasted less than 1,000 years. The regularities to be discovered operating in contemporary human life will be far more fleeting than any of these. But without long enough lasting regularities, there is not much hope for a science that can uncover them, much less enable us to exploit them.

Here is the problem facing any human science we might settle on for designing our futures: Anything like a law uncovered by a social or behavioral science will be a temporary equilibrium among adaptations (or their direct results). Every one of these local equilibria will eventually be broken up by arms races. Some sooner, some later.

Consider an example. It's the most robust "law" in international relations, perhaps even in the whole of political science: Democracies do not war with one another. Many political scientists claim that not a single clear-cut exception to this regularity has happened since democracies emerged at the end of the eighteenth century. Even though any number of countries have been at war with each other in any year since 1776, not a single pair of democracies have actually been at war with each other during this period. Apparently, the trait of being a democracy and the trait of not going to war with a democracy are, for the moment at least, coadaptive. This probably helps explain several things, like why democracies do better economically than market-economy dictatorships (fewer wars) and why the number of democracies seems to be increasing. It has also guided foreign policy—the U.S. and European encouragement of new democracies to ensure stability and peace.

Nothing is forever. We can be confident that somewhere or sometime, one democracy is going to find a way to exploit this regularity by attacking some completely unsuspecting fellow democracy lulled into a false sense of the permanence of peace among democracies. How can we be so confident? Mother Nature is forever searching through biological design space, looking for new variations on an existing adaptation that do even better. Nature seeks variations that are cheaper to make or more efficient to use or that otherwise improve on a solution to the design problem the environment poses. There is no way to stop blind variation. This goes for variations in human cultural adaptations as well as in genetically encoded adaptations. But human social design space is greater than the biological space genes search through. It is changing more rapidly, too. There are two reasons why the rate of cultural variation is much faster and cultural environments are changed much quicker, too.

First, biological evolution has to wait the 20-year human reproductive generation for a new genetic variation to start changing traits. Once a genetically encoded trait appears in an organism, it's stuck there for the organism's whole life. The leopard's lineage can change its spots by mutation and other tricks, but not the individual leopard itself. But cultural variations arrive continually, sometimes before the previous one has even had a chance to be selected for or against.

Second, once people and their traits become one another's selective environment, high-speed trait variation is converted to equally fast changes in the filtering environments. Nothing illustrates this process better than the changes in information technology since the personal computer came on the scene. People linking computers to one another provides an environment in which Web browsers emerge and get selected for and against (remember Netscape?). Now on every computer screen in the world, Google is locked in an arms race with Bing. (Check out how Google Images changed to copy Bing images.) Browsers themselves become the environment in which social network sites compete (remember MySpace?); social network sites become environments in which advertising, self-promotion, and blogging compete. It's nested Darwinian natural selection moving at ever-accelerating velocities, where rapidly changing filters select among relentlessly and randomly varying traits. This is why so much human cultural evolution looks more like fashion change than accumulating adaptation.

Here is another example: Only 50 years ago, economists thought that the Keynesian model of the economy captured the macroeconomic laws of the capitalist system. In most versions, the model consisted of three equations that showed how income, investment, and consumption were related, with implications for the interest rate, the money supply, and government taxing/spending policies. One reason the model looked right is that it seemed to enable economists of the third quarter of the twentieth century to fine-tune the macroeconomic variables of a nation's economy. The pattern of relationships between investment and savings, consumption and gross national income, the interest rate and the money supply had been figured out. At this point, economists thought that government could now control the economy to provide full employment. But the stagflation of the 1970s put an end to this apparently effective Keynesian economic "fine-tuning." What happened?

The Keynesian model ceased to work because it fell victim to an arms race. Its equations stated relationships between several economic institutions and their traits. These "institutions"—the interest rate, the money supply, the government budget, the propensity to consume, to hold money balances—had all arisen in modern society either as adaptations or as the immediate consequence of adaptations. No one understood these relationships till Keynes, so no government could exploit them to secure full employment before 1937, when Keynes's *General Theory of Employment, Money and Interest* was published. Once governments began exploiting the relationships between these adaptations, they began to change the environments that select for strategies in the behavior of businesses, labor unions—in fact, all economic agents. There was now a new filter selecting for new adaptive strategies. These were ones that had higher fitness in an environment that for the first time included governments using the tools that Keynesian macroeconomic theory provided. To the surprise of the Keynesian economists, after some years of Keynesian fine-tuning by the government, the tools their model provided ceased to work to provide full employment. All they got was higher inflation without growth: stagflation.

Why did this happen? Economists who rejected Keynes's theory had the answer: arms race. For a while, Keynes's theory got the macro-facts right about the economy and how it responds to governmental policy. Eventually, however, the businessmen and women, the labor union leaders, even the consumers on the street "got wise" to what government was doing in the economy to manipulate their behavior, and they started making different choices. The beautiful model of the capitalist economy that Keynes discovered ceased to work because the relationships it described broke down when they were exploited by the government. This had to happen once some of the institutions, groups, and individuals the model described began to change their behavior to exploit the other institutions and individuals it described. The result? About 10 or 15 years after it became widely known, the Keynesian model fell victim to an arms race.

But its replacement, new classical economics, didn't fare any better. This theory told us that people cannot be fooled in the way Keynes thought because they are rational. Moreover, markets inevitably regulate themselves owing to the counterbalancing actions of rational people who can't be fooled the way Keynes thought. But deregulated markets and the absence of Keynesian macroeconomic fine-tuning lasted just long enough to create its own arms races (between investment banks and their clients, for example). These new arms races unraveled new classical economics' policy recommendations and undermined its descriptions of economic reality. The reaction has been a revival of Keynesian thinking, but with quite different models of the nature of the economy. If it becomes the orthodoxy, "New Keynesianism" will simply give new hostages to fortune.

All such models, laws, and theories sought by the social sciences must share the same fate. There will be patterns to discover and to model and to offer to governments or companies to exploit in predicting or controlling people's behavior. But the patterns will hold for shorter and shorter periods of time, and they will always be unraveled by arms races. That makes the social sciences merely nearsighted, when history is almost completely blind.

THUCYDIDES (AND MILTON FRIEDMAN) TO THE RESCUE?

Nowadays, fewer and fewer historians hope to vindicate their discipline by its predictive uses. Pretensions to prediction are left to teachers of international relations, "grand strategy," and neorealism about the behavior of nations on the world stage. Many of these social scientists and policy wonks insist that to understand the future, we need to read and reread Thucydides's fifth-century BC classic *History of the Peloponnesian War*. It was there that the iron laws of human behavior were first elucidated.

Thucydides's contemporary followers will grant that there are transitory, ephemeral relationships in human affairs, ripe for exploitation in arms races. But underneath them all, and at all places and times, there are fixed law of economic rationality: everyone acts on self-interest; each of us looks out for number one; we maximize our own welfare, happiness, utility, preferences. It's individuals acting rationally that drive all the local equilibria and the arms races of economics, politics, and everything else in social life. This dogma is shared by Thucydides's latter-day protégés with the most distinguished (ersatz Nobel Prize–winning) members of the University of Chicago economics department.

Their doctrine is that there are laws that govern all human affairs: these are the laws economists have uncovered, the laws of rational choice. They are as disarmingly simple as they are far-reaching in their explanatory power. First, between any two choices, each individual always knows which (if either) he or she prefers. Second, if an individual prefers A to B and B to C, then that individual prefers A to C. Third, every individual chooses what he or she prefers most among alternative choices available. What could be simpler? What could be more obviously true (most of the time)? These laws have been known to social scientists at least in rough form since Thucydides assumed them to explain the behavior of his fellow Greeks. Economists have only refined them. The laws of rational choice are impervious to arms races. So we can rely on them to predict human affairs, *all* human affairs, forever.

Thucydides argued that these facts about human nature would enable anyone reading his *History* to understand all wars, international relations, and power politics everywhere. It was science, not mere storytelling. Economists think that the same "facts" about individuals' rational choices fix all the other facts about society. By aggregating individual rational behavior into markets, industries, and economies, economic science can provide foresight. It can even be employed to create stable institutions that won't perpetually give way to undermining arms races. That, at any rate, was the aspiration of economists up to the end of the twentieth century.

Not too many people believe this line any more. Current events in the financial sectors of the world's industrial economies have overtaken it. But even before the financial crisis of 2008, a great deal of cognitive science had already shown that no one, not even an economist, is much of an economically rational chooser. Economics, in fact, started to admit this fact in 2002 when it gave its pseudo–Nobel Prize to a couple of cognitive psychologists, Daniel Kahneman and Amos Tversky. They won the prize for proving that people not only violate the "laws" of rational choice, but that paradoxically it is often rational, or at least efficient, to do so. This is just what a Darwinian perspective on human choice would have suggested.

Kahneman, Tversky, and others who have contributed to the subject began by studying how people work their way through choices in laboratory conditions. By setting up experiments in which large numbers of subjects were forced to make choices, trades, guesses, and bets, Kahneman and Tversky were able to isolate rules of thumb, heuristic devices, and shortcuts that people actually use, instead of the logic and probability theory that rational choice requires. As if we didn't already know, humans often make judgments, guesses, trades, and bets that are not economically rational. They frequently give in to bias and stereotyping in judgment. They allow different but equally accurate descriptions of the same facts to shade their decisions. They are overconfident about some things and not as confident as the evidence would allow about others. They systematically take risks and make bets that rational choice theory can prove to be irrational. Equally often they refuse bets that any rational poker player should take. This is because people get by with these rough-and-ready rules for making choices, even though they can't articulate the rules if you ask them. Most of the time, people do better using these heuristics than they would by trying to use the principles of rational choice the economist has formulated.

People do better most of the time using these imperfect rules that fail to maximize utility or anything else for one reason. It is easier, faster, and cheaper in brain power to go through life using these approximations instead of the more precise, more correct methods of rational choice. It's only in the weird and uncommon experiments of the social psychologists that these heuristic rules betray us into obvious mistakes. Like the optical illusions that reveal how perception really works (as we saw in Chapter 8), it's trick questions that produce rationally "wrong" answers in the social psychologist's experiments. The errors people make reveal what rules of choice people actually use. They reveal to the experimenter how the subjects' brains are actually solving the problems they face (no surprise there for scientism). Like so much else in our mental lives, the rules that govern our choices and our actions are the results of processes of blind variation and natural selection. In the human struggle to survive in a threatening environment, rules of thumb and shortcuts in reasoning long ago triumphed over pure rules of rational choice. Rational choice is omniscient about what we should do, provided we have all the relevant information. In equipping us for survival, Mother Nature couldn't wait for the relevant information to come in. Instead she found a lot of quick and dirty solutions to problems that had to be solved immediately.

The way people actually choose reflects implicit rules of reasoning and choice that have probably persisted since the Pleistocene. They are more venerable and more reliable than almost any other pattern in human affairs that social science can uncover. Alas, nothing is forever. It is pretty clear that in at least some areas of modern life in the industrialized West, an arms race has been threatening to unravel the local equilibrium of people interacting with one another using these age-old shortcut methods of choice. That, in a nutshell, is what the financial crisis at the end of the first decade of the twenty-first century was about.

Suddenly, in the last 20 years, the environment has changed. The technology for crunching numbers and doing the rational calculation of risk and reward have become orders of magnitude cheaper and faster. By the late 1990s, perfect rational calculation strategies finally began to compete in real time with the imperfect, approximate heuristics that borrowers and lenders, investors and savers, consumers and producers have been using since time immemorial. In this competition, cheap and fast rational choice will take heuristic reasoning to the cleaners every time. For example, canny rational choice investment banks will help their heuristic reasoning customers buy mortgage-backed securities and then go out and sell the same securities short. The exploitation will become so effective that heuristic reasoners will either lose everything or be forced switch to rational choice in self-defense. The result has been to destroy many of the local equilibria of the financial markets in the West. How much of these equilibria in human relations will be unraveled by this arms race is anyone's guess.

Even if everyone becomes perfectly rational by the lights of the strictest Chicago school standard, human affairs will become increasingly unpredictable and therefore harder to steer into preferred directions. The reason is obvious. Since the scientific revolution began, technological advance and the science that produces it have been the most important source of the variations that break up society's local equilibria and trigger its arms races. They have increased their speed and their impact. They will continue to do so. The reason is obvious. No one can predict the next Nobel Prize breakthrough in physics or medicine or anything else for that matter. No one can scoop the hottest patent applications. So no one can predict or control the human future, no matter how reliable our discoveries about the basic patterns of human behavior.

Economists were wrong about rationality. But even had they been right about it, economists could do no better than identify local equilibria. Economics will be no better than other social sciences in providing an alternative to history's blindness. At most the human sciences will be able to see a little way into the future. They provide foresight. But they can do so only as far as they can be confident that no new arms race will break out to destroy the local equilibria they have been lucky enough to discover.

WINSTON CHURCHILL GOT IT
EXACTLY BACKWARD

Now we can see what's wrong with Winston Churchill's claim that "the farther backward you can look, the farther forward you can see." It's more than a little ironic that when he made this claim, he was overlooking the very thing that he spent almost a decade warning Britain about: the arms race. Of all things for Winston Churchill to miss.

Had Churchill's interest been ancient history or prehistory, missing the role of arms races might have been excusable. The farther back in time you look, the less important arms races are for human history or natural history for that matter. A couple of million years ago, at the point where hominins emerged, the pace of arms race change was glacial and almost entirely genetic. As hominin populations increased, hominin interactions with mega-fauna accelerated the arms race between them. Eventually, population growth, early toolmaking, and the resulting decrease in megafauna available to hunt led to serious competition between individuals and groups of hominins—the first significant human arms races. Traits and strategies that had worked for one group for hundreds of thousands of years came to be exploited by other groups and to disappear altogether, only to be replaced by other traits in other groups.

Once protolinguistic interaction emerged, say, 250,000 years ago, the rate at which arms races changed environments further increased. By the time you get to recorded history, changes have become so fast that there is almost nothing that studying genetically transmitted behavior can teach us about human affairs. And of course the arms races of the hunter-gatherer period, between tribes, within tribes, between genders, generations, and among individuals within all these groups have little to tell us about human affairs after the onset of agriculture. All of a sudden, looking back a million years can tell us almost nothing about the next 10,000. That's why Jared Diamond was able to explain so much about the period 8000 BC to AD 1500 in *Guns, Germs, and Steel* while neglecting the previous million years. By 200 years later, arms races were changing the selective environments so quickly that Diamond's theory was no guide to the past, let alone the present or the future.

Wind the tape of history through the stages of human "progress"—Mesopotamian hydraulic empires, Oriental despotism, feudalism, the Renaissance, the Industrial Revolution, the information revolution. As history unrolls, knowledge of the past becomes increasingly deficient as a basis for understanding the present and the future. The reason is the ever-accelerating rate of arms race interactions in that history.

By 400 years ago, scientific and technological change were increasing the size and dimensions of Mother Nature's selective design space so much and so fast that no one could keep up with it anymore. Almost nothing could any longer be anticipated in the move and countermove of arms races everywhere in human affairs.

HISTORY IS HELPLESS to teach us anything much about the present. The real lesson the history of arms races teaches is that there are no lessons in history. When it comes to understanding the future, history is bunk. So much for the persistent question of what the pattern or meaning of human history might be. There is no place history is heading, except toward the maximum-entropy heat death of the universe. We are not here for any reason, nor have we passed through any historical test for a reason. History is, to paraphrase Shakespeare, a tale told by an idiot full of sound and fury and signifying nothing. Just like Shakespeare's *Histories*, history, as stories, is mighty entertaining and sometimes even stirring. But when it comes to helping us understand our future or even the present, arms races make it bunk.

The only part of the past that can tell us much about the future is the very recent past, and the only thing it can tell us about is the very near future. At most the social sciences can uncover temporary truces that will be inevitably overthrown by an arms race. Since these truces are getting shorter all the time, the amount they can tell us is getting smaller all the time. Scientism must acknowledge that if history is blind, social science is myopic.

Chapter 12

— ◆ —

LIVING WITH SCIENTISM: ETHICS, POLITICS, THE HUMANITIES, AND PROZAC AS NEEDED

WHEN ADVERTISEMENTS LIKE THE ONE IN Figure 9 appeared on London buses in the fall of 2008, there were protests, of course. Just not the ones you might expect (especially in the United States). Many British atheists were unhappy about the qualification "probably" and said so. Scientism agrees. There is no reason to doubt atheism. What we know about physical and biological science makes the existence of God less probable than the existence of Santa Claus. And the parts of physics that rule out God are not themselves open to much doubt. There is no chance that they will be revised by anything yet to be discovered.

To be sure, there will be revolutionary developments in science. Superstring theory may give way to quantum-loop gravity; exceptions to the genetic code may be discovered; some unique function of consciousness may be identified. But there are some things that won't happen. Purposes and designs will never have a

FIGURE 9. Advertisement on a London bus

role in physics or biology. Perpetual motion machines and other violations of the laws of thermodynamics won't arise, not even if there turns out to be such a thing as cold fusion. And no clump of matter will just by itself be about another clump of matter. The parts of science that rule out theism are firmly fixed. Finally, it's not just probable that God doesn't exist. For scientism, it's as close to a sure thing as science can get.

Besides giving rock-solid reasons to deny the existence of the theist's God, science also provides equally compelling answers to the persistent questions that lead people to religion and mystery mongering. The answers that science provides are not as reassuring to most people as are the answers of religion and its substitutes. Should this fact worry those of us who reject theism because it conflicts with science? The short answer is no. There is no reason for us to be anxious about these answers. This last chapter explains why. It also draws out the implications of science for some of the moral and political issues that roil contemporary

life. Finally, it helps put in their right place the unforgettable stories that seduce us away from science. They turn out to be fun and
games masquerading as knowledge and wisdom.

Who Needs Secular Humanism, Anyway?

Some atheists worry that science's answers to the persistent questions will be psychologically disquieting, emotionally inadequate,
or completely unbearable for most people. They worry that science's answers to the persistent questions are just not enough to
satisfy most people—that we need more to live by than what science alone provides. If we can't have religion, we need a substitute that is as much like it as science can provide. Enter secular
humanism, a doctrine, dare I say, "designed" to do this job. It
hasn't worked.

Secular humanists embrace science—its methods and its
results—and seek to build meaning and value out of both. They
treat the core morality we share as true, right, correct, and really
morally binding on us, and they think that science can show why
it is true, right, and correct. This is something its advocates think
secular humanism has to do if it is going to compete with religion
for brand loyalty. Consumer satisfaction will also require that
science provide a meaning, purpose, or value for people's lives,
something that will make getting up in the morning worthwhile.
Finally, some of these secular humanists think that religion provides a sense of community that enables us to work together to
ameliorate the human condition. Since this is a good thing, secular humanism has to accomplish at least as much good as religion
does if it is going to displace religion.

Scientism recognizes that the ambitions of secular humanism
are unattainable. More important, they are mostly unnecessary

for leading a perfectly satisfactory individual and community life, the sort of life recommended by the adverts on the London buses.

Long ago, Plato showed that religion has no rational capacity to underwrite core morality. Yet his argument has never loosened the grip of core morality. Science provides the explanation of why we endorse core morality and why it needs no special rationalization—from religion or from science—for us to feel bound by it. Humans evolved to be moral creatures. That's what makes the nihilism we are committed to nice nihilism. What makes scientism nihilistic is its recognition that when science explains core morality, it also deprives it of any possible justification that will pass scientism's muster.

The core morality almost all human beings share doesn't need a justification and it can't have one. It doesn't need one to work because we have been naturally selected to act in accordance with it. So much for the secular humanist's mistaken hope that science can do for morality what religion tries and fails to do.

How about the psychological need to fill the vacuum with meaning and purpose—something religion is supposed to provide? *The Purpose Driven Life* is not a best seller for nothing. Even so adamant an atheist as Richard Dawkins has succumbed to the delusion that a substitute for religion is required and available from science. People ask Dawkins, "Why do you bother getting up in the morning if the meaning of life boils down to such a cruel pitiless fact, that we exist merely to help replicate a string of molecules?" His answer is that "science is one of the supreme things that makes life worth living."

Richard Dawkins gets misty-eyed when he thinks of the general theory of relativity or the symmetry of the double helix or how the invisible hand works to make everyone better off. So what? Why should we be like him? More important, does Dawkins have an argument or a reason or a basis to claim that science makes life worth living for everyone, or only for some people, or just for those smitten by science or scientism, or perhaps exclusively for Richard Dawkins?

It's hard to see how science itself could provide any argument for the supreme or intrinsic value of science or anything else for that matter. That something really is valuable or has meaning is never any part of science's explanation of why we value it. In fact, its explanation of why we value things also explains away the notion that they have some intrinsic value, independent of our wants, preferences, tastes, and so forth. We saw why this is so in Chapter 5. The argument works just the same for values that are supposed to make life meaningful as it does for norms. That goes for my values as much as yours or Dawkins's. Science can explain why we value things, but the same goes for values we reject as wrong. That's why scientific explanations of what we value cannot justify those values or serve as a basis to enforce them on others. Since science is the only possible source of justification, if it doesn't work to justify values, nothing does.

Nice nihilism undermines all values. This also goes for the silly idea of the existentialist philosophers, who realized that science rules out meanings or purpose and so insisted that we each had to create them for ourselves. In pursuit of this misguided idea, there emerged existentialists of many different kinds: Catholic, Protestant, Jewish, Muslim, Hindu, Zen, and every other kind of religious existentialist, as well as communist, socialist, fascist, and humanistic existentialists—existentialists for every kind of meaning or purpose that people wanted their lives to have. Existentialists didn't see the fatuousness of trying to create something that nature had ruled out as impossible. Creating purpose in a world that can't have any is like trying to build a perpetual motion machine after you have discovered that nature has ruled them out. Of course, it takes scientism to see this. Existentialists, like almost all philosophers, would have rejected scientism had anyone offered it to them. But secular humanism doesn't reject science. So, if it needs to vindicate an intrinsic value, goal, or purpose, such as revealing, or reveling in, the beauty of science or the beauty of the universe science uncovers, it's out of luck.

Luckily for us, Mother Nature has seen to it that most of us, including the secular humanists, will get up most mornings and go on living even without anything to make our lives meaningful. The proof is obvious. There is nothing that makes our lives meaningful, and yet here we are, out of our pajamas.

The notion that we need something to make life meaningful in order to keep living is another one of those illusions fostered by introspection.

For a long time now, Mother Nature (aka natural selection) has been operating on organisms to make them keep on living. The number one design problem that natural selection faced was how to maximize their chances of reproducing. By the time it got to mammals, the optimum solution was longevity. So it arranged their brains to keep their bodies out of trouble as long as possible, or at least till they stopped having offspring. By the time it got to us, natural selection had gotten the solution to this longevity design problem down so well that it wouldn't qualify as entirely quick and dirty anymore. Like other mammals, we are programmed to get out of bed in the morning, to keep on living. That raises for introspection the persistent question of why we do so, especially as it has the mistaken impression that with free will it's up to us whether we keep on living or not. Introspection can't provide a good reason to go on living because there isn't any. This is the one thing that at least some of the existentialists got right. But introspection keeps hoping, looking, trying to find a reason to go on. Since there really isn't one, those who look hard eventually become troubled.

Fortunately for our genes, introspection by itself can't often overcome natural selection. Even when it comes to the conclusion that there is nothing that makes life worth living, the result is almost never suicide or even staying in bed in the morning. Just ask Jean-Paul Sartre.

As with a justification for core morality, when it comes to making life meaningful, what secular humanists hanker after is something they can't have and don't need. What they do need, if meaninglessness makes it impossible to get out of bed in the morning, is Prozac.

People who stay in bed all day or who engage in self-destructive behavior or commit suicide don't do it because their lives lack meaning or even because they think their lives lack meaning. They commit suicide because the neural circuitry in their brain responds to intractable pain, feelings of depression, and all the other slings and arrows flesh is heir to. Often the circuitry responds by producing suicide notes along with and prior to the fatal act. These last gasps may even complain of the meaninglessness of the victim's life. Scientism assures us that such notes, as well as the conscious introspections they may report, are just by-products, side effects, produced by the brain, along with the self-destructive act itself.

Secular humanists recognize that religion provides the glue that binds people together into projects that sometimes ameliorate the human condition. So they hope to provide a substitute for this sort of fellowship in secular institutions. Those of us who embrace scientism may share the social "aims" of secular humanism, though we recognize that there is nothing objectively right about these "aims." Let's employ the illusory vocabulary of designs, goals, ends, and purposes for the moment. A careful scientific study of how religion accomplishes its crowd control and its social engineering may enable us to create secular institutions with similar good effects (at least until overtaken in arms races). It's just as likely to enable us to create institutions with consequences for humanity as harmful as those that organized religion has produced over the last several thousand years. But no one needs to buy into secular humanism to do this social engineering either. What is more, if scientism is right about most people's love of stories, it's not likely that Richard Dawkins will be able to sell people on the beauty of science as something we can build on as a substitute for religion. There is no really compelling story in the beauty of science and no convincing story in secular humanism either.

Most of us who have embraced atheism don't need secular humanism to be nice or to go on living. Since it won't work as a substitute among those who think they need religion for both, no one needs it at all.

Take Two Prozac and Call Me in the Morning

So, what should we scientistic folks do when overcome by *Welschmertz* (world-weariness)? Take two of whatever neuropharmacology prescribes. If you don't feel better in the morning . . . or three weeks from now, switch to another one. Three weeks is often how long it takes serotonin reuptake suppression drugs like Prozac, Wellbutrin, Paxil, Zoloft, Celexa, or Luvox to kick in. And if one doesn't work, another one probably will.

Once neuroscience has provided neurology—the medical specialty—with enough understanding of how the brain works, the docs will be able to deal with psychological problems almost as effectively as they now deal with problems of the other organs ("almost" because the brain is more complicated than the other organs). Psychological problems will always be with us. The Darwinian nature of everything biological assures us of that. As Darwin discovered, blind variation is the unvarying rule in nature. As a result, there will always be a wide range of brain hardwirings that combine with a wide range of environmental vicissitudes to produce a wide range of capacities and incapacities. No matter how much we try to homogenize upbringing, education, and health—mental and physical—there will always be people at the extremes. Some will be hopelessly depressed, maladjusted, and suicidal. Others will sail through life with not so much as a cloud in the sky. Each of us is located somewhere along the bell-curved distribution of psychological traits, dispositions, and abilities that nature and nurture conspire to create. Most of us will be reasonably well-adjusted, tolerably happy people, within two standard deviations from the mean between depression and euphoria.

What should you do if you feel the tragic sense of life, if you really feel you need to find the meaning of your life in order to keep living, and if you feel nothing will meet that need? Scientism tells you to treat introspection as a symptom. If it is the symptom of something serious enough to lead to bodily harm, pharmacology is the answer. If it is bearable, it may lead to some creative achievement, like Richard Burton's *Anatomy of Melancholy* or William Styron's *Darkness Visible*, two really enjoyable books about being miserable. Besides killing yourself or otherwise ruining your life, the really serious mistake is taking depression seriously as something of value by itself. Alas, people do talk and act that way. They often refuse to take their meds because, they say, it deprives their inner lives, their thoughts about the human predicament, of seriousness and authenticity. What's so valuable about the illusion that your thoughts have authenticity anyway? Even if everyone wanted it, that wouldn't make it valuable. That would only make it valued.

Certainly, scientism can't take authenticity seriously. Making heavy weather of what introspection seems to tell us turns out to be a big mistake. It may be responsible for a certain amount of great art, like *Finnegans Wake* or *Waiting for Godot*, highly entertaining to those who can sit through them. But taking introspection seriously creates a demand for satisfying narratives or stories, the search for ultimate meanings and cosmic purposes, and the quest for values in a world devoid of them. The quest is deep, heroic, and futile.

Scientism is committed to the mind's being the brain. It tells us that the direct route to mental health has to be by rearranging brain circuits. In most cases, we cannot do that yet. While we are waiting for neuroscience to advance far enough to do so, should we try psychotherapy? Well, it could help, but not the way most people think.

There are, of course, many kinds of therapy, many of them pseudoscientific spin-offs from Freudian analysis. Most of these just "double down" on the mistakes common sense makes when it takes introspection seriously. Some of these psychotherapies even take dreams seriously. But there are also scientifically serious approaches to talk therapy. For instance, various forms of cognitive-behavioral therapy are sometimes prescribed along with the pills. They might work. Stranger things have happened. Scientism has no problems with the improbable, so long as it's consistent with physics. However, if talk therapy does work, it will be like this:

Your therapist talks to you. The acoustical vibrations from your therapist's mouth to your ear starts a chain of neurons firing in the brain. Together with the circuits already set to fire in your brain, the result is some changes somewhere in your head. You may even come to have some new package of beliefs and desires, ones that make you happier and healthier. The only thing scientism insists on is that those new beliefs and new desires aren't thoughts *about* yourself, *about* your actions, or *about* anything else. The brain can't have thoughts about stuff. It's got lots of beliefs and desires, but they are not thoughts about things. They are large packages of input/output circuits in your brain that are ready to deliver appropriate or inappropriate behavior when stimulated. There is no reason in principle why the noises that your therapist makes, or that someone else makes (your mother, for example), shouldn't somehow change those circuits "for the better." Some of the changes may even result in conscious introspective thoughts that seem to be about the benefits of therapy. Of course, science shows that it is almost never that simple. It also shows that when talking cures work, they usually do so as part of a regime that includes medicine working on the neural circuitry. The meds reach the brain by moving through the digestive system first, without passing through the ears at all.

Even when talking cures have an effect, they almost never have the same effect on different patients. Imagine that everyone with the same complaint went to the same therapist, who said the same things to them. Just for starters, the noises would be processed by vastly different "speech recognition" neural circuits in all those brains. The slight and the not so slight differences between these circuits in each person's head would result in different outputs to the rest of each person's (also quite different) neural circuitry. And the differences in the rest of the circuitry would amplify the different effects. Even the therapist would begin to see differences in how the same therapy was affecting the patients on the couch differently. Some might remain deep in thought, while others might nod in agreement. Still others might grimace. And some just might get up and walk out.

On those comparatively rare occasions when people's behavior actually changes after therapy, with or without the benefit of psychotropic drugs, scientism is not completely surprised. After all, what has been changed—reprogrammed—are the input/output circuits in the brain. Talk alone probably won't change much. Still less will any change come from introspection's awareness of the "meaning" of the noises coming out of the therapist's mouth. When changes in brain circuitry and behavior do come, they may be accompanied by changes in conscious experience, even the feeling of willpower exercised. But they won't be caused by these experiences. (Remember your Libet.)

The play of silent markers across your conscious mind as you listen to the noises the therapist makes can't be thoughts about how the therapist wants you to modify your behavior. That's because thoughts can't be about anything. Your neural circuits, and so your behavior, may get modified as a result of the therapy, but it is an illusion that the change results from thinking about what the therapist said and consciously buying into his or her diagnosis. In therapy, as in everything else in life, the illusory content of introspective thoughts is just along for the ride.

SCIENTISM COOLS OFF THE HOT-BUTTON MORAL DISPUTES

Nice nihilism has two take-home messages: the nihilism part—there are no facts of the matter about what is morally right or wrong, good or bad—and the niceness part—fortunately for us, most people naturally buy into the same core morality that makes us tolerably nice to one another.

Understanding the second point is crucial. Like everything else subject to Darwinian natural selection, there is a wide range of variation in the degree of individual attachment to core morality. In every generation, a few people are so nice you can trust them always to do the right thing, and a few people are murderous sociopaths. It can't be helped. That's just how genes and environments fall out. But most of us are within two standard

deviations of the mean. There is enough niceness around to make
social life possible for almost all of us and agreeable for many.

So why is there so much disagreement about morality? Just
think about the moral issues about reproduction and sex that
have spilled out into the public sphere of the Western nations in
the last 50 years: abortion, stem-cell research, in vitro fertilization, gender screening, cloning, germ-line gene therapy, designer
babies, gay rights, same-sex marriage. It's no surprise that so
many of the moral issues of contemporary life involve sex. As
we have seen, that is a great deal of what morality is really about.
But there are other issues as well that people insist need to be
resolved: euthanasia, capital punishment, animal welfare, genetically modified organisms, human rights, affirmative action or
positive discrimination. Yet they all seem subject to intractable
disagreement.

Since there is no fact of the matter about right and wrong,
good and bad, none of the questions people spend so much time
arguing about have any correct answers. Scientism doesn't take
sides in these arguments. But even after we adopt scientism, we'll
inevitably take sides anyway. Because each of us, to a greater or
lesser extent, embraces core morality, each of us will always make
a lot of strong moral judgments. As Chapter 5 showed, disagreements about ethics and values, even between us and Nazis (if
there are any left after we exclude the psychopaths), are mostly
the result of harnessing the same core morality to vastly different factual beliefs about human beings. Most of the moral disagreements people have can be traced to differences about factual
matters. Since disagreements about matters of fact can at least in
theory be settled by science, and only by science, scientism has an
important role in moral disputes after all.

Norms of core morality get harnessed with a lot of different factual beliefs, most of them shown by science to be wrong.

Together, beliefs and norms produce the moral judgments most people can't stop making. Scientism gives us an advantage over most people when it comes to the moral judgments we are fated to make. Once science reveals the truths about human beings that may be combined with core morality, we can figure out what our morality does and does not requires of us. Of course, as nihilists, we have to remember that core morality's requiring something of us does not make it right—or wrong. There is no such thing.

Abortion, pro and con, provides a good example of the role scientism plays in our moral disputes. Some people think that abortion is impermissible because the fetus already has an immortal soul. It will be easy for scientism to refute this argument. No soul, immortal or otherwise, so no argument against abortion here. Some people think that abortion is permissible because the mother has a natural right—not just a legal right—to make final decisions about her own body. This argument, too, is one that scientism cannot take seriously. There are no natural rights—rights one has just by virtue of being human. To put it crudely, clumps of matter (and that's all we are) can't have natural rights just by virtue of their composition, shape, origin, and so forth, any more than one clump of matter (our brain) can be *about* some other clump of matter. So, no argument in favor of permitting abortion from the mother's natural rights.

Surprisingly, once you buy into scientism, settling the abortion problem turns out to be morally easy. Eventually, when all the relevant facts are in, we will be able to evaluate all the arguments in favor of or against abortion. It will be possible to figure out if any of the arguments pro and con are left standing—that is, whether any are supported by a combination of the facts and core morality. Consider how vast is the number of facts about abortions, with all their various causes and effects. Any one of them could be relevant to the question of whether abortion is or is not permissible. Almost certainly, when all these facts are decided, it will turn out that core morality doesn't contain any blanket prohibition or permission of abortion as such. Rather, together with the facts that science can at least in principle uncover, core morality will provide arguments in favor of some abortions and against other abortions, depending on the circumstances.

Of course, the antiabortion crowd won't like this conclusion. What they demand is a blanket prohibition of all abortion. As far as they're concerned, scientism has already sided with the pro-choice agenda. Not quite. Scientism allows that sometimes the facts of a case will combine with core morality to prohibit abortion, even when the woman demands it as a natural right.

Pretty much the same goes for most of the moral issues raised by scientific and technological change over the last generation, especially in the biomedical sciences. Stem-cell research involves destroying fertilized embryos, while in vitro fertilization requires that more embryos be created than are used. Both raise moral questions about whether potential human embryos have moral standing. No one is about to clone a human being, but lots of imaginative people have identified moral problems that this is supposed to raise; for example, does anyone have a right not to be genetically duplicated? Germ-line gene therapy could endanger future generations. Genetic enhancement and other costly innovations raise problems about equality of opportunity that never before existed. These problems don't have single-answer solutions dictated by core morality. Almost always, however, in specific cases where individuals have to make decisions for themselves, science and core morality together could in principle answer the moral questions they face. The trouble is that in most cases, the science is not yet in. Even worse, the rate of technological advance keeps raising new ethical problems even faster than science can settle the facts relevant to the old ones. For example, even before guidelines could be written governing the permissibility of experiments inserting genes in organs to correct malfunction, scientists were already inserting genes in sperm and eggs and switching whole genomes out of eggs to insert other ones. The science we need to combine with core morality to deal with new moral problems keeps falling further and further behind.

Of course, it's possible that core morality contains components that are incompatible with one another. After all, the difficulty we have in expressing its norms may reflect deep inconsistencies between some of them. More likely, in addition to providing variation in the degree of commitment to core morality, natural selection has also provided a range of moral norms inherited from the different environmental filters we and our lineages passed through and which to some degree conflict. Such conflicts won't be settled even when all the facts are in. These are the intractable conflicts of incommensurable moral differences that are among the strongest arguments for nihilism.

Under the circumstances of scientific ignorance, core morality together with people's reluctance to take risks may dictate even to scientistic people temporary blanket prohibition of practices like germ-line gene therapy or growing genetically manipulated organisms. But these decisions should not be misrepresented as scientific ones. Science is always neutral on what we should do. In these cases, as elsewhere, it's core morality that does the deciding.

Nice nihilism reveals that the apparently intractable debates about moral issues almost never really turn on moral disagreements. The two sides of a moral dispute usually fail to realize that they differ on factual issues. Often these differences are matters of church dogma, so they are treated by at least one side of the argument as things no scientific inquiry will decide on. Recall the role played by the immortal soul in the argument against abortion.

No science is going to get religious people to give up the notion that there is a soul. And if you think there is one, then it's not too difficult to convince yourself that it's immortal (in fact, we sketched an argument for this in Chapter 10). Once you believe that there is such a thing as an immortal soul and you put that belief beyond the reach of science, you can harness it together with core morality. The result of this gambit is a conclusion that no amount of science will shake. That's what really makes most moral disputes intractable.

In the face of an invincible refusal to allow one's mind to be changed by the morally relevant facts, there is not much we can do. Scientism encourages us not to treat those who make moral judgments we disagree with as evil. They are probably not even morally wrong. They are just benighted individuals wrong about the facts and thus confused about what our shared morality requires. They might be so benighted, so wrong, hold their views so deeply, and act on them so forcefully that we need to protect ourselves from them. But so long as we are not interfered with, scientism counsels tolerance of moral differences. We should patronize those we disagree with, not demonize them, even as they demonize us.

Along with tolerance of moral disagreement, scientism counsels modesty about our own moral convictions. We may think we've got the relevant facts and so hold firmly the conclusions they support. But science is mostly fallible, and the science we need to guide particular moral judgments is not as certain as the second law of thermodynamics or even the theory of natural selection. We could be wrong, sometimes quite wrong, about what we think are the morally relevant facts that, together with core morality, dictate our moral judgments. Even though scientism allows us to hold quite extreme views, it also counsels us always to hold them lightly, not firmly.

SCIENTISM DECONSTRUCTS
THE (DE)MERITOCRACY

Scientism is nihilistic, but we are not. The Darwinian process that got us here included steps that selected for a pretty strong commitment to a core morality. Even scientism can't shake our emotions or the moral judgments that they produce. Knowing that morality is only good for our reproductive fitness, and sometimes not so good for us, can't make us give it up. We are still committed to being nice. But when you combine our core morality with scientism, you get some serious consequences, especially for politics. In particular, you get a fairly left-wing agenda. No wonder most scientists in the United States are Democrats and in the United Kingdom are Labour Party supporters or Liberal Democrats.

The key to scientism's radical political agenda is its commitment to determinism. Above the level of the smallest numbers of fermions and bosons, the universe is almost totally deterministic. That means that everything we do is just the consequence of the laws of nature and events in the distant past. It's not up to us what went on before we were born, and we have no choice about what the laws of nature are. Therefore, none of the present and future consequences of the ways the laws worked with the past to bring about the present are up to us. That includes all of our actions and everyone else's, too. So, no free will anywhere.

How does determinism turn core morality into a political agenda?

Core morality tells us that important advantages and disadvantages in life should be distributed in accordance with desert (not to be confused with dessert); inequalities should be deserved. Core morality insists that gains in income and wealth should be earned, that freely exercised effort and ambition should be rewarded. That's what the word *meritocracy* is supposed to convey. The same goes for disadvantages. Punishment, including the deprivation of life or liberty, must also be earned. The meritocracy is also a "de-meritocracy." Core morality allows for inequalities in outcomes—wealth, happiness, fines, imprisonment—so long as they are earned or deserved. But all this is moot if nothing is earned or deserved.

The assumption that individuals usually have free will is clearly written into our criminal justice system. The law usually excuses people from a variety of crimes if it can be shown that they could not have done otherwise. If the act was not up to them, if they were not in full control of their bodies when their bodies harmed others, it was no crime. Crime merits punishment, but wrongs we do are not crimes unless committed freely. Wrongful acts freely committed earn punishment. This is part of our core morality.

But science shows that no one acts with free will. So, no wrongdoer ever earns punishment. That is an unavoidable conclusion that scientism draws from applying determinism to core morality. Once scientism leads us to give up free will, we need to completely rethink the moral justification of punishment. We need to rethink criminal law generally. That doesn't mean that scientism requires us to give up the law, the police, the courts, and the prisons. But scientism does give us good reason to rethink these institutions. If punishment needs a moral justification from core morality, it will have to find it in some principle other than the obvious one that freely committed wrongdoing earns punishment.

Of course, we may not need a moral right to deprive people of their freedom. Few people admit this, but scientism would have no trouble with such an admission. There are other parts of core morality that permit or even require locking people up—for example, to protect others and to deter, reform, rehabilitate, and reeducate the wrongdoer. But if we have to have a moral justification for inflicting pain, suffering, and other deprivations on someone, punishment's justification can't include that morally they deserve to be deprived or otherwise made to suffer. Desert requires free will, and there isn't any.

In effect, scientism's view of crime is like its view of disease. It must secure the reduction and elimination of crime the way medicine attacks illness. The prison, in our view, needs to be as much like a hospital as possible—with capacity for the incurably ill, the treatment of the curable, and the isolation of those who might spread their infection. But punishment is excluded. The problem for scientism is "preventive detention." Core morality and legal codes, for that matter, tell us that until people have freely chosen to do wrong, they have a right to be left alone. It is wrong to imprison people when they have not yet done anything wrong. They may never do anything wrong if they have free will. It's up to them. Scientism can't be so lenient. If we know that someone is going to do wrong, core morality requires that we take steps to prevent it, sometimes even detaining the potential wrongdoer when he or she has done nothing wrong. More than one government (left-wing and right-wing) has adopted this policy, alas. Scientism can at least temporarily excuse itself from endorsing such actions. Human behavior is determined, but we almost never can know with enough certainty that someone will do wrong if not detained. We don't have to put people in protective custody yet, but this is a problem all societies will face when neuroscience has advanced far enough.

There is another radical consequence that follows from scientism's denial of free will. As we have just seen, once you adopt determinism, you have to rethink the de-meritocracy; you can't treat lawbreakers as morally bad and worthy of punishment. But you must also entirely rethink the meritocracy, too. If you buy into core morality and scientism, you will have to accept some radical changes in the distribution of wealth and income. The morality of the meritocracy is based on the same principle as the de-meritocracy: criminals deserve what they earn by their character and their misdeeds; similarly, those who get rich by the free exercise of their character and their efforts earn their wealth. Given free will, the differences in outcomes between the unsuccessful criminal (punishment) and the successful rags-to-riches entrepreneur (wealth) are ones they have both earned.

Core morality tells us that people have a right to what they earn by their own efforts freely exercised. You may not always have a moral right to what you inherited from your parents or what you found on the street or won in the lottery. But core morality insists that you have a moral right to what you have earned. Inequalities, even large ones, between people are morally permissible, perhaps even morally required, when these inequalities are earned. It's because you earned your rewards in life that you deserve them. That's why you have a right to them and why taking them away is wrong. It is this part of core morality that Ayn Rand objectivists, libertarians, and other right-wingers tap into when they insist that taxation is slavery.

The trouble with such arguments is that nothing is earned, nothing is deserved. Even if there really were moral rights to the fruit of our freely exercised abilities and talents, these talents and abilities are never freely acquired or exercised. Just as your innate and acquired intelligence and abilities are unearned, so also are your ambitions, along with the discipline, the willingness to train, and other traits that have to be combined with your talents and abilities to produce anything worthwhile at all.

We didn't earn our inborn (excuse the expression "God-given") talents and abilities. We had nothing to do with whether these traits were conferred on us or not. Similarly, we didn't earn the acquired character traits needed to convert those talents into achievements. They, too, were the result of deterministic processes (genetic and cultural) that were set in motion long before we were born. That is what excludes the possibility that we earned them or deserve them. We were just lucky to have the combination of hardwired abilities and learned ambitions that resulted in the world beating a path to our door.

No one ever earned or deserved the traits that resulted in the inequalities we enjoy—greater income and wealth, better health and longer life, admiration and social distinction, comfort and leisure. Therefore, no one, including us, has a moral right to those inequalities. Core morality may permit unearned inequalities, but it is certainly not going to require them without some further moral reason to do so. In fact, under many circumstances, core morality is going to permit the reduction of inequalities, for it requires that wealth and income that people *have no right to* be redistributed to people in greater need. Scientism assures us that no one has any moral rights. Between them, core morality and scientism turn us into closet egalitarians.

This conclusion doesn't mean that we have to oppose all inequalities. It means that we have to reject all arguments for inequality that turn on the moral right to what we earn, together with the mistaken idea that we earn anything at all. Other parts of core morality provide some justification for limited inequalities in wealth, income, and other advantages between people, but mainly when these inequalities have spillover effects for everyone else. For example, core morality may morally justify paying doctors more than, say, movie reviewers. It is more difficult to qualify as a doctor and sometimes more unpleasant to be one. But it is also more important for all of us that the people most qualified by their talents and abilities become doctors. Of course, even if you accept this argument, and most people would, it may not seem to you like an argument from core morality at all. Rather, it looks like a practical or prudent argument for paying doctors more than others. Scientism won't have any trouble with such arguments, even if they are not really moral ones.

Scientism can even endorse some economists' arguments that inequalities are an indispensable part of the only economic system workable in a large society: free-market capitalism. There is a very good argument that only a free market can give people the right incentives to work efficiently and consume rationally. Suppose you combine this conclusion with the fact that people really do differ substantially in talents and abilities, ambition and industry. What do you get? The combination inevitably results in ever-increasing inequality. Even if everyone starts out with the same resources, after enough time has passed, free-market trade will make some people a lot wealthier than others. This is simply because they have skills that are in demand and the willingness to use them.

These inequalities, the economist may argue, are unavoidable. Mathematical economists have proof that the free market distributes scarce resources in the most efficient way to make people better off: it always produces the largest quantity of the kind of goods that people really want. No nonmarket economy can do this. The twentieth-century laboratories of centralized planning at its worst (the Soviet collectivization of farms? China in the Great Leap Forward?) and its best (Cuba or East Germany?) seem to have vindicated the mathematical economist's proof. Of course, this is not a moral argument for establishing a market economy. To make it a moral argument, you need to find some norm or rule in core morality that requires making most people as well off as possible. Is there such a rule?

Many people think there is a part of core morality that does require we make people better off if we can. Now we have a moral argument for inequalities even when morally unearned, because they are unavoidable in an institution, the free market, that provably makes most people better off. But if we take seriously the economist's argument for the benefits of a free market, we are going to have to engage in significant and regular interference redistributing wealth to keep it efficient.

The economist's proof that the free market is the best way to provide the most of what people really want requires that no one trading in the market become so rich and powerful that they can manipulate prices: no monopolist seller, no monopoly buyer (a monopsonist), nor any small number of buyers or sellers so powerful that they can get together to set prices above or below the free-market price. But every real market inevitably produces such "price setters." Why?

As already noted, there are significant inequalities in (unearned) talents, abilities, and ambitions among producers and consumers. Therefore, the free market will inevitably generate inequalities in income and wealth that grow larger and larger. These inequalities in wealth and power will eventually provide some producers or consumers with enough economic or political clout to start to set prices to benefit themselves at the expense of others. This is not a new observation, of course. In *The Wealth of Nations*, Adam Smith noted that businessmen invariably collude to set prices when they can. The result is the breakdown of the market's ability to make most people as well off as possible.

The only way to repair this breakdown is to level the playing field among producers and consumers. The unequal distribution of wealth must be eliminated or at least reduced to allow the market to return to its welfare-conferring competitive character. Just breaking up monopolies, of course, won't be enough. You have to break up the market power of individual consumers along with the producers. So, scientism plus core morality turn out to be redistributionist and egalitarian, even when combined with free-market economics. No wonder Republicans in the United States have such a hard time with science.

To the charge of being soft on crime, scientism pleads guilty. According to scientism, no one does wrong freely, so no one should really be punished. Prisons are for rehab and protection of society only. To the charge of permitting considerable redistribution of income and wealth, it must also plead guilty, and for the same reasons. Perhaps it should be clear now to many scientistic people why we are disproportionately sympathetic to Robin Hood. Scientism made us do it.

Scientism and the Two Cultures

In 1959 a British scientist and novelist, C. P. Snow, published an article about "the two cultures"—the sciences and the humanities—in which he worried about the ignorance of scientists and humanists about each other's culture and their alienation from one another. Snow sought to bridge the divide between these two cultures. Each, he thought, provided distinctive understanding, knowledge, wisdom. There had to be a way of vindicating the claims of each without sacrificing the insights of the other.

We have seen that this can't be done. Despite their pretensions to equal standing, the humanities can't compete with science when it comes to knowledge of reality, including human reality. There is only one kind of knowledge, one kind of understanding, and there is no such thing as wisdom. What looks like wisdom is either knowledge or good luck.

So, how should we treat the humanities?

To begin with, we can't take their views of science seriously.

As Snow observed, scientists are in general keener to learn about the other culture. They certainly know a lot more about the humanities than humanists know about science. Snow made an invidious comparison between scientists' acquaintance with Shakespeare and humanists' ignorance of the second law of thermodynamics. (The physicist who discovered the quark must have been a serious consumer of the humanities. He found the word *quark* in *Finnegans Wake*.)

In fact, Snow went on to describe humanists as little short of proudly illiterate about science. As a result, he wrote, "So the great edifice of modern physics goes up, and the majority of the cleverest people in the Western world have about as much insight into it as their Neolithic ancestors would have had." Snow was much more on target than he realized.

Driven by physics and by the second law in particular, science has built up an account of reality that we can be confident is fairly accurate, if not complete. This reality looks nothing like what humanists think about nature. Humanists are literally, nonmetaphorically trapped by the worldview of our Neolithic ancestors. As we have seen, since well before the late Stone Age, people were acting on the notion that understanding comes from interpretation of other people's actions in terms of motives and meaning. It was a useful illusion then and for a long time after. In fact, much of contemporary society is still organized around that illusion, and for a long time it was hard to shake even by science.

Physics has had ever-increasing success in explaining phenomena that since Neolithic times people mistakenly thought were in the domain of interpretation, meaning, or purpose. Only after Darwin's achievement in 1859 did the threat begin to be taken seriously by humanists. A great deal of the intellectual history of the last 150 years can be understood as the struggle between purpose and cause, between meaning and mechanism, first in the realm of biology and then in human affairs. It has been a somewhat one-sided debate: while humanists have been following Kant and constructing arguments to show that what the sciences aim to accomplish is impossible, the scientists have been hard at work actually accomplishing it.

In the struggle to maintain their intellectual supremacy, the humanists had the great advantage that everyone could understand their explanations, while few people could understand the explanations science provided. However, despite its impenetrable mathematics and its inability to tell stories, science has been relentlessly pushing the humanities off the playing field. Its technological impact inevitably secured for science the material resources, the influence, and the social standing that first equaled and then exceeded the interpretative disciplines—from history and cultural anthropology through literature, philology, criticism, and art, to mythology and theology.

How were the humanities to limit the writ of science and even regain their ascendancy? Two bold strokes suggested themselves. First, the humanities could help themselves to the scientific study of science itself to denigrate its claims to knowledge. Second, they could make themselves look more like the sciences. The fact that these two stratagems were at cross-purposes did not occur to every humanist.

First, humanists sought to show that science provided no more objective knowledge than did any other system of inquiry or, for that matter, any system of inquiry suppression, like religion. The strategy here was to turn the institutionalized fallibility of science against science itself: if earlier scientific theory was shown to be wrong by later scientific results, well then probably these later theories are mistaken, too. What if later scientific theories could be shown to be no closer to the truth about reality than earlier theories? Then humanists would be able to rebut the claim that science progresses and the humanities merely change. Humanists found an unexpected source for such arguments in the work of a historian of physics, Thomas Kuhn.

In *The Structure of Scientific Revolutions*, Kuhn introduced the term *paradigm shift* to explain how major scientific theories succeed each other. (The "paradigm" meme went viral in a perfect example of Darwinian cultural evolution.) Kuhn noticed that when paradigms shift in science, new problems are solved, but sometimes older, previously solved problems are reopened. Since weighing gains against losses in such shifts is a matter of comparing apples and oranges, there is no single yardstick for measuring scientific progress, Kuhn thought. Thus, hanging on to an older superseded theory cannot be judged completely irrational. As a result, Kuhn suggested, a new paradigm finally triumphs in a science only when its older generation dies off.

This was a history of science made in heaven for those eager to deny the objectivity of science. To Kuhn's horror, they used his analysis that there is no single yardstick for measuring scientific progress to conclude that there is never any yardstick at all. Therefore, the success of new theories in science was more political than epistemic. In the 1970s, Kuhn was the most heavily cited author in all the humanities as scholars sought to identify the deforming roles of ideology, prestige, power, and material rewards in determining paradigm shifts. This argument, it was hoped, would turn each successive scientific theory into just another tenet of political or religious faith—sustained by the masses and in the interests of the elect. The argument was convincing to many in the humanities themselves. They had long recognized changes of doctrine in their own disciplines as merely the result of a craving for novelty and outrageousness. If the epistemology of experimental science was no more progressive than what drives theory change in, say, literary theory, then literary theory's epistemology—its "way of knowing"—was no less reliable either.

But the argument inspired by the radical interpretation of Kuhn suffered a fatal weakness. The trouble was that the humanist's version of Kuhn couldn't explain away the real miracles—the track record of technological successes in science—that neither religion nor the humanities could provide. The only way to explain this difference in successful application between scientific and humanistic "ways of knowing" is to invoke the objectivity of science by contrast with the humanities.

The second broad stratagem for securing the standing of the humanities was to try to make them look more scientific—to turn the humanities into *sciences of interpretation*. Making commonsense folk psychology into a scientific theory is a tradition that goes all the way back to Sigmund Freud in the late nineteenth century. Freudian psychodynamic theory is just the illusory folk psychology that introspection foists on us, but now pushed into the unconscious part of the brain. According to Freud, conscious introspection is frequently wrong when it tells us what packages of thoughts about our wants and about our circumstances motivate our behavior. The real causes are unconscious packages of different thoughts about ourselves and others. Sometimes all it takes is a Freudian slip to reveal the real thoughts about your mother and father that motivate your conduct toward them. More often, years of daily psychoanalysis are required to figure out what you are really thinking about, to uncover the real meaning of your actions.

Freud's theory had its share of technical terms—*libido, cathexis, superego, transference, repression*. These, together with the fact that Freud was a physician, gave it the air of a scientific theory. It had three other features destined to make humanists fond of it: it was easy to understand because it was just a version of the folk psychology they already understood, it was iconoclastic, and it was sexy.

There is another reason that Freud's theory became fashionable among humanists seeking to reveal the real meaning of actions, works of art, historical epochs, and so on. Over time, the standard folk psychology inherited from Neolithic times wasn't getting any better at explaining action, while scientific theory was persistently getting better at explaining and predicting phenomena in its domains. Compared to the ever-increasing explanatory precision and predictive power of scientific theory, interpretation in terms of motives just never really got any better from Homer and Thucydides to Hegel and Toynbee.

Chapter 10 made it clear why the blunt instruments used by us conspiracy theorists can't get any better. They will remain forever fictions useful for navigating social life. Interpretation is the articulation of this useful neural circuitry in introspection. It is without any prospects of providing deepening understanding of human affairs. Humanists were unwilling to give up interpretation. They also recognized that real science secures influence and resources in modern life, in spite of the fact that its theories are hard to understand and getting stranger all the time. This led some humanists to try to imitate the outward appearances of science. They began to frame a succession of increasingly wacky interpretative theories of human affairs, each one replete with technical terms and neologisms that no layperson could understand.

The journey starts with the New Criticism of F. R. Leavis, which rejects the author's conscious intentions, whether known or not, as irrelevant to the meaning of her or his work. Instead, interpretation required a study of meanings imposed on the author by language—a social force that exists independent of the people who speak it. Then, once the fashionability of the unconscious was established, literary theory took a detour from Vienna and headed for Paris, were it combined formalism and Jacques Lacan's Hegelian-Freudian psychoanalysis to end up with Jacques Derrida's conclusion that there is nothing to interpret except other interpretations. On the way from Freud's Vienna and Leavis's Cambridge, the science of interpretation passed through semiotics, existentialism, phenomenology, hermeneutics, formalism, ethnomethodology, colonial and subaltern theory, structuralism, post-structuralism, historicism and new historicism, reader-response theory, and feminist and queer theory. What all these "-isms" and "-ologies" have in common is an often heavily disguised commitment to the Neolithic conspiracy theory of human behavior that managed to get us out of the Pleistocene and into the Holocene about 10,000 years ago. This hoary old theory, as we have seen, gives center stage to narratives, histories, plots, conspiracies, and other ways of stitching motives into stories. Narratives will always be with us.

By the 1980s, these humanist stratagems—trying to use science's fallibility against itself, denigrating science as merely political, and pretending to be scientific—transformed C. P. Snow's "two cultures" into the "science wars." Scientists tried to bridge the gulf between themselves and the humanities, but they were ultimately unwilling to surrender the standard of predictive success based on experiment as the basis for claims to knowledge. Thus, they found themselves accused of attempted intellectual hegemony and ideological imperialism. They were accused of failing to see that their standard of predictive success was itself without independent objective basis. What is more, humanists argued, Kuhn and others had shown that there was no such thing as objective knowledge. The enterprise of science was also an arena of subjectivity. The humanities were a domain of knowledge different from but in no way inferior to science's way of knowing.

No scientist could really take these charges seriously; in fact, outside of the lecture hall and the seminar room, neither could the most interpretatively besotted postmodernist. Theirs was a doctrine repudiated by its adherents every time they got on an airplane, had an X-ray, or washed their hands, for that matter.

When it comes to ways of knowing, scientism must plead guilty to charges of hegemonic ambitions. There is only one way to acquire knowledge, and science's way is it. The research program this "ideology" imposes has no room for purpose, for meaning, for value, or for stories. It cannot therefore accommodate the humanities as disciplines of inquiry, domains of knowledge. They are not the source of truths about human affairs, to which real science must reconcile its results. There may be two cultures, but only one of them is free from illusions and qualified to tell us about reality.

That doesn't mean that scientism has nothing to say about the humanities, beyond curbing their pretensions. The same facts that put science in a position to show why the humanities are a scientific dead end also show why they are an important source of satisfaction, happiness, and psychological reward universal to human experience.

Recall from Chapter 9 how Mother Nature secured our survival and eventual triumph in the evolutionary struggle. She disposed of a major threat—bigger, stronger, faster, meaner predators—by turning us into teams, making us conspiracy theorists, experts in the interpretation of the conduct of others, lovers of stories. The way natural selection turned us into conspiracy theorists was by hitching the psychological feeling of pleasure, satisfaction, relief from curiosity to the formulation of minimally predictive hypotheses about other people's motives, what they wanted and what they believed about how to get it. The humanities thus were not second nature, but first nature to us. No wonder scientists are more committed to bridging the gulf between their culture and the humanities than vice versa. We are all hardwired humanists. Perhaps only a few of us can successfully shed our humanist cloaks and gird on scientific armor.

The humanities will always be with us, at least as long as our psychology retains the shape it assumed in the late Pleistocene. Our continuing fascination with narrative reflects this makeup. This passion for plot-finding is forever being combined with the artist's eternal search for something new, surprising, outrageous, and otherwise attention getting. The result is criticism—diverting, enjoyable speculation about the meaning of art. Criticism, whether of literature, music, or the visual arts, is interpretation, storytelling. It is storytelling about art. Art, of course, is not always storytelling. In abstract expression or stream of consciousness, it rejects narrative. But when the critic seeks to understand it, the result is inevitably a story, a narrative about the artist or the artist's time. At its best, this narrative provides as much pleasure and diversion as good art does itself.

When it comes to real understanding, the humanities are nothing we have to take seriously, except as symptoms. But they are everything we need to take seriously when it comes to entertainment, enjoyment, and psychological satisfaction. Just don't treat them as knowledge or wisdom. Don't feel the need to take sides about deconstruction, postmodernism, Freudian/Marxist structuralism in literary criticism, the dialectic or the eschatology of history, what Marlowe or Bacon or the Earl of Oxford or perhaps even Shakespeare were up to when they wrote *Hamlet*. Just sit back and try to enjoy the outrageous stories spun by those who think they are finally providing the true interpretations on the basis of the right theories about human motives—conscious or unconscious. Scientism encourages you to treat the study of the creative arts as itself a creative art. We don't judge paintings or poetry by their predictive power and explanatory adequacy. Scientism tells us to judge humanistic scholarship devoted to the study of these human creations exactly the same way. If that is not enough for the humanists, if they are not satisfied with producing entertainment, well then, there is nothing for it but trading in their tools for those of the cognitive neuroscientist.

THE MORAL OF THE STORY

The Atheist's Guide to Reality is not an advice or how-to or self-improvement book. There are far too many of these books tempting gullible people who think that all you need to change your life is a convincing narrative. But there are some things that scientism should have us take to heart and make use of, bending our lives in the direction of less unhappiness, disappointment, and frustration, if not more of their opposites.

Before outlining some of these take-home messages, it's important to make clear why scientism isn't fatalism. Yes, it's committed to determinism and does deny us free will; and yes, it may put a whole new spin on our purposes, projects, and plans; and yes, it has to plead guilty to nihilism where values are concerned. But fatalistic it is not!

Fatalism is very different from determinism. Fatalism tells us that no matter what happens, the outcome is unavoidable. It claims that no matter what route life takes you down, all roads lead to the same place. Determinism is quite a different matter. If the universe is deterministic, then where you end up depends on where you start out (plus the laws of nature). Start at different points, and almost every time you will pass through altogether different places and come to a different end. Determinism does not dictate that you'll end up in the same place at all. Of course, we are all going die. The difference between fatalism and determinism is this: If fatalism is right, you'll die of the same thing no matter what you do. If determinism is right, how you die, what you die of, depends on what you did in life. (Did you smoke, overeat, wear your seat belt?) That's a big difference. Some deaths are worse than others. Which we experience will be determined, but is not fated.

Science tells us that the only thing that really is fated is the heat death of the universe. The second law insists that all roads lead to maximal disorder in the universe at the end of time. In fact, the second law says that maximal disorder *is* the end of time, since after that point, there won't be any asymmetries, any one-way processes left in nature. Physics tells us that state of completely evened-out flatness without any energy differences is about 100 billion years off. So, scientism doesn't have to worry about it. Almost everything else in the history of the universe, including our histories, will be determined but not fated. (This is important for any chance this book has of climbing up the best seller list.)

Everything that happens in your life is determined. That doesn't mean that reading this book can't make a difference to your happiness, well-being, or adjustment to reality. That you bought, borrowed, or otherwise acquired this book was determined. So was its effect on you, if any. If your brain is organized in roughly the same way mine is, there are neural circuits that have produced disquiet in you, along with the illusion of thoughts about the persistent questions. Reading this book has rearranged a large number of neural circuits in your brain (though only a very small proportion of the millions of such circuits in your brain). If those rearranged neural circuits change their outputs in certain ways when triggered by inputs seeming to pose the daunting questions, then this book will have worked. The process will be the same one psychotherapy employs when it works. It will have changed your neural circuitry, unconscious and conscious. You will acquire the correct information about the matters that keep you up at night. You will almost certainly undergo the conscious illusion of thinking about these questions in a new way, as finally having been answered.

Don't take narratives too seriously. That is the most obvious moral of our tour through science's version of reality. By now you can see why this advice is important and also hard to follow. After all, the human brain has been shaped by millions of years of natural and cultural selection to be addicted to stories. They are almost the only things that give most of us relief from the feeling of curiosity. Scientism has nothing against stories. It just refuses to be an enabler. Stories are fun, but they're no substitute for knowledge. In fact, the insistence on packaging information into narratives is an obstacle to understanding how things really work. Scientific findings, along with the models, laws, and theories that explain them, can't be squeezed into the procrustean bed of a good detective story, or any other kind of story for that matter.

When politicians or political commentators try to sell you on a narrative become suspicious. Even if their stories are sincere, the plot is probably distracting them and you from the real issues. Things are always more complicated than any story we can remember for very long, even if the story happens to be true. Being able to tell a story that voters can remember is almost never a good qualification for elective office.

This advice goes double for anyone trying to sell you on religion. But if you have read this far, you don't need to be warned off stories with spooky plots that always end well for the good guys and badly for the bad guys. Religion and some of those who make their living from it succeed mainly because some of us are even more given to conspiracy theory than others. But none of us is entirely immune. We need continually to fight the temptation to think that we can learn much of anything from someone else's story of how they beat an addiction, kept to a diet, improved their marriage, raised their kids, saved for their retirement, or made a fortune flipping real estate. Even if their story is what actually happened, the storytellers are wrong about the real causes of how and why it happened. Learning their story won't help you figure out the real causal process from rags to riches, from misery to happiness. And in many cases, the real links in the chain of their story have already been broken by an arms race, often one no one has noticed.

It's hard to follow the advice against taking narratives seriously when we seek to understand the past. After all, what is left from the past besides its artifacts and its stories? In some cases, there are other traces left, much more reliable than stories, that will enable us to reconstruct history. Gene sequence differences, slight differences between dialects and languages, and other quantifiable variables are already allowing biological anthropologists to uncover large swaths of human prehistory and even to correct written histories of settlements, migrations, technological advances, and military conquests. But even what these scientific means uncover can't really amount to more than entertainment. The narratives about what actually happened in the past have no more value for understanding the present or the future than the incomplete and even entirely mythic narratives that they might replace. History, even corrected by science, is still bunk.

Once you adopt scientism, you'll be able to put lots of the strife and controversies about politics into perspective. You will also be able to cease taking seriously aesthetic and ethical judgments that offend you. When it comes to politics, you will be able to sidestep disagreements in which other people try to force you to choose just by pointing out that the dispute is at least in part a factual one, and the facts are not in. You will be able to undercut some arguments just by pointing out that they make assumptions about reality that science has already shown to be false—for example, that humans have souls or that there is free will or that most people are selfish.

Of course, some disputes, especially about the meaning of works of art, literature, and music, are ones in which all disputants are wrong, for in these cases the argument is about whose illusion is correct. When the answer is none, the argument is hard to take seriously as anything but a game. Games are fun, and gamesmanship is the (naturally selected) function of many of the disagreements that divert the chattering classes.

When it comes to your own life, scientism makes no unqualified prescriptions. If you enjoy being unhappy, if you really get off on the authenticity of the tragic view of life, if you are not inclined to break harmful habits that will shorten your life or cause your body grief in the future, scientism has nothing much to say. You are at the extreme end of a distribution of blind variations in traits that Mother Nature makes possible and exploits. To condemn these extreme traits as wrong, false, incorrect, bad, or evil is flatly inconsistent with nihilism.

On the other hand, if you are within a couple of standard deviations of the mean, you will seek to avoid, minimize, or reduce unhappiness, pain, discomfort, and distress in all its forms. If so, scientism has good news. There is an ever-increasing pharmacopoeia of drugs, medicines, treatments, prosthetic devices, and regimes that will avoid, minimize, or reduce these unwanted conditions. Take them. And if you feel guilty for seeking surcease from the thousand natural shocks that flesh and especially gray matter are subject to, well there's probably a drug that reduces such guilt feelings, too. Which of these treatments work, and which do not? That's an easy (or at least an unambiguously answerable) question, too. The treatments that survive rigorous experimental testing are the ones to try. You can write off any treatment whose provider excuses it from double-blind controlled experiments on the grounds that you have to believe in it for the treatment to work. Even placebos pass the double-blind test.

We can organize our own lives in the absence of real purpose and planning. We do so by reorganizing the neural circuitry that produces these very illusions of design and forethought. If reorganizing our brain is needed, scientism commends a very ancient "philosophy." The really scientistic person will cultivate an Epicurean detachment. This is a disposition recommended by Epicurus, a Greek philosopher of the fourth century BC. His views about the nature of reality were about as close to correct as one could get by pure reason alone in Plato's time. He believed that everything was basically atoms moving on determined paths forever. The physical facts, he rightly held, fix all the facts, and that made him an atheist. Epicurus held that there was nothing more to the mind than physical matter and that immortality was out of the question. He equated the morally good with pleasure and evil with pain. A tranquil self-sufficient life along with your friends was the key to securing the good and avoiding evil. That made Epicurus a nice nihilist, though he didn't realize it. The tranquility he commended requires that we not take ourselves or much of anything else too seriously. Epicurus was no fatalist, and he wasn't a stoic. That's another ancient prescription for living that counseled indifference to pain and pleasure—definitely not Epicureanism. Epicureanism encourages a good time.

Scientism has nothing against having a good time either. In fact, it observes that we were selected for being Epicureans. It serves our genetic interests most of the time. Of course, our brain has become powerful enough to see through the stratagems of Mother Nature. We can get off the Darwinian train and stop acting in our genes' interests if we want to. There can't be anything morally wrong with that (recall nice nihilism) if that's what we want to do.

There is one last persistent question that this book has been silent about. It was one that concerned Epicurus: *Should we fear death? Is it a bad thing?* This question is quite different from the easily answered question, "Is dying bad?" The answer to that question is obvious: prolonged painful dying, like any unpleasant experience, is very bad and should be avoided. Epicurus's question was about being dead. His answer was no. There really is nothing to fear about death. Scientism will be sympathetic to his answer. It may even be able to take Epicurus one better.

Epicurus was famous for arguing that death is nothing to us, and nothing to fear when it arrives, because when it does arrive, we aren't around to experience it. The event of dying is like a revolving door: we go out of existence just as our body dies. We never even get to meet death face to face. It's impossible to do so, since death is the end of our existence, and if we can't exist, we can't be disturbed, discomfited, or otherwise made unhappy by death. So, death is nothing to fear.

Most of the commonsense objections to this argument start by forgetting that death—the termination of our lives—is an instantaneous event quite different from dying—a process that might take a long time and be quite unpleasant. That process is something to fear and to avoid. But becoming dead and being dead, those are two things Epicurus thought no one should waste time worrying about now. We are not around to suffer any harm from death. Another misconception about Epicurus's argument is that it is neutral regarding longer lives versus shorter ones. Epicurus recognized that most people are better off postponing death and living longer. Premature death—a shorter life—is usually to be feared. But death, the event itself, he convincingly argued, is no cause for alarm.

An argument like Epicurus's is a magnet for smart alecks, of course. Clever philosophers have long contrived counterarguments. Some try to show that bad things that happen to your reputation after death can harm you even if you are dead. Others argue that post-death survival, even infinitely long immortality, is a good thing, or at least something people might want. They conclude that by depriving you of that, death harms you.

Scientism helps Epicurus respond to these arguments and perhaps even strengthens his original one. The self, the person, the "I" inside the body is an illusion, along with all those others. That means that even if there is a loophole in Epicurus's argument that death is something you shouldn't worry about, science still backs him up: there isn't really any "you" or "me" or "him" or "her" to worry about death, post-death harm, boringly endless post-death existence, or anything else.

Epicurus wasn't right when he argued that understanding the nature of reality is by itself enough to make a person happy. Alas, some people do get everything right about the universe and our place in it and remain dissatisfied. Satisfying themselves that science answers all the persistent questions correctly, they are still troubled. You, gentle reader, may be one of these people. Fortunately for such people, Epicurus was almost right. If you still can't sleep at night, even after accepting science's answers to the persistent questions, you probably just need one more little thing besides Epicurean detachment. Take a Prozac or your favorite serotonin reuptake inhibitor, and keep taking them till they kick in.

THE ATHEIST'S GUIDE
TO REALITY:
THE BACKSTORY

MOST OF THE SCIENCE THIS BOOK USES IS SO WELL established that no physicist or biologist feels the need to argue for it. But there is some wonderful science writing that explains this background. This backstory identifies the scientists who have the best take on reality and/or communicate it most effectively. Providing the real substance of science in ways people can grasp is extremely difficult. The authors recommended by this backstory successfully convey substance because they have found a way to do so without storytelling.

Besides books, one great place to start if you want to know more about almost any of the science made use of here is *Wikipedia*. Don't ever take my word for it. If you have questions about the science, check *Wikipedia*. Almost a decade ago, a scientific study revealed that *Wikipedia* was then at least as accurate as the *Encyclopædia Britannica*. Nowadays, it's probably better. It's certainly more up-to-date. Many of the articles in *Wikipedia* come with wonderful illustrations.

Wikipedia is usually a reliable source when it comes to philosophy as well. Put a phrase like "causal closure of physics" into your favorite search engine, and you are likely to see a *Wikipedia* result that offers an accessible introduction with reliable references. If you want to take a deeper look at a philosophical issue arising from science, check the website for the *Stanford Encyclopedia of Philosophy*—the online source for the current state of play in academic research by philosophers.

THE NATURE OF REALITY

The best panoramic pictures of the frontiers of physics are found in Brian Greene's *The Elegant Universe* (1999) and *The Hidden Reality: Parallel Universes and the Deep Laws of the Cosmos* (2011). Not only does he manage to avoid stories, but Greene has a way with examples that makes even superstring theory accessible. He also makes clear what the really outstanding questions are that face physics. The most important thing Greene does is demonstrate how powerfully and precisely clever experiments and intricate observations made by astronomers and high-energy physicists continually confirm theories about what will happen on scales vastly too small and too large to grasp.

A brace of Nobel Prize–winning physicists have taken up the challenge of conveying the nature of reality in story-free terms that don't talk down to the nonphysicists. The first of these was the great iconoclast, Richard Feynman. His *QED: The Strange Theory of Light and Matter* (2006) shows how much is explained by the theory he put together, quantum electrodynamics (whence QED). But Feynman is frank about the deep problems inherent in a coherent interpretation of quantum mechanics. In *QED*, he wrote: "What I am going to tell you about is what we teach our physics students in the third or fourth year of graduate school. . . . It is my task to convince you not to turn away because you don't understand it. You see my physics students don't understand it. That is because I don't understand it. Nobody does." Fortunately, the part of physics we need, all physicists understand.

Steven Weinberg's *Dreams of a Final Theory* (1993) reveals the inevitability of quantum mechanics' and general relativity's take on reality, while explaining the difficulty physicists face reconciling them. If you read one of Greene's books first, you'll come away optimistic about physics' eventual ability to do so.

Stephen Hawking's *A Brief History of Time* (1998) doesn't tell us what we need know to understand time: how the second law of thermodynamics makes it and every other one-way process work. But Sean M. Carroll has done the job in *From Eternity to Here* (2010). Hawking's later book, however, *The Grand Design* (2010, with Leonard Mlodinow), sketches the multiverse theory and explains why physicists have no time for the "Why is there something rather than nothing?" question or its Goldilocks answer, the "anthropic principle."

How Physics Fakes Design

The single best guide to Darwinian natural selection and its key features is Richard Dawkins's aptly titled *The Blind Watchmaker* (1986). Dawkins has written many books that combine important scientific originality with great accessibility. But the one supplement to this book particularly worth reading is *The Ancestor's Tale* (2004), in which evolutionary history is traced back from our species all the way to the primeval slime. The book is a long tour through details that are fascinating in themselves and that leave no doubt that Darwin was the Newton of the blade of grass.

Daniel Dennett's magisterial *Darwin's Dangerous Idea* (1995) settles most of the latter-day controversies within evolutionary biology and among its fellow travelers. This book has done more even than Dawkins's to reveal how Darwin's theory is a universal acid that eats through all cant (as well as Kant) about nature. But don't trust the last three chapters, where Dennett tries to prevent the acid from eating through our values.

"The Heavy Hand of Entropy," Chapter 2 of Sean Carroll's *From Eternity to Here*, already praised, is a great introduction to the second law of thermodynamics for purposes of biology as well as physics.

Thermodynamic randomness makes molecular self-assembly possible, and with it the emergence of adaptation from zero adaptation. Self-assembly is an idea pioneered by Stuart Kauffman, a serious scientist with a knack for popularization. In *At Home in the Universe: The Search for Laws of Self-Organization and Complexity* (1995), he develops these notions in a way that nonphysical scientists can grasp. Why he thinks self-assembly is an alternative to Darwinian processes of order production remains unexplained.

The websites of the nanotechnologists give vivid examples of how molecules, especially DNA molecules, can self-assemble into almost any shape under the sun and therefore into shapes that replicate themselves. To find the most up-to-date pictures (some lab is always coming up with a better picture), just Google "DNA cube." While you're online, you can even find Lord Kelvin's scientific screed against Darwin by searching "On the Age of the Sun's Heat."

The *Wikipedia* site for the Miller-Urey experiment has a nice diagram of its setup, a clear explanation of the results, and the even more impressive results of a reanalysis of their original data 56 years later. Turns out Urey and Miller actually synthesized 22 amino acids, not the 5 they originally thought. The Internet has many other diagrams and photos of the original experiment and the others it inspired.

IKEA DIDN'T MAKE NATURAL HISTORY

Humans have 24,000 genes. Fruit flies have 14,000. And they are pretty much the same ones. One startling discovery of the last 20 years is how a small number of differences in the number and arrangement of the same gene sequences produce the incredible range of diversity and complexity in living things. Peter Lawrence gives the details in *The Making of a Fly* (1992). How complex adaptations arise from zero adaptation just through random minor changes in molecular biology is obvious but breathtaking. How this works in many other species is reported in Sean B. Carroll's *Endless Forms Most Beautiful* (2005). The title comes from Darwin's elegant observation, quoted in Chapter 3. (Note that this Sean Carroll is a different one altogether from the Sean Carroll of *From Eternity to Here*. Science can be confusing.)

The single biggest mystery in evolutionary biology is not how to get adaptation from nothing. The real problem is explaining the profligate wastefulness of natural selection: why evolution resulted in sex. It's everywhere and yet it is so wasteful of the very thing reproduction is supposed to spread: information and order. Sex should have been selected against. The best treatment of this mystery belongs to the most important biologist since Darwin, W. D. Hamilton. See his *Narrow Roads of Gene Land*, volume 2: *Evolution of Sex* (2002). A less mathematical presentation can be found in John Maynard Smith and Eörs Szathmáry, *The Origins of Life: From the Birth of Life to the Origin of Language* (1999).

There is a wonderful graph of the major extinctions at http://www.astro.virginia.edu/class/oconnell/astr121/guide22.html.

The *Wiki* site for "atmosphere of Earth" has an equally clear graph showing the transition from a time when oxygen was a poison for most living things on Earth.

The most earnest attempt to reconcile religion and science, and especially Darwin and God, comes from the Catholic theologian John Haught, *Making Sense of Evolution: Darwin, God and the Drama of Life* (2010). Father Haught is a good guy, having testified against "intelligent design" in the courts. But he gets his Darwinian biology wrong in just the way the less learned reconcilers do.

If you really want to check on Bishop Ussher's calculations, there is a good introduction at "Ussher chronology" on *Wikipedia*.

MORALITY: THE BAD NEWS AND THE GOOD

Plato's problem for sermonizing about morality is developed in his dialogue, the *Euthyphro*. It's in almost every collection of Plato's dialogues. There are lots of translations from Plato's classic Greek available online.

J. L. Mackie really began making moral philosophers take evolutionary biology and nihilism seriously in *Ethics: Inventing Right and Wrong* (1977). Richard Joyce followed Mackie's "error" theory of ethics 30 years later. *The Evolution of Morality* (2006) updated the evidence that morality is an adaptation and showed why that fact is no reason to believe it, even when it is the cause of our believing it.

Shaun Nichols's *Sentimental Rules: On the Natural Foundations of Moral Judgment* (2004) brings together the neuroscientific evidence and the evolutionary factors that shape universal core morality. His book with Joshua Knobe, *Experimental Philosophy* (2008), shows how the hardware and software of the brain—shaped by cultural and natural selection—generate pretty much the same moral judgments in everyone. Further evidence for how everyone carries around roughly the same morality is being illuminated by functional magnetic resonance studies of the brain, as described by Joshua Greene in *The Moral Brain and How to Use It* (2011)

How bad is Mother Nature at selecting for true beliefs? How good is she at selecting for false ones? Daniel Dennett and Ryan McKay examine these questions in their paper "The Evolution of Misbelief," in *Behavioral and Brain Sciences* (2009). You can find it online for free and for a fee. They show that evolution is good at selecting false beliefs when they have beneficial consequences for our posterity—just why you'd expect Mother Nature to select for core morality along with other false beliefs.

Before the Dawn (2006), by Nicholas Wade, introduces what we are beginning to learn about human prehistory by the combination of paleoarcheology and human gene sequencing. Clever use of gene sequence data can detail the earliest arrivals of humans everywhere and where they passed through on the way. It can also tell us how widespread cannibalism was—very; when we began to wear clothes—70,000 years ago; how one of our favorite foods— the dog—domesticated us; and whether we had sex with Neanderthals. This subject is moving so fast—two new human species in the last 10 years—that the most convenient way to stay on top of it is to read the *New York Times* (where Wade reports). *How Humans Evolved* (2008) is a textbook by two important evolutionary anthropologists, Joan Silk and Robert Boyd, so full of beautiful and instructive illustrations it's practically a coffee-table book.

It's now commonplace in every social science (except maybe economics) that altruism and unselfishness were inevitable among puny creatures like our ancestors if they were going to survive long enough to produce us. The best combination of sociobiology and comparative human/primate ethology that makes this obvious comes from Sarah Hrdy, *Mothers and Others: The Evolutionary Origins of Mutual Understanding* (2009), and Michael Tomasello, *Why We Cooperate* (2009).

The impact of evolutionary game theory in biology traces back to John Maynard Smith, *Evolution and the Theory of Games* (1982). The prisoner's dilemma's role in how cooperation must have been selected for was first made clear by Robert Axelrod in *The Evolution of Cooperation* (1984). J. McKenzie Alexander's *Structural Evolution of Morality* (2007) gives all the details. And if you are really keen, his website enables you to run your own simulations of all the games that select for moral norms as optimal strategies. Cross-cultural experiments reveal much the same thing, using "cut the cake," the "ultimatum game," and other games. Rob Boyd, Joseph Henrich, and others' work in 15 non-Western societies show this, as reported in Joseph and Natalie Henrich's *Why Humans Cooperate: A Cultural and Evolutionary Explanation* (2007).

The role of the emotions in the evolution and enforcement of core morality is developed by Jesse Prinz in *The Emotional Construction of Morals* (2007). Richard Nisbett and Dov Cohen's *Culture of Honor: The Psychology of Violence in the South* (1996) is a lovely study of how local ecologies shape moral norms and how they harness the emotions to impose them on individuals. Robert Frank's *Passions within Reason* (1988) links emotions to the design problem of credible commitment in strategic interaction that they solve.

NEVER LET YOUR CONSCIOUS BE YOUR GUIDE

Blindsight has been troubling philosophers ever since it came to their attention. Check out references to it in the *Stanford Encyclopedia of Philosophy* online. Lawrence Weiskrantz has been writing about the phenomenon for at least 25 years. His latest book is *Blindsight: A Case Study Spanning 35 Years and New Developments* (2009).

Libet's experiments are well described in an article on *Wikipedia*, with references to later discussions. Many of these are written by those eager to wriggle out of the conclusion that we don't have free will. By contrast, in *The Illusion of Conscious Will* (2002), Daniel Wegner carries Libet's argument further and adds some more empirical findings to show that the will is an illusion of consciousness. Libet's results have been strongly substantiated by recent work using fMRI brain imaging, reported in "Unconscious determinants of free decisions in the human brain," a paper by C. S. Soon, M. Brass, H. J. Heinze, and J. D. Haynes, in *Nature Neuroscience* (2008). Remember, our take on Libet is merely that his experiment shows that we can't trust introspection. We have lots of other reasons to distrust consciousness.

The visual illusions in Chapter 7 are used with permission of Dale Purves. For more and better ones, together with links to his further work and the theory of how we see things, check out his website (http://www.purveslab.net/seeforyourself/), especially the link labeled "See for yourself."

There is a huge literature on "confabulation"—false memories—especially about the self. A good place to start is William Hirstein, *Brain Fiction: Self-Deception and the Riddle of Confabulation* (2005).

THE BRAIN DOES EVERYTHING WITHOUT THINKING ABOUT ANYTHING AT ALL

The problem of the Paris neurons and the infinite (and multiplying) regress of *about*ness is often called "homuncularism." The "homunculus"—Latin for little human—was the undetectably small human shape in the sperm, which was thought to grow into the human shape of the fetus and infant. Explaining the form and development of a very complex thing as the result of the growth of something equally complex but much smaller doesn't cut it in embryology. The same goes for psychology; you can't explain the *about*ness of one part of the brain by assuming the *about*ness of another. The problem is to explain "original intentionality."

The temptations of homuncularism in contemporary psychology were first diagnosed in the development of psychological theories of vision and mental imagery by scientists like Stephen Kosslyn and Zenon Pylyshyn. Get a handle on the problem at "Mental Imagery" in the *Stanford Encyclopedia of Philosophy*. The issue goes much deeper than just visual imagery storage. One graphic way to see the problem is in John Searle's famous essay "Minds, Brains, and Programs," in *Behavioral and Brain Sciences* (1979; online, too), where the expressions "original intentionality" and "derived intentionality" got their recent currency.

A generation of naturalistic philosophers tried to solve the problem of "original intentionality"—showing how neural circuits could be *about* stuff—using the only tool available: Darwin's theory of natural selection. Just as blind variation and environmental filtration produce adaptation in nature, so, too, do they produce adaptation in brain circuits. True. Could neural content be a very finely tuned adaptation? This idea got started with Daniel Dennett's *Content and Consciousness* (1969) and reached full flourishing in Ruth Millikan's *Language, Thought and Other Biological Categories* (1984), along with Fred Dretske's *Explaining Behavior* (1991). Too bad it didn't work, as Jerry Fodor (among others) showed in *A Theory of Content and Other Essays* (1990). Fodor carried this argument much too far in *What Darwin Got Wrong* (2010).

Besides his best-selling autobiography, Eric Kandel has written a great book with Larry Squire on how the brain stores information, and does so without any *about*ness. The book is *Memory: From Mind to Molecules* (2008). A lot of his technical papers on somatic neurogenomics can be found on his personal website. You are probably familiar with rats and people, but not Kandel's lab pet, the sea slug, *Aplysia californica*. Google-image it just for fun: it's an escargot as big as your foot.

Watson, the supercomputer that plays *Jeopardy!*, is the star of a couple of IBM websites and the darling of more than one article in the *New York Times*. But the details of the software Watson is running are as proprietary as Google's search protocol.

FAREWELL TO THE
PURPOSE-DRIVEN LIFE

As early as 1960, the great American philosopher Willard Van Orman Quine had recognized the impossibility of thought being about anything and had begun developing its implications in *Word and Object*.

Steven Pinker's *The Language Instinct* (1994) is a gateway to recent work in linguistics, cognitive psychology, and neurogenetics. His best sellers *How the Mind Works* (1997) and *The Blank Slate* (2002) argue for a sophisticated evolutionary account of several cognitive capacities critical for speech. More recently, *The Stuff of Thought* (2007) shows how language reflects cognition (even though language misleads us about how cognition does it all).

Psychologists are increasingly able to test hypotheses about the infant mind by clever experiments on babies as young as a few weeks. Philippe Rochat's *The Infant's World* (2001) reports on the trail he blazed with inspired use of cutting-edge technology and careful attention to the slightest behavioral changes.

The way our brain has been shaped to make us prefer narratives and to anthropomorphize everything is something evolutionary psychologists noticed long ago. Darwinian processes have selected the human mind for rejecting Darwin's theory, just another example of how natural selection is not much good at uncovering truths. What this book has been calling our tendency to engage in conspiracy theory, to see whodunits everywhere, cognitive scientists call the *hyperactive agency detector*. Several of them trace the universality of religions to overshooting by the quick and dirty adaptation for figuring out the threats and opportunities caused by other people's behavior. Todd Tremlin, in *Minds and Gods: The Cognitive Foundations of Religion*, develops this theme in detail.

You've Got to Stop Taking Yourself So Seriously

Freaky Friday was made in 1976, remade in 1995, and again in 2003, each time by Disney. If you missed any of these, there is a 2010 remake. In addition, there are variations in which a boy and his dad trade places (*Vice Versa*) and about 100 other such films and TV programs listed under "Body swaps" on *Wikipedia*. Conceptually, the worst of these films is *Being John Malkovich*, worst because it is about the best illustration of the homunculus problem ever made into a major motion picture.

It was David Hume who first figured out why there is no enduring self. He was so disconcerted by the discovery that he had to distract himself: "I dine, I play a game of backgammon, I converse, and am merry with my friends; and when after three or four hours' amusement, I would return to these speculations, they appear so cold, and strained, and ridiculous, that I cannot find in my heart to enter into them any farther." Now we know why he had to do so. Blame Darwin, or rather the process he uncovered.

Antonio Damasio's *The Feeling of What Happens* (1999) came out for three selves. His *Self Comes to Mind: Constructing the Conscious Brain* (2010) develops the neuroscience of this ever-so-useful illusion further. But nothing the brain produces qualifies as one or more selves numerically identical over time.

Thomas Nagel's famous article "What Is It Like to Be a Bat" (1974) is available online. There is a wonderful modernized translation of Leibniz's *Monadology* at the Early Modern Philosophy website (www.earlymoderntexts.com) by Jonathan Bennett, the great historian of philosophy and analytical philosopher.

The best antidotes to these subversive texts are in a series of books by Vilaynur S. Ramachandran, including *The Emerging Mind* (2003), his Reith lectures on the BBC, *A Brief Tour of Human Consciousness: From Impostor Poodles to Purple Numbers* (2004), and (with Sandra Blakeslee) *Phantoms in the Brain* (1998). Ramachandran's latest book, *The Tell-Tale Brain* (2011), is also good on blindsight, mother's face neurons, and confabulations of consciousness.

History Debunked

Arms races started in the genome and have accelerated ever since. Even if human affairs were not the domain of Darwinian adaptation, it would still be the area of ever-lasting arms races. The beginning of the story is given in Austin Burt and Robert Trivers's *Genes in Conflict* (2006). The last chapter in the history of arms races will probably end with human extinction.

At its outset, human history might have been predictable just because the arms races were mainly biological. That's what enabled Jared Diamond to figure out how and why western Europeans came to dominate the globe over a period that lasted 8,000 years or so in *Guns, Germs, and Steel* (1999). Though he doesn't acknowledge it, Diamond is only applying an approach to human history made explicit by sociobiologist E. O. Wilson in *On Human Nature* more than 30 years ago (1978) and more recently by Peter Richerson and Robert Boyd in *Not By Genes Alone* (2006). For an illuminating example of the process of gene/culture coevolution that they identify, read Gregory Clark's explanation for why the Industrial Revolution first took hold in Britain in *A Farewell to Alms* (2007).

Once human culture and human accumulation began to depend on technological change, its unpredictability made telling the future scientifically as difficult as reading tea leaves—for Darwinian theories as well as all others. The refusal of economics as a science to deal with the impact of technological change is detailed in David Warsh's *Knowledge and the Wealth of Nations* (2006). What he doesn't realize is that it can't be done, even if you try.

The outrageous notion that humans have been selected for acting rationally, which is supposed to give economists the right to assume that they do, stood behind much of the orthodoxy of twentieth-century economics. It produced such quaint results as Gary Becker's *Economic Approach to Human Behavior* (1977) and innumerable successors. None of them seemed to pay any attention to the revolution in behavioral economics. But even if we take seriously the results of cognitive scientists like Gerd Gigerenzer (with Peter Todd), *Simple Heuristics That Make Us Smart* (1999), or Daniel Kahneman and Amos Tversky, *Choices, Values and Frames*, we really won't do any better when it comes to predicting the future. Arms races will always be with us.

It was Friedrich Hayek who realized that neither human intentions nor human planning can produce those enduring human institutions that have a capacity to withstand arms races. Institutions do so only because they are the products of the same evolutionary processes that make arms races inevitable. Some of these insights can be found in his *Individualism and Economic Order* (1976), available online.

LIVING WITH SCIENTISM

Sam Harris, of atheism fame, gets the role of science in settling moral disputes nearly right in *The Moral Landscape: How Science Can Determine Human Values* (2010). But he mistakenly thinks that science can show the resulting moral agreement to be true, correct, or right. It can't. Science has no way to bridge the gap between *is* and *ought*. That is why secular humanism can't do the job secular humanists wrongly think needs to be done. The end of Philip Kitcher's wonderful introduction to Darwin and its impact on theism, *Living with Darwin: Evolution, Design, and the Future of Faith* (2007), tries its best to make a case that there is a real religious need that something like secular humanism should take seriously.

The overwhelmingly powerful argument that determinism and moral responsibility are just logically incompatible was given its most powerful contemporary expression by Peter van Inwagen in *An Essay on Free Will* (1983). His argument should remind us of Kant's dictum that attempts to reconcile determinism and free will are "wretched subterfuges," and "word jugglery." The subterfuge goes back to Hume. To check out latter-day proposals for how to reconcile free will and determinism, read Daniel Dennett's *Elbow Room* (1984) or *Freedom Evolves* (2003).

Some moral philosophers are luck egalitarians. They argue that luck—good or bad, shouldn't be allowed to have any impact on "distributive justice"—roughly how much money and other good things people have and how much they are paid. That should be determined only by their ambitions and wise choices. Susan Hurley explores these ideas in *Justice, Luck, and Knowledge*

(2003). Of course, there aren't any free choices, and ambitions are as much luck as native talents are. The only argument against real egalitarianism is that it will make everyone worse off. That economist's argument is hard to refute. For a partial antidote, read *Meritocracy and Economic Inequality* by the greatest American economist, Kenneth Arrow, with coauthors Steven Durlauf and Samuel Bowles (who also participated in the cross-cultural studies of cooperation recorded in Henrich and Henrich's *Why Humans Cooperate*, mentioned earlier).

C. P. Snow's lecture *The Two Cultures and the Scientific Revolution* (1960) was reissued on its 50th anniversary. Less enduring was the *ad hominem* attack on it and on Snow by the progenitor of preposterous twentieth-century literary theory, F. R. Leavis, in *Two Cultures? The Significance of C. P. Snow* (1963). For a properly jaundiced view of literary theory from Leavis to Derrida, read the second edition of Terry Eagleton's *Literary Theory* (1996).

Little of Epicurus survives, but what does is available online. The greatest Epicurean work, *De Rarum Natura*, or *On the Nature of Things*, was actually written in the first century AD, about 350 years after Epicurus's death, by Lucretius. This great Latin work in the form of an epic poem is available online in English. If Lucretius had not used the title, I would have taken it for my own.

INDEX

Page numbers in *italics* refer to illustrations.